# THE FUTURE OF THE DOLLAR

A volume in the series

**Cornell Studies in Money**

edited by Eric Helleiner and Jonathan Kirshner

*A list of titles in this series is available at www.cornellpress.cornell.edu.*

# THE FUTURE OF THE DOLLAR

EDITED BY

## Eric Helleiner and Jonathan Kirshner

Cornell University Press
Ithaca and London

First published 2009 by Cornell University Press
First printing, Cornell Paperbacks, 2009

Printed in the United States of America

Library of Congress Cataloging-in-Publication Data

The future of the dollar / edited by Eric Helleiner and Jonathan Kirshner.
    p. cm. — (Cornell studies in money)
  Includes bibliographical references and index.
  ISBN 978-0-8014-4825-6 (cloth : alk. paper) — ISBN 978-0-8014-7561-0 (pbk. : alk. paper)
  1. Dollar, American.   2. Monetary policy—United States.
3. Monetary policy.  4. Foreign exchange.   5. Currency question.
6. International finance.   I. Helleiner, Eric, 1963–   II. Kirshner, Jonathan.   III. Title.   IV.   Series: Cornell studies in money.

  HG540.F89 2009
  332.4′973—dc22

2009008775

Cloth printing     10  9  8  7  6  5  4  3  2  1
Paperback printing   10  9  8  7  6  5  4  3  2  1

To Charles Kindleberger and Susan Strange,
pioneers in the interdisciplinary study of international money

# CONTENTS

# FIGURES AND TABLES

# PREFACE

This book began with a simple question: What is the future of the U.S. dollar as an international currency? Since we could not agree on the answer, we thought it might be interesting to invite a number of distinguished scholars to share their views in a set of lectures and a workshop at Cornell University and the Centre for International Governance Innovation in Waterloo, Ontario. The answers proved much more interesting than we had anticipated. Many of these scholars had studied the dollar's international role over several decades, but they disagreed—often profoundly—about its future. Although some saw the dollar remaining as the world's key currency for years to come, others anticipated a dramatic scaling back of the dollar's global role in the near future.

The significance of these disagreements only grew as the project evolved. When we launched the project, little did we know that it would unfold against the backdrop of the worst international financial crisis since the 1930s. Since this crisis was centered on the United States itself, the dollar's future global role quickly became a popular topic in the media and financial press. Would the crisis mark the final dethroning of the U.S. dollar? Or would predictions of its demise end up just as inaccurate as those that had accompanied other major international financial crises since the early 1970s?

This book does not attempt to provide a definitive answer to these questions. Instead, it provides a range of perspectives on the dollar's future as an international currency. Rather than declare one perspective "the winner," our goal has been to try to understand why scholars can disagree so profoundly about the topic. In so doing, we hope this book contributes not only to contemporary debates about the dollar's future but also to broader scholarship on the organization of international money. We also hope the framework we present helps readers come to their own conclusions about the kinds of variables they should look for to adjudicate debates on this topic.

We have incurred many debts in putting this book together. We are, of course, particularly grateful to the contributors to the book for their support for the project and their diligence in meeting deadlines. A number of scholars also provided very insightful and helpful feedback on the chapters and the book, including William Grimes, Hubert Zimmerman, Steve Nelson, and two anonymous reviewers. For their help in the preparation of the manuscript, we would like to thank Kausar Ashraf and Troy Lundblad. As always, Roger Haydon provided excellent feedback and advice. And finally, for their financial support, we would like to thank the International Political Economy Program at the Mario Einaudi Center for International Studies at Cornell University, the Centre for International Governance Innovation in Waterloo, the Social Sciences and Humanities Research Council of Canada, and the Trudeau Foundation.

ERIC HELLEINER, WATERLOO, ONTARIO
JONATHAN KIRSHNER, ITHACA, NEW YORK

# CONTRIBUTORS

DAVID P. CALLEO is University Professor, Johns Hopkins University, Dean Acheson Professor and Director of the European Studies Department at its Paul H. Nitze School of Advanced International Studies.

BENJAMIN J. COHEN is Louis G. Lancaster Professor of International Political Economy in the Department of Political Science of the University of California, Santa Barbara.

MARCELLO DE CECCO holds the Chair of History of Money and Finance at the Scuola Normale Superiore di Pisa, Italy.

ERIC HELLEINER is CIGI Chair in International Governance and Professor in the Department of Political Science at the University of Waterloo.

HAROLD JAMES is Professor in the Department of History and Professor of International Affairs, Woodrow Wilson School of Public and International Affairs at Princeton University, and Marie Curie Professor at the European University Institute.

JONATHAN KIRSHNER is Professor of Government and Director of the Peace Studies Program at Cornell University.

RONALD I. MCKINNON is William D. Eberle Professor of International Economics at Stanford University.

HERMAN SCHWARTZ is Professor and Director of Graduate Studies in the Department of Politics at the University of Virginia.

# THE FUTURE OF THE DOLLAR

# 1

# THE FUTURE OF THE DOLLAR

## Whither the Key Currency?

Eric Helleiner and Jonathan Kirshner

The U.S. dollar's status as the leading international currency has been an enduring feature of the post-1945 world order. The greenback has provided the monetary foundation for the international economy and its worldwide role has both reflected and reinforced America's global preeminence. But questions about the future of the dollar's international standing are now heard with increasing frequency, and predictions of an impending erosion of the dollar's global status have now become commonplace. To take only one example, it used to be possible to enter the Taj Mahal for $15—now dollars are not welcome.

We have of course been down this road before—the demise of the dollar has been predicted by observers for decades, and U.S. government officials have spent sleepless nights worrying about the imminent collapse of the dollar and the subsequent implications for American power and the world economy—in the '60s, in the '70s, and in the '80s.[1] Yet the sky, sometimes almost stubbornly it seemed, would simply not fall. In defiance of the conventional wisdom, Richard Cooper stated plainly that "at the end of this decade the position of the dollar will not be very different from what it is now." That was

[1] For a good and representative tip of this iceberg, see Gavin 2004, 59–88; Zimmermann 2002, 105–26; Strange 1972; Bergsten 1975; Triffin 1978–79; Calleo 1982; Krugman 1984.

1973. The prediction was right on the mark—and Cooper is still keeping his powder dry, currently siding with those who do not see fundamental weakness in the dollar-centric international monetary order.[2]

And indeed, it is important to acknowledge that there are good reasons why the dollar has been so attractive, including the enormous size and institutional depth of the U.S. economy, its capital markets, economic growth, vitality and profitability, and, importantly, its political stability and unmatched physical security. It is also important not to confuse the value (or exchange rate) of the dollar with the extent of its international role. Predictions of the imminent erosion of the dollar's international position have invariably coincided with periods of dollar depreciation. Today's situation is no different. Past experience reminds us that the dollar's global role rests on broader foundations than its value at any given moment.

Given the inaccuracy of past predictions, how seriously should we take those who question today the dollar's future as an international currency? This book explores this question. It is, of course, impossible to predict the future with any certainty. But in the context of growing public interest, this book is designed to highlight the important contributions that scholars have been making, and can make, to the debate about the future of the dollar's international position. This book does not aim to marshal consensus in favor of one view. Indeed, we have deliberately invited contributions from distinguished scholars who have reached quite different conclusions about the issue. Some of the contributors are firmly in the "declinist" camp, while others believe the dollar's international role is sustainable. Our objective is to arrive at a clearer understanding of why scholars, especially those who have written with such authority and wisdom on monetary affairs and the international role of the dollar, can disagree so widely about this question in the contemporary context.

These disagreements, we suggest, stem from the fact that analysts draw on distinct underlying theoretical models that employ quite different sets of assumptions about the mechanisms by which currencies achieve and maintain an international position. These differences, along with alternative views about how to relate contemporary developments to specific models, account for the varying predictions. The goal of this book is not to try to persuade readers that one or another of these perspectives is the more convincing. Our aim instead is to uncover the bases for their disagreements in order to help readers make judgments for themselves. Identifying the sources of these dis-

---

[2] Cooper 1973, 4; 2005.

agreements, we hope, is a useful contribution to the debate as well as to scholarship on international monetary affairs more generally.


## The Dollar's International Role and Its Significance

Before examining these distinct models, let us first clarify the nature of the
subject itself. What does it mean to say that the dollar is an international currency?[3] Benjamin Cohen outlined six international roles of the dollar that
correspond to the three basic functions of money as well as a distinction between public and private use.[4] As a *medium of exchange*, it is used by the private sector to settle international economic transactions or by governments
as a vehicle currency to intervene in foreign exchange markets. As a *store of
value*, the dollar might be held as an asset by either foreign private actors for
investment purposes or by governments in the form of their official foreign
exchange reserves. Finally, as a *unit of account*, it might be used by market actors as a quotation currency for international trade and investment transactions, or by governments for either this purpose or as an anchor for pegging
the national currency.

In all of these respects, the dollar has been by far the world's most important international currency throughout the postwar period, and it remains in
a preeminent position today. As a medium of exchange, one indicator of its
dominant role is the fact that the dollar continued to be used on one side of
about 86 percent of all foreign exchange transactions at the time of the last
Bank for International Settlements survey of foreign exchange trading—
whereas its nearest rivals, the euro and yen, have shares of only 37 percent and
16.5 percent respectively.[5] As a store of value, the dollar still made up 64 percent of the world's official foreign exchange reserves at the end of 2007, compared to about 26.5 percent for the euro and below 5 percent for the yen. The
dollar's shares in 2006 of international bank deposits (48%) and the stock of
international debt securities (44%) also remained above those of the euro
(28% and 31%), with the yen again very far behind.[6] In addition, the dollar
continues to be by far most popular currency in which to denominate international trade, with the euro used prominently only in trade with the euro
area itself. As an official unit of account, the dollar is used as the anchor cur-

---

[3]  The following three paragraphs draw from Helleiner 2008.
[4]  Cohen 1971.
[5]  Bank for International Settlements 2007a.
[6]  Bertuch-Samuels and Ramlogan 2007; European Central Bank 2008.

rency in almost two-thirds of all the countries in the world that peg their currency in various ways, while the euro is the anchor in only about one-third (and they are almost all in Europe or in French-speaking African countries).[7]

One further indicator of the dollar's global role is its use *within* many countries' domestic monetary systems. Earlier literature on international currencies often assumed that all states maintained an exclusive national currency within the territory they governed and that "international" monetary transactions took place largely between these "territorial currency" zones. In the contemporary age, however, the lines between domestic and international have become increasingly blurred as territorial currencies have eroded in many parts of the world. In this context, many have highlighted how the dollar's international status today stems from its role as a medium of exchange, store of value, and unit of account not only in "inter-national" economic activity but also at the domestic level in "dollarized" countries such as Russia or many parts of Latin America.[8] The phenomenon of "euroization" is largely restricted to countries on the geographical edges of the euro zone.[9]

Given the various possible functions of an international currency, one might question whether it is possible to make any concise generalizations about the dollar's future. As we shall see, differing predictions on this subject do indeed sometimes reflect the fact that analysts are focusing on different aspects of the dollar's international role. Declinists are more likely to highlight the store of value functions, while their critics often cite its medium of exchange and unit of account functions. This raises the question of whether the distinct international functions of the dollar could increasingly experience a different fate in the future.[10] Some—including Marcello de Cecco in this book—suggest that they could. States and private actors could continue to rely heavily on the dollar as an international medium of exchange, while actively diversifying their reserve portfolios. At the same time, too wide a divergence is probably unlikely since each of the functions of an international currency tend to reinforce the others in important ways.[11]

Why should we care if the dollar's international role were to fade? Because the dollar has acted as the monetary foundation of the postwar international economic order, any diminution of its role raises the prospect of international economic instability. Some draw a lesson from the interwar period, that a more multipolar international monetary system will inherently be more un-

[7] Bertuch-Samuels and Ramlogan 2007.
[8] See esp. Cohen 1998.
[9] European Central Bank 2008.
[10] For a discussion of the relationship between the reserve and vehicle roles of international money, see Roosa and Hirsch 1966, 3–6.
[11] See, for example, Krugman 1984; Chinn and Frankel 2005.

stable than a hegemonic one. Others, however, argue that a multipolar currency order may be more stable since no one leader can exploit its hegemonic position. But even advocates of this latter position usually acknowledge that the transition phase from hegemony to multipolarity is likely to bring many risks for the international economy.[12]

Since the U.S. dollar's global role has helped boost U.S. hegemony in the postwar period, any decline in that role will also have important distributional consequences among states in the international system. What precise benefits has the dollar's role provided the United States?[13] To begin with, when foreigners have held dollars, they have provided the equivalent of an interest-free (in the case of Federal Reserve notes) or low-interest (in the case of U.S. Treasury securities) loan to the United States. According to some estimates, in recent years this "seigniorage" profit has totalled over $20 billion per year (Cohen 2008, 258). The dollar's international role has also reduced exchange rate risks for U.S. firms involved in international commerce, and U.S. banks have gained a competitive advantage in dollarized financial markets because of their privileged access to the Federal Reserve's resources.

The dollar's global role has also strengthened the capacity of the United States both to delay and deflect adjustments to its current account deficits.[14] The power to delay has stemmed from the greater ease the United States has in financing its deficits because of the dollar's international role. The power to deflect the costs of adjustment onto foreigners has partly reflected the ability of the United States to depreciate the currency in which it has borrowed funds from foreigners. At the same time, the depreciation of the dollar has also generated political pressures for expansionary policies within countries dependent on dollar-based markets, policies that in turn have helped the United States correct its trade position by expanding exports. Countries that tried to resist this "dollar weapon" by supporting the dollar usually found themselves pursuing expansionary policies anyway because of the difficulties of sterilizing accumulating dollar reserves. Through these channels, U.S. policymakers were able, since the early 1970s, to indirectly prompt foreigners to absorb much of the burden of adjustment to U.S. current account deficits.[15]

In addition, the international position of the dollar has bolstered the U.S. state's coercive power in more direct ways. Countries relying on the dollar are vulnerable to the United States because of their dependence on access to U.S.-based dollar clearing networks. The United States has exploited this vulnera-

[12] For these debates, see, for example, Einzig 1935; Rowland 1976; and Walter 1991.
[13] See chapter 8 for a more detailed discussion.
[14] For the distinction between the power to delay and deflect, see Cohen 2006.
[15] See, for example, Henning 1987, 2006; Kawasaki 1992.

bility effectively as a tool of both foreign policy (e.g., vis-à-vis Panama in the mid-1980s) and to encourage cooperation with U.S. regulatory goals (e.g., anti-money-laundering regulations).[16] The dollar's role also has given the United States a uniquely important role in international financial crisis management. As the sole producer of dollars, the United States has an unparalleled ability to make advances of dollars to foreign governments or to private financial institutions during crises.

Finally, the dollar's international position may also boost U.S. influence in some less tangible ways. To some, the dollar's global standing acts as an important symbol of U.S. influence worldwide.[17] Others highlight how the worldwide use of the dollar may transform the interests of foreigners in subtle ways that encourage them to support the United States. By encouraging commerce with the United States, for example, the dollar's international role may strengthen domestic economic actors in foreign countries that advocate closer ties with the United States. Similarly, as foreign governments accumulate dollar reserves, they acquire an interest in the stability and value of the currency in ways that may encourage a certain identification of their interests with those of the United States.[18]

In short, the dollar's international role has generated substantial economic and political benefits for the United States. To be sure, there have been some costs too. The ability of U.S. monetary authorities to conduct monetary policy has been compromised. The United States has also become more vulnerable to a dumping of dollars in the event that foreigners suddenly find a more attractive, alternative international currency. The risk of this kind of external constraint was highlighted by the British experience with its "sterling overhang" after World War II. Overall, however, there is no question that the dollar's international standing has provided an important boost to the U.S. economic and political position in the world. For this reason, any decline in the dollar's international standing will erode U.S. economic and political influence, with important consequences for Americans and for the rest of the world.

### Three Distinct Models

Will it happen? And why is there so little agreement on the answer to this question? We have already noted that contrasting views on the dollar's future

---

[16]  For the former, see Kirshner 1995. For the latter, see Helleiner 1999.

[17]  Cohen 2004; Helleiner 2003a, 2003b.

[18]  Kirshner 1995 describes these transformations of interests as a kind of "entrapment" that can result from participation in a dollar-based international currency system.

sometimes simply reflect a focus on different aspects of its international role. But more importantly they stem from fundamentally different sets of assumptions about the mechanisms by which currencies achieve and maintain international standing. We argue that there are three distinct sets of such assumptions that dominate the literature on the future of the dollar: those embodied in *market-based, instrumental,* and *geopolitical* approaches to the subject.[19] Within each of these distinct approaches, we also highlight how there are often sharp disagreements that stem from different interpretations of how contemporary real-world developments relate to these underlying assumptions. In highlighting these distinct schools of thought, we recognize that many scholars—including the contributors to this book—employ a mix of these approaches in their analyses of the dollar's future. We believe, however, that it is useful to isolate each approach in order to identify the sources of contrasting views.

### Market-Based Approaches

*Market-based* approaches are found most frequently in the writings of economists.[20] They assume that the dollar's future as an international currency will be largely determined by market actors making judgments about the inherent economic attractiveness of the dollar vis-à-vis other currencies. The attractiveness of any currency as an international medium of exchange, store of value, and/or unit of account is most commonly associated with three factors: confidence, liquidity, and transactional networks.[21]

Currencies that inspire confidence in their stable value are more likely to be used by market actors at the international level, particularly as a store of value. This kind of confidence, in turn, will stem from the past record and sound macroeconomic fundamentals in the issuing country as well as more intangible political variables such as the issuer's domestic political stability or global power. British sterling inspired confidence abroad for many of these reasons during its nineteenth century heyday, and this confidence then eroded gradually in the twentieth century in the face of Britain's economic troubles and declining power, as well as the various sterling devaluations from the 1930s onward.

---

[19] The three sets of assumptions are by no means exhaustive—we have highlighted them only because they are the most prominent views.

[20] Some portions of this section are drawn from Helleiner 2008.

[21] For a detailed survey of recent writing about the economic determinants of international currencies, see also Lim 2006. This recent literature builds on earlier economic writings around the time of the collapse of the Bretton Woods exchange rate system, e.g., Cohen 1971a; Swodoba 1969; Kindleberger 1967.

In the contemporary context, those predicting the U.S. dollar's decline as an international currency suggest that a similar fate awaits the greenback. Estimates about the future value of the dollar are based on expectations regarding its internal and external price—that is, expectations about the inflation rate and the exchange rate. Anticipating future inflation is a tricky business, wrapped up in intangibles such as "credibility," but the very large and sustained U.S. federal budget deficits—currently projected far into the horizon—warn of the threat of future inflation. More straightforward if still a bit murky in the particulars of when and how much, the massive imbalances in American external accounts strongly suggest that the dollar is more likely on a long-run trajectory of depreciation rather than of appreciation.[22]

Beyond these indicators looms the larger concern of whether the U.S. current account position is sustainable. American trade deficits have spent the twenty-first century shattering record after record, surpassing $750 billion in 2006, and as a percentage of GDP, the U.S. current account deficits reached annual levels at or above 5 percent, by a considerable amount the highest levels in U.S. history (although they headed lower in 2007 as the U.S. economy entered the recession). Total U.S. net external liabilities, about 25 percent of GDP in 2005, are projected to reach 50 percent in 2015 and 100 percent by 2030. These are alarming figures. Most other countries would find their backs to the economic wall under such circumstances.[23] Obviously, the United States is very much not "most other countries," and the American economy is not most other economies. For a variety of reasons, the United States will be able to sustain external deficits for longer and at higher levels than would other countries. But many question whether the United States can sustain such deficits and debts indefinitely.[24]

The dollar has of course faced similar challenges at various moments since the breakdown of the Bretton Woods exchange rate system in the early 1970s without its international status eroding. But one thing that kept the dollar on its perch in the past was that those disenchanted with the dollar had nowhere else to go—whatever shortcomings it might have had, the dollar was the only game in town. With the emergence of the euro, however, many believe that the dollar is finally facing its first real competitor. For the first time in the postwar period, confidence in the dollar is eroding in an environment where a credible alternative currency exists, a currency that is managed by a central

---

[22] See Bergsten and Williamson 2003, 2004.

[23] For developing countries, as a rule of thumb, net external liabilities of 40% are considered a "crisis threshold"—the point at which the imbalance will trigger a financial crisis.

[24] Obstfeld and Rogoff 2004, 1, 5, 7, 18; Mussa 2005, 175–76, 186, 194–95, 201–3; Cline 2005, 3, 66, 85, 99, 154, 168–71, 275–77; Edwards 2005, 2–3, 11–12, 26, 40–42.

bank with a much stronger mandate than the U.S. Federal Reserve to pursue price stability as its central objective.

Others within the market-based approach are less certain that confidence in the dollar will erode so quickly. U.S. current account deficits could improve, especially in light of the country's deflating asset bubble and economic slow-down. More generally, the enduring military power and domestic political stability of the United States boosts market confidence in the dollar, while un-certainties about European political cooperation undermine confidence in the euro. George Tavlas also argues that foreign confidence in the dollar has been linked to deeper structural economic factors that contribute to the relative sta-bility of its exchange rate over the longer term, such as the fact that the United States is subject to relatively few external economic shocks and is able to ad-just easily to these shocks.[25] Pierre-Olivier Gourinchas and Hélène Rey argue that confidence in the dollar has been sustained because the United States, de-spite its record external debt, continues to earn a higher return on its gross ex-ternal assets than it pays in external liabilities (primarily because it enjoys a risk premium on borrowing). If, however, the United States began paying more for its gross liabilities than it was earning on its assets at some point in the future, they suggest that foreign confidence could begin to erode.[26]

The international use of a currency is also bolstered if the issuing country has very liquid and open financial markets. These markets make the currency an attractive one in which to hold assets and in which to transact for market actors. In the nineteenth century, the liquidity of London's financial markets played a major role in boosting sterling's international standing as a store of value, medium of exchange, and unit of account. Similarly, in the last few decades, the unparalleled depth and openness of U.S. financial markets has been a central pillar for the dollar's international role.

The fact that Japan and Germany were unwilling during the 1970s and 1980s to transform their financial systems along U.S. lines also provides much of the explanation for why the yen and deutsche mark did not challenge the dollar's international role in a significant way in that period. The underde-veloped and regulated nature of Chinese financial markets today ensures that the renminbi is very far away from becoming an international currency. Many economists argue that the euro today, however, poses more of a challenge to the dollar because it is backed by an integrated European financial space that increasingly rivals U.S. financial markets in size, depth, and sophistication. But others argue that euro-zone financial markets remain quite fragmented,

---

[25] Tavlas 1997.
[26] Gourinchas and Rey 2005.

and, in the absence of a single fiscal authority, crisis management remains decentralized and there is no central European equivalent to the all-important U.S. Treasury bill market.[27]

The third determinant of international currency standing identified by market-based approaches relates to the extensiveness of the issuing country's transactional networks in the world economy. The more extensive the networks, the more likely foreigners are to use the country's currency in their international trade and investment activities. Even when foreigners do not have direct links with the issuing country, they will be tempted to use its currency because the country's worldwide transactional networks guarantee the currency's broad acceptability. Charles Kindleberger was among the first to highlight this link, arguing that the choice of an international currency was made "not on merit, or moral worth, but on size."[28] Some economists have since shown empirically how changes in a country's share of the world product and trade influence the international role of the country's currency in areas such as reserve holdings.[29] More generally, others have argued that the most important reason for the dollar's enduring international role is the overwhelming size of the United States within the world economy or the global reach of its corporations.[30] Some economic historians have also found evidence from the late nineteenth century that trade size is a powerful driver of currency leadership.[31]

These empirical studies focusing on country size in fact understate the significance of transactional networks. As Paul Krugman has noted, there is a kind of "circular causation" encouraging a leading international currency to become even more prominent over time because people find benefits in using a currency that is used by others.[32] These network externalities mean that an international currency can assume a global role that is well out of proportion to the issuing country's size in the world economy. They may also lead a currency to retain its international standing for a long time after the issuing country's position in the global economy has contracted. A number of economists have cited this inertia of incumbency to explain why sterling's decline as an international currency was so slow and prolonged.[33]

Will the same inertia slow the erosion of the U.S. dollar's international

---

[27] For these debates, see, for example, Cohen 2004; Schinasi 2005; Galati and Wooldridge 2006; Bertuch-Samuels and Ramlogan 2007; Papaioannou and Portes 2008.
[28] Kindleberger 1967, 11.
[29] Chinn and Frankel 2005.
[30] For the former, see Bergsten 2005. For the latter, see Frank 2003.
[31] Flandreau and Jobst 2005.
[32] Krugman 1984, 272.
[33] See, for example, Krugman 1984; Bergsten 2005.

standing? Some believe it will,[34] but others have suggested that the possibility should not be overstated. Barry Eichengreen notes that network externalities may be influential in preserving the dollar's international role as a medium of exchange in realms such as foreign exchange trading, but they are less relevant to the dollar's function as a store of value where economic incentives in fact encourage diversification for risk-aversion purposes. He also argues that the power of network externalities may be diminishing as financial markets become ever more sophisticated in ways that reduce the costs of using many currencies and switching between them.[35]

Even if inertia is significant, there could come a point when the continued usefulness of the dollar's international role is suddenly questioned. Krugman notes that this was the experience for sterling and he predicts that the dollar too could reach a "critical point, leading to an abrupt unraveling of its international role."[36] In their analysis of the determinants of official reserves, Menzie Chinn and Jeffrey Frankel argue that such a point could be reached if the euro zone expanded well beyond the economic size of the United States by including all EU members, particularly if this development coincided with a further depreciation of the dollar.[37]

In sum, there is no clear consensus that emerges from *market-based* approaches to the study of the dollar's future. Although some predict that the dollar's international role is about to decline dramatically, others foresee little change in its status in the coming years. These disagreements reflect the different weighting placed on the relative importance of the variables of confidence, liquidity, and transactional networks as well as on different interpretations of the significance of current developments. What binds together analysts within this approach, however, is the assumption that the dollar's future as an international currency will be determined primarily by its inherent economic attractiveness to market actors as a medium of exchange, unit of account, and store of value. As Edwin Truman puts it, "It is important to appreciate that the choice of an international currency today is made by the private sector via market forces, not by the public sector by government decisions or fiat."[38]

---

[34] Bergsten 2005, 34; McKinnon 2005a, 247.
[35] Eichengreen 2006.
[36] Krugman 1984, 272.
[37] Chinn and Frankel 2005.
[38] Truman 2005, 63n17.

### Instrumental Approaches: Bretton Woods II and Monetary Anchors

In making this point, Truman was critiquing a second prominent approach that we call the *instrumental* approach. It gives more attention to the role of public authorities in determining the dollar's international role. Analysts in this school of thought suggest that the dollar's future as an international currency will be strongly influenced by choices made by foreign governments about whether to continue to peg, formally or informally, their currencies to the dollar and to hold dollar reserves. These decisions, in turn, are seen to center around their instrumental calculations of some specified broader economic benefits that stem from this support for the dollar.

One of the most prominent examples of this approach comes in writings of Michael Dooley, David Folkerts-Landau, and Peter Garber who drew a parallel between the contemporary situation and the Bretton Woods era of the late 1950s to 1971.[39] In the earlier "Bretton Woods I" era, Japan and western European countries pegged their currencies formally to the dollar, and they acquired larger and larger dollar reserves as their economic recovery accelerated. In the view of Dooley et al., these countries gave official support to the dollar's international role because this allowed them to maintain undervalued currencies vis-à-vis the dollar, thereby boosting their exports, particularly to the United States. At the same time, the United States accepted this situation because the foreign financial support was cheap and useful to the country's broader ambitions in this period.

Since the early 1990s, Dooley et al. suggest that a new "periphery" of countries, primarily in East Asia, has offered growing official support to the dollar in a similar manner. This "Bretton Woods II" is a looser international monetary arrangement; most of these countries have adopted more informal pegs to the dollar. But according to Dooley et al., the motivation has been similar. These countries have set out to pursue an export-oriented development strategy that relies on deliberately undervalued currencies and access to the buoyant U.S. market.[40] Within a relatively short time, these countries have accumulated massive dollar reserves—Japan, China, Taiwan, and South Korea alone hold well over *two trillion* dollars—which have provided crucial foreign support for the international position of the dollar in a manner that is remi-

---

[39]  Dooley, Folkerts-Landau, and Garber 2003, 2005.
[40]  Dooley and Garber 2005 also develop an argument that dollar reserves are being accumulated by foreign governments such as China's as a kind of collateral to encourage foreign private investment in the country. As Eichengreen 2006 notes, however, there is little evidence for this thesis and it also does not apply well to large dollar holders such as Japan or South Korea where there is no real risk of expropriation of foreign assets.

niscent of the 1960s.[41] The United States is also portrayed as upholding its end of the bargain by keeping its markets open to East Asian exports, a position that is said to reflect the lobbying influence of U.S. businesses with plants in China as well as a broader recognition of the benefits stemming from cheap imports and low-cost foreign funding for its deficits.

A different variant of the *instrumental* approach has been put forward by Ronald McKinnon. While sharing the Bretton Woods II school's assumption that the dollar's international position is heavily dependent on the decisions of foreign governments to maintain dollar pegs and reserve holdings, McKinnon rejects Dooley et al.'s "mercantilist" interpretation of their behavior. Instead, he suggests that foreign governments have pegged to the dollar and accumulated dollar reserves as a way of gaining a *monetary anchor* for their countries' macroeconomic policies and price levels.

He argues that the incentives to embrace the dollar as a monetary anchor are particularly strong for countries experiencing inflation and where domestic monetary policy is complicated by underdeveloped or malfunctioning financial markets. This was the situation experienced by many European countries and Japan after the war and McKinnon argues that their most efficient route to domestic price stability was to fix their currencies formally to the U.S. dollar. To maintain these pegs, the monetary authorities of these countries accumulated dollar reserves. More recently, he argues that many Asian and other developing countries have embraced a soft peg to the dollar for a similar reason.

What is the future of the dollar's international role from the perspective of either the "Bretton Woods II" or "monetary anchor" version of the *instrumental* approach? As with the *market-based* approach, there is no consensus answer. The source of disagreements centers around the question of whether foreign governments will continue to perceive the broad economic benefits described above from supporting the dollar. From a monetary anchor perspective, as long as the United States maintains price stability and thus remains a trustworthy monetary anchor, foreign governments such as China will maintain their dollar pegs and continue to accumulate dollar reserves indefinitely. But if the United States begins to experience inflation or the dollar devalues dramatically, these foreign governments will be more likely to cut their links with the dollar, seriously undermining its international role.

A Bretton Woods II perspective also anticipates that foreign official support of the dollar could last a long time; Dooley et al. suggest that the trade-based system as it currently operates may survive for many more years. From

---

[41]   Genberg et al. 2005; Murray and Labonte 2005; Burdekin 2006; Truman and Wong 2006.

this standpoint, neither official dollar reserve holders abroad nor the United States have reason to upset the existing arrangement given the mutual economic benefits it provides. Although some have described the relationship as a "balance of financial terror," Dooley and Garber suggest that it is better characterized as one of "mutually beneficial gains from trade."[42]

Others who accept the underlying assumptions of the Dooley et al. version of the Bretton Woods II model are less certain. If the U.S. market became less important to East Asian exporters—either because of a reorientation of their trade or the U.S. recession—this might undermine the economic rationale for foreign governments to continue supporting the dollar.[43] Skeptics also highlight how the dollar's depreciation would raise the opportunity cost of holding massive dollar reserves. They call attention to the enormous size of the financial losses incurred by countries such as China and Japan to their enormous dollar holdings whenever the dollar depreciates.[44]

One further trigger for an unraveling of the Bretton Woods II arrangement could come from the United States itself. Growing protectionist pressures in the United States today call into question the *willingness* of the United States to provide an open market to the export-oriented, dollar-supporting countries. More generally, focusing solely on *foreign* perceptions of the sustainability of the dollar order overlooks the fact that, as Andrew Walter has argued, monetary orders are often toppled by the hegemon in the driver's seat, as opposed to the disgruntled passengers. American presidents, David Calleo notes, have never hesitated to abuse the international monetary system in order to pursue domestic economic goals.[45] Bretton Woods I was brought down by similar pressures, which culminated in President Richard Nixon's sudden imposition of import surcharges in August 1971. There is now considerable support within the United States for unilateral protectionist measures against countries that are deemed to be keeping their currencies artificially low, with China now as the main target. Back then, U.S. allies responded to the Nixon shock by largely accepting U.S. policy preferences and a move to a pure dollar standard. But if the United States were to repeat this kind of policy today, the Chinese government and others might be prompted to reevaluate the larger economic benefits of their support for the dollar standard.

---

[42] Dooley and Garber 2005, 148.

[43] Gray 2004 highlights the importance to the U.S. dollar's standing of the United States acting as the key locomotive in boosting world aggregate demand.

[44] See, for example, Goldstein and Lardy 2005, 9.

[45] Walter 1991; Calleo 1982.

## Geopolitical Approaches

The final prominent approach to the question of the dollar's international future shares the assumption of the *instrumental* notion that states will play a key role in determining the dollar's future as an international currency. But its conception of their role is different. Often put forward by international relations scholars, this approach assumes that governments' backing for an international currency can be linked to broader geopolitical motivations and power considerations. For IR scholars, and especially realists like Robert Gilpin, "every international monetary regime rests on a particular international order," and it is impossible to understand how and why the international financial order operates, and why it might unravel, without close attention to those international political foundations.[46]

Susan Strange was an earlier pioneer of this *geopolitical* approach in her writings about the future of sterling as an international currency in the early 1970s. She highlighted how sterling always derived at least part of its global standing from the global power of the British state. This was most obvious in British colonies where backing for sterling reflected Britain's political domination over these territories. But it was also apparent among independent countries that were members of the sterling area, many of which backed sterling's international role as part of a set of broader political relationships—particularly security relationships—with Britain. At the time, Strange called on scholars to devote more attention to the significance of the relationship between high politics and support for international currencies: "The coincidence of close monetary and close military relations is sufficiently common that it is odd how little it has been remarked upon, either by economists or political commentators."[47]

Marcello de Cecco was one of the first scholars to explore the political underpinnings of the supposedly "automatic" functioning of the classical gold standard in his book *Money and Empire: The International Gold Standard, 1890–1914*. Strange's research agenda was also taken up by many scholars examining the dollar's international position during the Bretton Woods system and after. Historians have shown how the holding of dollar reserves by key countries such as West Germany during the 1960s was linked explicitly to broader bilateral security relations with the United States.[48] With the breakdown of the Bretton Woods system, U.S. officials sought to preserve the dollar's international role once again through the use of diplomacy, this time

---

[46] Gilpin 1987, 119.
[47] Strange 1971b, 18.
[48] See, for example, Gavin 2004; Calleo 1982; Zimmermann 2002.

involving key military allies such as with Saudi Arabia after the oil shock of 1973.[49] Other scholars have highlighted the fact that one of the most consistent supporters of the dollar's international role since the 1960s has been Japan, one of the closest military allies of the United States.[50]

As foreign holdings of dollar reserves have mushroomed since the turn of this century, the question of the relationship between geopolitics and the dollar's international role has arisen again prominently. The *instrumental* approach explains growing foreign support for the dollar on the basis of economic goals, but the *geopolitical* approach explores how this support may be linked to deeper political motivations and relationships. To date, scholars have produced little evidence of any explicit high politics deals between the United States and dollar- supporting countries. But this is not to say that implicit understandings are not in play. Some of the key official support for the dollar today comes from countries—such as Japan, South Korea, and members of the Gulf Cooperation Council—who rely heavily on the United States for military protection.[51] Even the continuing support of countries that are not close allies, such as China, may derive from the political motivations of keeping relations with the United States on good terms.

What predictions for the dollar's international future emerge from a geopolitical approach? Again, there is no clear consensus. On the one hand, the political base of support for the dollar today seems more fragile in geopolitical terms than in the past. In the previous two modern episodes of addressing disequilibrium in the dollar and global currency disorder—the U.S. closing of the gold window in 1971 and the coordinated depreciation of the dollar via the Plaza Accord in 1985—two factors, no longer present, helped frame monetary conflicts by assuring some level of *political* commitment to the dollar. First, all of the main players in both 1971 and 1985, in Western Europe and Japan, were political allies of the United States. Second, many of those allies were also essentially military dependencies of the United States.

But the resolution of the current (even larger) global macroeconomic imbalances—whether by hard landing or soft—will be coordinated (or not) with less of this political safety net and in the absence of an instinctive bias to rally politically (if through gritted teeth) around the maintenance of a global dollar order. In future monetary negotiations and during currency crises, included in prominent seats at the table will be states that are military adversaries of the United States (in particular, China), and by allies, especially in Europe, that are no longer bound to the Americans by anti-Soviet glue, wary

---

[49] Spiro 1999.
[50] Murphy 2006; Posen 2008.
[51] For Japan, see Murphy 2006.

of aspects of American power, foreign policy, and unilateralism, and harboring currency ambitions of their own.

On the other hand, concerns about China's role also may overlook the extent to which Chinese policymakers see their country's rise taking place within preexisting—that is, U.S.-led—global institutional structures.[52] Also reinforcing this countercase is the fact that the dollar's chief rivals have their own geopolitical difficulties. Political rivalry in Asia will complicate the emergence of either the Chinese yuan or the Japanese yen as potential rivals to the dollar. The more plausible euro also comes with its own assortment of political baggage. Adam Posen also has argued that the inability of the euro-zone countries to project geostrategic influence beyond their immediate neighborhood will inhibit the euro's challenge to the dollar elsewhere.[53]

The fact that the United States is the overwhelmingly dominant geopolitical power in the world bodes well for the dollar's enduring international position. Indeed, the British showed how it was possible to bolster their currency's international standing through explicit bargains with other states. If the United States chose to bolster the dollar's international position through negotiation and by putting pressure on foreign governments, it can draw on unparalleled power resources to do so.

## Arguments of the Chapters

Predicting the dollar's future as an international currency is thus far from a straightforward exercise. Distinct sets of assumptions about how currencies achieve and maintain international standing can generate very different projections. And even when these assumptions are shared, there can be further disagreements about how to relate them to contemporary developments. The three broad approaches outlined above, and the disagreements within them, are summarized schematically in table 1.1.

With this framework, we are able to locate the arguments of the chapters that follow. As we noted initially, the purpose of this book is not to come to a definitive conclusion about the future of the dollar, but rather to uncover the roots of disagreement between scholars on this issue. The authors of these chapters disagree not just about whether the dollar's international role is sustainable or not. Within the "declinist" camp, there are also disagreements about how quickly the dollar's role could erode. Within the "sustainability"

---

[52] Ikenberry 2008.
[53] Posen 2008.

TABLE 1.1.
Contrasting approaches to the dollar's future as an international currency

| What future for the dollar's international role? | Determinants of international currency standing | | | |
|---|---|---|---|---|
| | Market-based | Instrumental | | Geopolitical |
| | | Bretton Woods II | Monetary anchor | |
| Sustainable | • Dollar still relatively more economically attractive vis-à-vis confidence, liquidity, transnational networks<br>• Inertia | • Mutual gains from existing situation | • U.S. price stability | • U.S. power<br>• Geopolitical rivalries in other regions |
| Decline | • U.S. deficits/debt<br>• Euro's stability; size of eurozone economy and financial markets<br>• tipping points | • Foreign de-coupling from U.S. economy<br>• Foreign financial losses on dollar holdings<br>• Risk of U.S. protectionism | • U.S. inflation and depreciation | • Loss of alliance glue<br>• Growing political reaction against dollar hegemony |

camp there are differences as to how easily the dollar order could be upset, or how crucial it is that some public policies be modestly adjusted to assure continued smooth sailing. All of these disagreements stem from differences in both the underlying assumptions about the determinants of international currencies and specific interpretations of contemporary developments. Each perspective identifies key variables to monitor, and each suggests, implicitly or explicitly, the reasons why things might turn out differently. The monetary anchor perspective, for example, holds that the current system *should* be sustainable—but recognizes that policy blunders, like protectionism and misguided exchange rate conflict, might bring the system down.

Harold James (chapter 2) is a dollar optimist, and makes the strongest statement in anticipation of continuity in international monetary affairs and the dollar's international role in this book. He places great emphasis on the influence of market forces, and, with regard to such, sees the dollar's woes as exaggerated and the strength of the American economy underappreciated by the dollar pessimists. James also has confidence in contemporary central bankers and their ability to assure monetary stability in general and the dollar as a reliable store of value in particular; it is likely as well that any crisis that does emerge will be managed and ultimately defused. He finds the Bretton Woods II hypothesis compelling, the euro limited and relatively uncertain in its appeal, and is skeptical about the importance of overt political pressure in sustaining the monetary order. Instead, the dollar will continue to stand on the inherent attractiveness of the U.S. economy—its size and stability and ability to serve a safe haven in times of both geopolitical and economic distress, and its ability to provide an outlet for the large amounts of capital generated by high savings rates abroad. James shares with observers such as Richard Cooper the wisdom of those who have heard the cry of wolf so many times in the past—as James notes, the dollar's share of international reserves fell from 73 percent in 1978 to below 50 percent by the end of the 1980s, but then rebounded to 71 percent at the turn of the century. As long as the United States remains the world's largest concentration of political and military might and economic potential, and James sees little reason why it won't, the dollar will remain the world's currency.

Ronald McKinnon (chapter 3) is also a dollar optimist (if somewhat more qualified than James). As noted above, McKinnon's chapter articulates a distinct instrumental perspective where the key cog in the machine is not a mercantilist trade strategy, which implies, to some extent, the potential for conflict, but rather a strategy rooted in macroeconomics, through soft pegs to the dollar in order to assure domestic monetary stability. Central to this perspective is the argument that exchange rate adjustments will have little practical effect on the trade balance, which is largely a function of differential savings rates between states. In this interpretation of the relationship between Asian and American economies, and of U.S. current account deficits, there is no reason to believe that these arrangements cannot continue indefinitely.

McKinnon is agnostic as to the significance of America's military, commercial, or political hegemony—in his view, as long as the United States maintains price stability and thus remains a trustworthy monetary anchor, McKinnon believes foreign governments such as China will maintain their dollar pegs and continue to accumulate dollar reserves. At the same time, he predicts that if the United States began to experience inflation or the dollar is devalued dramatically, these foreign governments would cut their links with the dollar as it ceased to serve as a useful monetary anchor. McKinnon therefore shares James's optimism about sustainability, and expresses confidence in the U.S. Federal Reserve as the guardian of the greenback, but unlike his fellow optimist he does see danger in the inadequate U.S. savings rate. Worse, the whole system could come tumbling down if the American political system misinterprets its trade deficits as an exchange rate problem rather than a consumption problem, and turns toward protectionism, which McKinnon recognizes as an all-too-real possibility.

Eric Helleiner (chapter 4), Herman Schwartz (chapter 5), and Marcello de Cecco (chapter 6) occupy a middle ground, expressing more qualified and ambiguous expectations about the future of the dollar. Helleiner and Schwartz articulate the basis for the dollar's sustainability but are wary of visible dangers, while de Cecco, drawing on historical analogy, is more suggestive of change.

Eric Helleiner explores how politics influences the international role of currencies by revisiting and extending the distinction between "top" and "negotiated" currencies that Susan Strange developed in her seminal study, *Sterling and British Policy* (1971). In the coming years, Helleiner believes that the dollar is likely to remain the dominant top currency; that is, a currency whose international standing is derived from the kinds of economic factors identified by *market-based* analyses. His reasoning is that the political foundations of the economic factors that sustain the dollar's top currency status are stronger than those of any potential challenger currency. Where the dollar is more vulnerable, Helleiner suggests, is with respect to its partially negotiated status. Negotiated currencies are currencies whose international role is supported by foreign governments for reasons that do not stem from the currency's inherent economic attractiveness, such as those identified by the Bretton Woods II and geopolitical approaches. Helleiner suggests that the political considerations and relationships that support the dollar's negotiated status are potentially more fragile, both from the side of follower states and from the United States itself. If a challenge to the dollar's international position is to emerge, it will most likely to stem from these political sources.

Schwartz and de Cecco each suggest novel interpretations of the international role of the dollar and the sources of possible changes to that role, offering insights that broaden our understanding of the future of the international monetary order. For Schwartz, the booming U.S. housing market was the crucial element in the resurgence of the American economy (and the international status of the dollar) in the 1990s. The housing boom, facilitated by the distinct structure of the relevant U.S. financial markets, both attracted foreign capital and contributed to America's relatively strong economic performance, a virtuous cycle that further bolstered the appeal of the dollar to market actors as well as governments in developing Asia driven by Bretton Woods II motivations. From a market-based approach, Schwartz holds that despite the problems the American economy may currently face, top currency status rests on relative, not absolute, economic performance, as this is the metric that investors focus on. Thus, although the housing wave has now crested, and the level of U.S. consumption is indeed problematic, dollar primacy will be sustained by the relative attractiveness of the U.S. economy as long as it grows relatively faster than its would-be European rivals. Schwartz also finds support for the dollar following the logic of the Bretton Woods II machinery for developing Asia, and he also argues that the breadth and composition of housing debt within the country has broadened anti-inflationary sentiment in the United States, a key variable for the sustainability of the dollar order identified by James and McKinnon.

De Cecco is similar to Schwartz in stressing uncertainty about the future, but ultimately he is clearly more pessimistic about the fate of the greenback. From a historical angle, he throws new light on the dollar question by exploring an analogy not with the interwar period (which has naturally attracted the attention of many scholars as the most recent example of a leaderless, contested international monetary order) but instead with an appeal to the period before World War I. Then as now, the leading currency was under pressure; then as now, new large industrial economies were emerging on the scene; and then as now, de Cecco argues, the international monetary order was devolving from hegemony toward an odd duopoly, with the leading currency uneasily coexisting with a nonnational, attractive reserve asset—then gold, now the euro. The period before the Great War was also characterized by financial fragility and threatened by a mercantilist-protectionist turn, two factors arguably present today as well. These lessons of the past suggest a darker future vulnerable to political conflict and financial crisis, regardless of the specific destiny of the dollar.

Benjamin Cohen (chapter 7), David Calleo (chapter 8), and Jonathan Kirshner (chapter 9) are more pessimistic about the trajectory of the dollar's international role. For Cohen, market factors are key and monetary preferences sticky, and thus the dollar enjoys considerable advantages in sustaining its position of primacy. But he also considers the persistent buildup of America's debt unsustainable, and concludes that this will result in a gradual cumulative erosion of the dollar's appeal, which will create opportunities for competitors to the dollar. However, Cohen does not see a viable candidate capable of even coming close to filling the dollar's international role for the foreseeable future, and thus he anticipates a leaderless currency system. Such a system will invite rivalry for currency leadership, as states will bid for greater international influence by extending the reach of their currencies not only in the global marketplace but vis-à-vis foreign governments. Cohen anticipates that the Middle East and Asia will be likely monetary battlegrounds, featuring vigorous skirmishes and challenges to the dollar in those regions that will fortunately fall short of active economic conflict.

Calleo is in general agreement with Cohen on the economic issues involved, but emphasizes, in discussing causes and consequences, geopolitical factors. In particular, Calleo notes the absence of the strategic safety net of cold war imperatives that protected the dollar in the past. The dollar has suffered repeated rounds of pressure for decades, Calleo argues, because of U.S. foreign policy ambitions and unwillingness to pay its geopolitical bills or perhaps the United States has simply been unable to resist the temptation that the key currency role of the dollar has afforded in this regard. But the Vietnam War and the cold war and most recently the ambitions of unipolarity each stretched that ability to the breaking point. With the surge in post-9/11 military spending, Calleo now sees all the economic and political variables pointing in the wrong direction: the dollar is being left vulnerable by the Bush tax cuts reversing the Clinton surpluses, falling American savings rates, the current subprime mortgage crisis, and the emergence of a plausible alternative reserve currency, the euro. Calleo also expects that the continued depreciation of the dollar will recast assessments about its attractiveness, and that China will also find it unwise to indefinitely accumulate vast quantities of dollars. All of the arrows, it would seem, point in the direction of states disengaging, to some extent, from their relationship with the dollar.

Kirshner is perhaps the most pessimistic of all, anticipating a diminution of the dollar's international role, as he sees the erosion of all of the foundations that support the international role of the dollar—the vulnerabilities implied by the dollar's accounts, the emergence of a potential peer competitor to the dollar, and a change in the political foundations of the international monetary order, from one managed by political friends and military allies to one negotiated by political adversaries and even potential rivals. With Cohen, Kirshner sees the U.S. current account deficit (and Bretton Woods II) as unsustainable and thus anticipates the emergence of competitors; like Calleo, he places great emphasis on the political foundations of the international monetary order, and in particular the absence of geopolitical imperatives on the part of others to bolster the dollar in times of crisis. Kirshner parts company with his fellow dollar pessimists with his expectation that the most likely outcome is a sudden, rather than gradual, change in the dollar's international role, emphasizing, à la de Cecco, the high risk of financial crisis in the contemporary system (although his underlying expectations remains pessimistic—even in the absence of such a crisis, he expects the greenback's relative international role to diminish gradually over time). Kirshner's chapter also takes the opportunity to consider most explicitly the stakes, for international politics and especially for American power, of a diminution of the dollar's international role, should that occur.

TABLE 1.2.
Expectations about the future of the dollar

| What future for the dollar's international role? | Determinants of international currency standing | | |
|---|---|---|---|
| | Market-based | Instrumental | Geopolitical |
| Sustainable | **James** <br> Helleiner | **McKinnon** <br> James | |
| Uncertain | **Schwartz** <br> De Cecco <br> McKinnon | Helleiner <br> Schwartz | Helleiner <br> De Cecco |
| Decline | **Cohen** <br> Calleo <br> Kirshner | | Cohen <br> **Calleo** <br> **Kirshner** |

These arguments can be loosely mapped onto the framework outlined above. This is not to suggest that all of the authors can be easily placed within one of the specific boxes outlined in table 1.1. Most cannot be so easily categorized. Instead, they draw on a unique mix of the perspectives outlined above. However, this mapping does offer a useful guide to the general perspectives of the contributors, and where they identify and position key variables. In table 1.2, each author is mapped according to intensity of position, with their principal causal mechanism in bold and a secondary causal mechanism also noted.

Although the authors don't agree on the dollar's future, they do agree that the stakes are high. A decline in the dollar's international role would be an important signal of the unraveling of the postwar international economic order. To be sure, this order has already been challenged on so many different fronts since the 1970s, from the trade realm to investment rules to financial regulation. And yet, despite enormous change in the international political economy over this period, the dollar's preeminent status has endured. Are we now finally at a turning point? This book does not provide a definitive answer, but we hope it helps to clarify different ways in which the question can be answered. In turn, as noted in the concluding chapter, we hope that readers come away with a clearer sense of the kinds of judgments they must make in order to decide which future scenario is more likely.

# 2

# THE ENDURING INTERNATIONAL PREEMINENCE OF THE DOLLAR

Harold James

Economic historians and historians of international relations are both fascinated by the story of the international monetary system, but they have quite different research interests and designs as well as a contrasting vision. Economic historians are interested in the way money functions as a measure of value, while international relations specialists think more in terms of the use of money as a tool for power politics. Most economists now believe that (unlike for most of the twentieth century) with their help, central bankers have come to a superior understanding of monetary policy with the result that an appropriate choice of targets (usually inflation targets) can lead to monetary stability. In this view, there is a widespread awareness of both the costs of inflation and a sophisticated understanding that apparent benefits from inflation are illusory, because rational agents respond immediately to signs of inflation. Political scientists, on the other hand, think of money as a political weapon that might be used in the advancement of the higher objectives of power politics. Such views still have a large resonance in the policy community, but not among central banks. Surprisingly, the two academic approaches are brought together only rarely, with the result that economists and economic historians on the one hand and political scientists on the other may use very similar methods but appear to live in completely different worlds.

An increasingly attractive modern conventional wisdom sees parallels between the development of the two major post-1945 monetary regimes: the par value or Bretton Woods system that had its heyday in the 1960s, and the flexible rate regime that succeeded Bretton Woods but only reached its own golden age in the 1990s.[1] These parallels are:

1. the hegemonic role of the U.S. dollar, with the dollar as the major reserve currency
2. the deliberate use of the exchange rate regime by rapidly growing economies (Germany and Japan in the 1960s, the Asian economies after the 1990s) to secure employment growth via export promotion
3. the widespread demand for dollars, permitting the financing of U.S. current account deficits for very long periods of time, though perhaps not indefinitely
4. the strategic dominance of the United States
5. expectations of a coming financial crisis on the part of those who are suspicious of or hostile to the strategic dominance of the United States.[2]

Given that the architecture of the system before and after the structural shift of 1971–73 was completely different, the striking parallels might suggest the classical realist answer that power politics shape the behavior of the international monetary order irrespective of institutional design. This chapter proposes a different answer, namely that economic fundamentals (in particular the emergence since the end of the cold war of a surge in world savings) has created the conditions for a new preeminence of the dollar. The new movements of capital create the potential of financing large current account deficits, not just in the case of the United States but of other economies with similar proclivities (notably Australia and the United Kingdom). With this, an expansive fiscal policy is tempting, which allows military as well as other types of expenditure, and lays the foundation for a security regime that is a vital prop for confidence in the dollar.

---

[1] Dooley, Folkerts-Landau, and Garber 2003. For a recent survey of the debate, see Wachtel 2006. Eichengreen 2006 gives a more sceptical view without succumbing to undue alarmism.

[2] Other chapters in this book give these elements different weights and emphases. On point two, McKinnon sees the use of the exchange rate by Asian emerging economies primarily as a nominal anchor that in the Chinese case was originally an effective policy response to the bout of uncontrolled inflation in the late 1980s; after almost two decades of responsible monetary policy, however, it is not clear that this anchor is needed or that it does not entail a high risk of imported inflation. On point four, Kirshner suggests that China has a much more antagonistic relationship with the United States than Germany and Japan did in the 1960s, but other commentators see China's economic and exchange rate strategy as bringing it into a U.S.-dominated world economy (see Ikenberry 2008).

## The Central Role of the U.S. Dollar in the International Monetary System

The U.S. dollar had a central role in the agreements of Bretton Woods, in that other currencies were to have a par value fixed in either gold or U.S. dollars, under Article IV, Section 1(a). This occurred as a result of American insistence, and in contrast to the early drafts that envisaged a new synthetic international reserve currency.

The consequence was that other countries, exhausted and devastated by World War II, were legitimately worried by that the United States might impose its monetary preferences on them. In the initial postwar period, there was widespread concern that the dollar would be a permanently scarce currency, and that this would produce a world deflation, similar to that which had resulted from the interwar gold standard.[3] By the second half of the 1960s, exactly the opposite argument was made: namely that the United States was forcing inflation on the rest of the world.[4] The international monetary system, according to this account, was a mechanism for transferring the U.S. budget deficits that resulted from the Vietnam War and President Johnson's Great Society program into dollar claims held as international reserves. In consequence, the United States could import goods and services (including those required by its military presence overseas) without really having to pay a price for them, at least for the moment. According to the Belgian economist Robert Triffin's diagnosis, there were two contrasting dangers:[5] one, that the buildup of dollar claims would go on until the point where investors panicked because they would realize that the claims were unredeemable; the other, that U.S. monetary authorities would not expand their money provision sufficiently to meet the world's demand for dollar liquidity.

A frequent criticism, expressed particularly by French policymakers in the late days of the Bretton Woods regime, was that the world was using a "defective clock" as its standard, and would be much better off using a more reliable or constant measure of value, such as gold. In the late 1960s, gold did indeed look like a store and measure of value superior to paper currencies, where political pressure seemed to lead to endemic high inflation and to a tendency to move to even higher levels. From the 1980s onward, however, monetary policy was better understood by central banks, and there was a more general awareness of the benefits of shielding central banks from political pressures to misbehave. The new policy consensus reduced world inflation levels, and paper seemed more stable than gold or silver, now largely demon-

---

[3]  Balogh 1949.
[4]  Rueff 1967; Sohmen 1969.
[5]  Triffin 1960.

etized, whose prices moved quite sharply. Incidentally, the conclusion that paper could be more stable than a commodity such as a precious metal, where prices might be affected by the chance of new discoveries, had been reached at the beginning of the twentieth century by some writers, notably the German economist Karl Helfferich.

After the collapse of the fixed exchange rate regime in 1971–73, no legal obligation existed to define the value of currencies in terms of dollars. Every decade since then has produced new worries about the American position and its allegedly inherent unsustainability. At first, the dollar exchange rate remained (largely for trade reasons) a key issue of concern. At the first economic summit at Rambouillet in 1975, French president Valéry Giscard d'Estaing denounced flexible exchange rates as a "decadent" idea that fostered the abuse of monetary standards.[6] In the late 1970s, the persistence of high inflation in the United States and dollar weakness was a crucial motivation for French and German leaders to move forward with monetary integration at the European level. In the mid-1980s, a high valuation of the dollar (following from a combination of an anti-inflationary monetary policy and a highly expansive fiscal policy) made other countries worried that the U.S. political system would respond to the erosion of jobs in manufacturing with trade protection. This concern was used as a lever by the United States to prize open (or "liberalize") other economies, notably in Japan but also in western Europe. In 1988 Robert Triffin renewed his critique of the "fantastic US deficits and capital imports" which were "unsustainable as well as unacceptable" and revived the idea of a substitution account denominated in European Currency Units (ECUs). In the early 1990s, Robert Z. Lawrence announced the "end of the American dream" as a consequence of falling labor productivity rates.[7]

The world in reality still remained a dollar-based system, in part because the United States was still the world's largest single market, and perhaps consequently the overwhelming majority of commodity prices were denominated in dollars, and in consequence there existed an obvious rationale for many countries to continue to hold reserves in dollars. In fact, the dollar share of international reserves, which had fallen from 73 percent in 1978 to below 50 percent by the end of the 1980s, surged again to a peak of 71 percent in 1999–2001, before a modest fall to 66.5 percent in 2005 and 63.8 percent by the third quarter of 2007.[8] A large part of the changes, however, represent simply valuation effects following from the rise of the dollar in the 1990s and its

[6] Triffin 1998, 41–43; James 1996.
[7] Lawrence 1994, 2–6.
[8] IMF figures. See also Wooldridge 2006.

subsequent fall, rather than decisions to shift portfolios even when the dollar exchange rate fell as rapidly as it did in the course of 2007. The implications of such analysis are comforting to the longer term position of the dollar.

Yet the replacement of the dollar as the reserve currency has been widely predicted, by Barry Eichengreen as well as by some of the contributions to this book (notably that of Marcello de Cecco), who see the rise of the euro as an alternative store of value. The euro is indeed for Eichengreen the major reason why the Dooley/Folkerts-Landau/Garber Bretton Woods II interpretation is implausible, and why the analogy with the 1960s should not be convincing: "The difference today is the euro. The large, liquid market in euro-denominated government securities provides an attractive alternative to holding United States treasury bonds for the central banks of emerging markets."[9] But there are more uncertainties about the future of the euro than about that of the dollar. The relationship between the European Central Bank and the European Union is sometimes strained. Financial sector regulation is still managed on a national rather than a European level, making the threat of financial stability relatively greater. There is no provision at the EU level for the fiscal action necessary in managing bank failures. There are also macroeconomic difficulties in the euro area. Differentials in wage costs in the Mediterranean countries (notably Spain and Italy), where labor markets contain some inflationary pressure, are likely to make for higher levels of unemployment and for discontent that is focused on the common currency.

Most important, there are much more "attractive alternatives" than euro-denominated securities that do not involve much of a shift from the dollar. A new generation of financial analysts has convinced central bankers that they can begin to behave more aggressively, and more like normal, commercial, financial institutions (as central banks actually did behave in the nineteenth century). A more likely alternative to traditional dollar reserve assets is thus a diversification by central banks to a much broader asset portfolio. Many central banks have been quietly experimenting, but the purchase in May 2007 of a 9.9 percent stake in the U.S. buyout fund Blackstone for $3 billion by the People's Bank of China marks a major shift in the world of central bank reserve management. In particular, the new approach escapes from the reserve management problem that seemed to come with holding large dollar reserves: that an attempt to diversify would be too costly to undertake in most circumstances, because it would depress the dollar exchange rate as the Chinese central bank sold its dollar holdings, and would thus lead to large balance sheet losses. In the new approach, sales of U.S. Treasury bills would be com-

[9] Eichengreen 2006, 26.

pensated by purchases of other dollar assets, including debt instruments of government agencies, securities, real estate, and hedge and buyout funds. The U.S. dollar as managed by an independent central bank is likely to remain a reliable store of value, against which the performance of the new alternative assets can be judged. Most important, the dollar's position in the international system does not depend on explicit political pressure. In this narrow sense the often-mentioned link between U.S. security and strategic preeminence is a chimera.

In the Bretton Woods regime, the United States on occasion instrumentalized security policy in order to persuade countries to hold dollar reserves: the Germans, for instance, had to be persuaded that the American military presence required some offset in the form of a commitment not to liquidate German dollar reserves.[10] Britain more explicitly used its imperial connections in order to oblige its former empire to hold sterling balances. But after the end of Bretton Woods, the choice to hold reserve balances was much less easily influenced by the reserve centers, and consequently the role of sterling as a reserve currency ended. The holding of dollar reserves, by contrast, represented not a choice of the United States, but of other countries, or an outcome of market behavior. The task is thus to understand why such choices were made.

## Export Promotion by Means of Exchange Rate Policy

The fact that the United States was the world's most important market created an incentive for countries that wanted to industrialize via the promotion of exports (and also saw the export economy as a major machine for the creation of jobs) to maintain an undervalued currency against the dollar, in order to make their exports more attractive. These countries had considerable price inflation, which was frequently rightly or wrongly blamed on inflation imported from the international monetary system. They could have had greater price stability, but that would have required a currency appreciation. The choice not to do this meant forgoing a part of the new prosperity that the postwar world had to offer, in particular the opportunity to purchase cheaper goods abroad and to stimulate the consumer economy. This strategy was relatively uncontested in Japan in the 1960s, while in West Germany it created a controversy between interest groups and banks associated with manufacturers for export who wanted to resist U.S. and international pressure to revalue

---

[10] See Gavin 2004, and Zimmermann 2002.

the deutsche mark, and those who argued that a revaluation would raise incomes and increase living standards. In the Great Coalition government that ruled the Federal Republic from 1966 to 1969, the former position was taken by the Christian Social finance minister, Franz Joseph Strauss, and the latter by the Social Democratic economics minister, Karl Schiller. American policymakers complained that they were prisoners of the Bretton Woods system, since uniquely they had no mechanism for altering their own exchange rate.

But the dollar remained a hostage of the international monetary system after the transition to generalized floating. The maintenance of a low exchange rate has also been a development tool in Asian "emerging markets." South Korea in the mid-1980s was the subject of U.S. complaints that the won had been artificially undervalued in order to create an export boom after a soaring bilateral trade surplus with the United States.[11] The Korean model was widely seen in other Asian economies as offering a blueprint for an "Asian economic miracle," and the same sort of exchange rate policy was widely adopted in the 1990s by countries seeking to enter world markets.

The most controversial of these issues, which raised more political problems than Korea's 1980s strategy, has been the Chinese pegging of the renminbi. The outcome contributed to an expanding bilateral trade surplus with the United States, which might have been reduced if the renminbi had been allowed to appreciate.[12] The American trade problem generated political controversies even more extreme than those in previous episodes (Japan in the early 1970s or mid-1980s, or Korea in the 1980s), because the possibilities for U.S. pressure on China are much more restricted than in the case of Japan or Korea, which had (and continue to have) a security dependence on the United States. In addition, the threat of U.S. protectionism, which was a powerful tool in previous bargaining about substantial bilateral imbalances, looks less realistic now because of the extent of global interconnectedness. U.S. pressure, as well as lectures from the International Monetary Fund on what China's contribution to solving the problem of "global imbalances" might be, have made little difference. In July 2005, the People's Bank of China indicated that it would move to greater exchange rate flexibility, and undertook an initial 2.1 percent revaluation of the renminbi. But the move was soon followed by a real *depreciation,* with faster export growth as a consequence. Some commentators, notably Cheung, Chinn, and Fuji, have produced arguments that would support the Chinese position, namely that in the light of a number of institutional factors, including the large extent of nonperforming loans, public

---

[11] See James 2006; Boughton 2001a.
[12] The IMF's April 2007 *World Economic Outlook* suggests a greater degree of sensitivity by the U.S. current account to exchange rate alterations: see esp. 100–102.

sector corruption and inefficiency, the renminbi is actually not overvalued.[13] However, no one in China is likely to explicitly support this interpretation, and no one in the United States is likely to believe such an argument given the size of the bilateral trade deficit.

China accumulated reserves at an increasingly rapid pace—a steady $200 billion a year (the 2001 figure was $219 billion), rising slowly to $412 billion in 2003, and then to $826 billion in 2005 and $1,046 billion in 2006 and accelerating at such a pace that by September 2008 they stood at almost $2,500 billion. These are held mostly in dollars, and while there are signs that the People's Bank of China would prefer a more balanced portfolio, it is locked in by the realization that any large-scale unloading of assets would produce a dollar collapse with a substantial price to be paid by the holders of dollar assets. In other words, the dollar regime is compelled by self-interest rather than external pressure. The question then arises: Under what circumstances will the perception of self-interest (outside the United States) change? The answer depends on the extent to which the United States continues to be widely regarded as a stable country, with secure property rights, which can consequently act as a "safe haven" in times of both geopolitical and economic stress.

## Security and the United States

The question of the current account is inevitably political. The current account only matters because of the existence of separate currencies controlled by distinct political entities. There may thus be massive differences in savings and investment levels between New Jersey and California, corresponding to a flow of funds or a current account "imbalance," but no one really notices or minds, because these states are in a single currency area. If there were one world currency, as some writers such as Robert Mundell and, in a more nuanced form, Richard Cooper have advocated, then there would also be no need to debate the current account position of the United States, even though the real effects of a Chinese "undervaluation" would still be noticeable as a surge in job creation but reduced wealth levels (with the opposite effect in the United States). Indeed, precisely this effect can be seen in contemporary Europe's monetary union, in which Germany has an "undervalued" currency and creates jobs, while suffering low income growth. The currency union takes away the political dynamite (unless enough people notice what is happening). But with a separate currency, the surplus or deficit is political, and

[13] See Cheung, Chinn, and Fujii 2007.

there may as a consequence be pressures for an alteration of the exchange rate policy. In this sense, the current account does matter.

There are two ways of approaching the story of the current account, which must arithmetically produce identities: first, as the outcome of the levels of savings and investment, in which a surplus of savings produces a current account surplus and the export of the difference between savings and investment, and a savings deficit needs to be financed by inflows from abroad; and second, as the result of the accumulation of payments for goods, services, and as investment income.

The current account position of the United States reflects a long-term shift. In 1946, the current account surplus was 3.9 percent of GDP, with a merchandise trade balance of $6,697 million and a (nonmilitary) services balance of $1,043 million. The United States had built up a substantial creditor position in the world economy, which became even bigger over the course of the next thirty years as American corporations pumped investment into countries all over the world, and transformed the local economies of western Europe and Japan. Net investment income in 1946 amounted to $560 million. By 1971, when the international monetary system built around the fixed exchange rate (Bretton Woods) regime collapsed, the current account had shrunk to a small deficit, equivalent to 0.1 percent of GNP, and there was a negative merchandise balance ($-2,260 million), a small surplus on services, and very substantial earnings from the investment assets built up overseas over the previous twenty years ($7,272 million). In 1985, when tight monetary policies combined with a big fiscal deficit had sent the dollar to a spiky peak, there was a large current account deficit of $118,155 million, or 2.8 percent of GDP, and a surge in earnings from investment ($25,723 million). At this point, the U.S. became a net debtor, and a major recipient of foreign inflows, but the earnings on investment remained very high through the 1990s, as the U.S. debtor position became ever more extreme.

The large-scale capital movements that supported the U.S. dollar in the 1990s and 2000s were only in part the consequence of the reserve policies of the Chinese and other Asian central banks. The flows present a puzzle. Usually, most economists assumed, capital should flow from rich to poor countries where there was a greater potential for technological catch-up. Although such flows characterized much of the 1970s, they did not take place (on a net basis) when the real era of modern globalization began, in the 1980s. From the mid-1980s, the United States became a net debtor (as it had been before World War I), and by the millennium the United States accounted for some three quarters of the world's net capital imports (the other big borrowers were the United Kingdom and Australia).

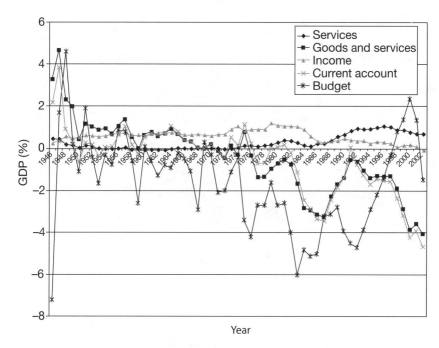

**Figure 2.1.** U.S. current account and budget balance, 1946–2002 (share of GDP)
Calculated from data in *Economic Report of the President,* 2004

   The large and apparently counterintuitive inflow of capital to the United States was at first explained by many analysts as an idiosyncratic response to the Latin American debt crisis of the early 1980s, which appeared to reverse the direction of capital flows. Subsequently other essentially short-term reasons have been given: the attractions of the U.S. stock market, then the real estate boom. They also reflected massive private capital flows: in the 1990s, apparently as a response to the buoyancy of the U.S. stock market, but also as a consequence of a preference by some investors for security. The phenomenon has been in existence for such a relatively long term (over twenty years) that some more structural explanation might be called for, rather than the concatenation of a series of more or less chance influences. The long-term propensity of the late twentieth-century United States to import capital could be explained either through supply factors (changes in the global supply of savings, as a result of more widespread development outside the established industrial countries) or as a result of demand factors (why the United States appears to be so attractive).

   First, the supply of savings: the amount of money that can move interna-

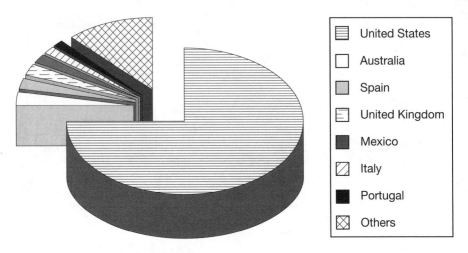

**Figure 2.2.** Capital importers in 2002
International Monetary Fund, International Financial Statistics Database

tionally has increased as a result of the emergence of new players in the global economy. In the 1990s, the pool of world savings increased dramatically, leading some influential policymakers to speak of a global savings glut that was likely to depress the cost of borrowing permanently.[14] The Asian newly industrialized countries (NICs) (Taiwan, Singapore, Korea) saw a reduction in savings rates in the 2000s, although this was compensated for by lower investment levels, so that funds continued to flow out. For the NICs, the saving rate from 1990 to 2000 had been 33.5 percent of GDP; by 2006 it was 31.3 percent. But lower income countries ("developing Asia") had big increases in savings: from 32.9 percent to 42.2 percent. Especially quickly growing but politically unstable and insecure countries experienced dramatic rises in their savings rates, as citizens felt unsure about their future and unable to rely on state support mechanisms. Again, the paradigmatic case is that of China, where, although consumption rose in absolute terms, consumption *rates* fell as incomes rose: by 2005, Chinese households consumed less than 40 percent of GDP, and Chinese households moved to very high savings rates (of around 30 percent). With simultaneous high saving by the government and by enterprises, the outcome is a large amount of capital in search of security. But the savings surge, and the accompanying positive current account balance is not

[14] The phrase became widely repeated after it was used by Federal Reserve governor Ben Bernanke in a speech to the Virginia Association of Economics in Richmond on March 10, 2005: http://www .federalreserve.gov/boarddocs/speeches/2005/200503102/default.htm.

just a Chinese peculiarity, but can be found in most Asian, South Asian, and Middle Eastern economies. For the Middle East, the savings rate rose from 24.2 percent in the 1990s to 40.4 percent in 2006. In the latter case, the surge in oil prices has been responsible for the growth in savings, but in Asia it reflects the combination of stronger growth and increased precautionary saving.[15]

On the demand side, money flows to the United States not for higher returns but because of the greater security that the United States offers. One apparently odd fact makes the deficits more sustainable than most analysts believed they should be: the yield on U.S. assets for foreigners, the price paid by the United States for its borrowing, is substantially lower than the yield for Americans on their foreign holdings. This is the reason why the balance on investment income continues to be so surprisingly resilient and large. Gourinchas and Rey calculate that for the whole period from 1960 to 2001, the annualized rate of return on U.S. liabilities (3.61%) was more than two percentage points below the annualized real rate of return on U.S. assets (5.72%), and that for the post-1973 period the difference is significantly larger (3.50% and 6.82% respectively).[16] The yield difference reflects not miscalculation or stupidity on the part of foreign investors, but a calculation in which they buy security in return for lower yields. The primary attraction of the United States as a destination for capital movement is the unique depth of its markets (which generate financial security) and the political and security position of the country. Very few other countries share the reputation of the United States as a stable and secure haven in which property rights are powerfully protected. This is why inflows to the United States may increase after global security shocks, as they did after September 11, 2001, as well as after the financial shocks of September 2008 even though they had emanated from the U.S. financial system. Currency analysts in consequence like to speak of the dollar having a smile: it is turned up in the corners, in that it reacts positively to very good news but also to very bad news; and turned down in the middle, when a merely average economic performance by the United States briefly convinces the world that everywhere else is also stable.

---

[15] Figures from IMF 2007, Statistical Appendix, table 43.

[16] This was a point made very effectively by Tim Congdon: see Lombard Street Research Ltd., *Monthly Economic Review*, November–December 2002, 5: "The analyses of unsustainability, and total unsustainability, based on the familiar theory of debt dynamics have been dumbfounded." For a fuller analysis, see Gourinchas and Rey 2005. Also Caballero, Farhi, and Gourinchas 2006. Haussmann and Sturzenegger 2006 make a slightly different case for longer term sustainability based on invisible exports and assets. Buiter 2006 and Gros 2006 point out that the reason for the difference in returns lies almost entirely with the difference in yields on direct investment, often reflecting tax reasons to overreport earnings outside the United States and to underreport U.S. earnings.

The United Kingdom has similar characteristics to the United States, with a substantial difference between high returns on external assets and lower yields on external liabilities. Australia has similar returns on assets and liabilities, while in Spain (another country with a large current account deficit that needs to be financed by external inflows) the assets yield less than the liabilities. It might thus be concluded that the British and American position is fundamentally more sustainable than that of Spain, while Australia lies somewhere in the middle.

In addition, Fogli and Perri have recently observed that the business cycle volatility of the United States has fallen substantially since the early 1980s (the so-called great moderation) and that this fall was not as pronounced in other major economies. Reduced volatility reduces the incentives to accumulate precautionary savings, with lower savings as a result and consequently a permanent equilibrium deterioration of the balance of payments that should not be regarded as malign. Fogli and Perri estimate that this effect accounts for around a fifth of the current U.S. external imbalance.[17]

The United States needs the inflow of surplus savings from elsewhere, because of a dramatic fall in the U.S. savings rate, above all in the level of personal savings. Here again, a relatively long-term development is under way, with personal saving falling from 10.1 percent (last quarter of 1970) to 6.9 percent (1990), and then a much more rapid decline in the 1990s (to 1.9% in 2000) continuing in the 2000s (2005, 0.8%).[18] This fall has been so dramatic that it leads many commentators (including Kirshner, Calleo, and Schwartz in this book) to see it as the major driver of today's "global imbalances."

It is worth thinking further about what allows countries like the United States and the United Kingdom to attract money with low rates of return, and about the motivation that drives the inflows. There exist two types of capital market centers in the modern era of globalization. Some small dynamic intermediaries attract large inflows, but also recycle funds and have large current account surpluses: for 2005, Hong Kong, 11.4 percent of GDP; Singapore, 28.5 percent of GDP; or, in Europe, Luxembourg with 9.7 percent of GDP and Switzerland with 13.8 percent of GDP. The larger intermediaries, by contrast, are major capital importers, the United States with a current account deficit of 6.4 percent of GDP, Australia with 6.0 percent, and the United Kingdom with a more modest 2.2 percent. They are also countries that have a lifestyle and clusters of specific skills, in high-value-added sectors, as well as high-quality institutions of higher education, that attract substantial numbers of

---

[17] Fogli and Perri 2007.
[18] Bureau of Economic Analysis, *National Income: 2001,* table 21, "Personal Income and Its Disposition."

skilled immigrants. Such immigration substantially raises their potential and probable growth rates. These large countries rely not only on their size but on their image as homes to the "good life." Their attractiveness is an essential component of their security assets, and their desirability also helps to make them secure in both a political and economic sense.

The role of migration in this story is one that is relatively neglected in the literature on what makes for security and stability. Immigration often is associated with optimism on the part of the migrants, and one of the consequences of a more generalized optimism is a belief in higher future returns. Again, such attitudes will tend to produce lower rates of savings, as people make a wager on a better tomorrow (even though the immigrants themselves may save in order to make remittances). By contrast, emigrant societies (especially those with the low birth rates characteristic of much of Europe and Japan) are worried about falling future returns, and consequently the motives for precautionary saving are much stronger.

The U.S.-style good life is not simply a commitment to high levels of consumption. Contrary to popular assumptions, particularly outside the United States, the consumption story that drives the growing current account imbalance is not fundamentally the result of an addiction to outrageous forms of conspicuous consumption such as sport utility vehicles.[19] (Though there are some odd statistics that seem to bear parts of this thesis out: Americans spend more on jewelry today than on shoes.)[20] But expenditure on food and clothing as a proportion of income has fallen quite dramatically over recent decades, expenditure on housing remains more or less constant, and the big growth has been in spending on education and health. Many academic economists (who have an obvious interest as educators) would like to reclassify these as forms of investment in human capital, and it is probably true that the continued innovative capacity of the United States depends on quality education. Such a link between higher education (investment in human capital) and economic growth is the subject of much research.[21] Good education promotes inflows of high-skill labor (an inward brain drain), that has picked up notably in the last decades of the twentieth century. Thus a 2005 study by the U.S. Committee on Science, Engineering and Public Policy showed that the proportion of doctorates granted to non-U.S. students in science and engineering rose from 23 percent in 1966 to 39 percent in 2000. We can also get much or at least some benefit by attracting highly educated people from other parts of the world; and the export of people trained in American universities

[19] Though see Bradsher 2002.
[20] See Underhill 2004.
[21] A good survey is Ehrlich 2007.

is a vital part of Joseph Nye's idea of "soft power."[22] Highly educated continental Europeans have become extremely mobile and leave their countries, often for Anglo-Saxon destinations. In consequence, London has become the fourth largest French city, with an estimated four hundred thousand French citizens in London and the South East.[23] Australia has become a similar magnet for highly dynamic and educated Asians. But the United States remains the most popular destination for the world's educated mobile elite.

Another element of the overconsumption theory arises out of the contemplation of the link between fiscal issues and the current account. Some part of the story can be explained by government dissaving, rather than by household choices. This link is more obviously and directly political. Government spending on the military is a form of consumption, and in the Vietnam era, in the Reagan defense buildup, and in the post-9/11 era this was a current issue in international discussions of the stability of the monetary and financial order. In all these cases, the defense buildup went hand in hand with domestically oriented fiscal expansion, to create the Great Society, or for Reagan and Bush II to cut taxes. It is as if the United States could not gather the domestic support for defense or war without buying social content at home. Federal spending is thus part of a large package that underpins in the broadest sense the security of the United States, and capital markets respond to that higher sense of security.

The conceptualization of the U.S. position as a banker or international intermediary was first made in the 1960s, when some American economists (Despres, Kindleberger, and Salant) presented a hypothesis on why the apparently deteriorating U.S. external payments position was in reality more sustainable than it seemed. The United States was in the position of a bank, taking short-term deposits whose owners wanted security, and earning a return by lending these deposits out long term and to riskier borrowers. We tend to trust bigger banks more, as we think that they are better able to absorb shocks. Such a position contains two sets of risks: first, that the lenders (depositors) might come to think of the United States as in some way less secure; second, that they might be worried about the bank's lending policy and the solvency of its borrowers. The modern equivalent to Kindleberger et al.'s 1960s analogy of the United States with a bank would be that the United States is the equivalent of a global hedge fund, taking risks elsewhere on substantial leverage in the belief that the world as a whole is becoming more secure and hence that risk premiums will fall over the long term. The link between global

---

[22]  Nye 2004.
[23]  See Favell 2008.

enrichment, peace, and American superior strategic capability was made in a very striking way in the September 2002 National Security Strategy. Conversely, doubts about the U.S. image in the world since 2003, in the aftermath of the Iraq War, have helped to make the United States look less stable and secure.

The 2006 announcement by the People's Bank of China that it would try to diversify its reserve portfolio into a much broader class of investments is a recognition of the continuing logic of U.S. preeminence. It is also an indication that the world's fastest-growing and most dynamic economy sees the United States as a world hedge fund, and that it would like to share in some of the profitability of that hedge fund. The 2007 credit market crisis did not lead to any reassessment. On the contrary, the sovereign wealth funds of emerging markets saw it as an opportunity to buy some control over the levers of global finance as firms such as Citigroup, Bear Stearns, UBS, and Merrill Lynch needed new capital injections. The Singapore fund Temasek explained its decision in terms of the "underlying strength of Merrill Lynch's franchise."[24] Even a year later, after the financial meltdown of September 2008 that destroyed the American investment banks, Asian houses were looking to pick up pieces from the wreckage at favorable prices.

The ability to take bets on the American economy and the American financial franchise depends on the assessment of others that the United States is indeed stable, and that worldwide pacification through the actions of the U.S. and its allies is a strategy that is paying off. Thus, in the first place the ability of the United States to finance its deficits depends on the continued perception that it is a high-growth and high-productivity economy and that it is politically and militarily secure. That confidence could clearly be shaken by a series of terrorist attacks on U.S. territory, particularly were they to employ atomic, biological, or chemical (ABC) weapons. It is also possible to see how financial attacks can be mobilized in the "Great Game" of great power rivalry. There are historical precedents from the classical world of European great power politics in which countries used speculative financial attacks against their rivals in order to obtain a security advantage. France in the 1911 Morocco crisis tried in this fashion to instrumentalize a run on the German market, while in the mid-1930s German agents encouraged speculation against the French franc. In both cases, the hope was that a financial crisis would not only shake the rival but also and most immediately force fiscal action, which would involve a cutting back of defense expenditure.

Conversely, however, the security of the United States depends on the con-

---

[24] "Temasek in $4.4 bn. Merrill Vote," *Financial Times*, December 27, 2007.

tinued inflow of capital, as a sudden adjustment would be unbearably painful and intolerable politically. This is why the sustainability discussion is so central to estimates of the future path of the international order (as Calleo and Kirshner make very clear in their contributions to this book). A vicious cycle would commence, in which an end to the capital inflow would reduce the political stake of other countries in American stability, and that would prompt even more rapid outflows. It is this nightmare scenario that lies at the heart of Kirshner and Calleo's pessimism, as well as of the influentially gloomy commentaries and websites of Nouriel Roubini, Kenneth Rogoff, and Brad DeLong. So it is worth looking back at previous nightmare scenarios.

In the post–Bretton Woods world, there have been several moments when the United States no longer appeared to be so secure, and when a political as well as an economic logic drove the movement of capital out of the United States. At these moments of shock, capital outflows seemed to be related to the questioning of the solidity of U.S. institutions. The first of such crisis moments was the breakdown of the par value system in the early 1970s, which coincided with the U.S. attempt to extricate itself from a failed war in Vietnam.

In the late 1970s, a second oil price shock seemed to raise new questions about the stability of the United States. Again, there were major outflows, and a rapid depreciation of the dollar.

Developments since 2001 bear some analogies to these earlier moments of doubt about the permanence of U.S. stability. As in previous episodes there are apparently unrelated sources of doubt: the failure of U.S. grand strategy throughout the world, but also the response of U.S. lawmakers to the corporate scandals at the turn of the millennium, which produced a pendulum shift toward much heavier and more complex corporate regulation, in particular the Sarbanes-Oxley Act. There was an initial halt to the growth of foreign-owned assets in the United States after the stock crash, but since 2003 the inward surge began again. There is currently little sign that the United States is or should be perceived as more vulnerable to crisis than Europe or the rapidly growing Asian economies. In particular, we know from historical observation of the United States in the late nineteenth century or Japan in the 1960s and 1970s, or Korea in the 1980s and 1990s, that fast-growing economies are hit by dramatic crises and current account reversals.

## American Vulnerability to Crisis

Since the early 1960s, alarmists have believed that the position of the United States in the international monetary system was unsustainable. One of the first to sound the alarm was Melchior Palyi.[25] In the mid-1960s the French economist Jacques Rueff took up this theme, and impressed President de Gaulle with the urgency of the situation. De Gaulle's criticism of the United States seems a peculiarly timeless instance of the European view that could have been made at any point over the past forty years: "The United States is not capable of balancing its budget. It allows itself to have enormous debts. Since the dollar is the reference currency everywhere, it can cause others to suffer the effects of its poor management. This is not acceptable. This cannot last."[26] Such critiques of the American role were taken up again in the mid-1980s, and once more after the turn of the millennium. The financial crisis of 2007–08 produced a new wave of assertions of European superiority as the German finance minister announced that the United States would lose its role as "financial superpower," and French president Nicholas Sarkozy announced that "laissez faire is finished."[27] The criticisms usually come from people who have doubts about the value of the good life as practiced in its modern epicenters. For them, the good life is associated with the projection of power, the instigation of inequality, and the canonization of consumption and cupidity.

There is an obvious contrast between the American and the British imperial experience, and the resilience of the British Empire owed a great deal to its long-term current account surplus position from the mid-nineteenth century to World War I. The "cannot last" issue raises the link between the capacity to borrow and its dependence on continued economic dynamism. In the late nineteenth century era of open capital markets, inflows to high-growth countries (such as the United States or Australia) were sustained over very long periods of time, above all because (then as now) capital inflows were accompanied by migration flows in which labor moved over large distances and across national frontiers into higher productivity occupations. The result generated income gains both in the senders and the receivers of the migrations.

The question about sustainability then turns into one about the probability of continued growth rates that are higher than those of the rest of the industrialized world. For much of the 1990s foreign capital inflows reflected a foreign view that the peace dividend, fiscal prudence, and technological dynamism represented an ideal environment. In the years after 2001, this environment clearly deteriorated, and some analysts began to argue that the United States was increasingly "decoupled" from the rest of the world, and in particular from the dynamic Asian economies.[28]

[25] Palyi 1961.

[26] Peyrefitte 2003, 664. See also Gavin 2004, 121.

[27] "Lessons from a Crisis," *Economist,* October 4, 2008, 55, U.S. edition.

[28] The concept of "decoupling" obtained widespread circulation in September 2006 in a report by Jim O'Neill of Goldman Sachs.

Growth rates are threatened by long-term fiscal problems arising both out of military commitments and the burdens of ensuring social security for an aging population: in this the United States shares (in a less extreme form) a problem that is also emerging in the aging industrial societies of Europe and Japan.[29] Every forthcoming election produces pressures on politicians to promise more spending. The deterioration of the fiscal position at the beginning of the millennium was a transnational phenomenon: the average general government fiscal balance for all the advanced industrial economies in 2000 was exactly in balance, while in 2004 the figure had slid to a deficit of 3.9 percent. The U.S. position, with a change from a 1.3 percent surplus (2000) to −4.9 percent, looks like an extreme example of the transformation, but Germany moved from 1.3 percent to −3.9 percent, France from −1.4 to −3.4 percent, and Italy from −0.6 to −2.9 percent, while Japan stayed with very high deficit levels, showing only a slight improvement (−7.5 changing to −6.9).[30]

Fiscal problems thus pose a long-term threat to the capacity of not only the United States but also of other large industrial countries to sustain growth and hence capital inflows.

The liquidity produced by the new large international transfers of capital has produced a trap, in which it is easy for the large advanced countries to borrow very cheaply. Even in the short term there are some question marks. Central banks increasingly look to place their reserves in higher yielding or more commercial investments than in the traditional short-term Treasury bills. The People's Bank of China is actively discussing such a diversification: if realized, it would make the funding of U.S. and other debt more costly. Private investors in emerging markets are also likely to be increasingly sophisticated and interested in the yield on their assets.

Maybe it is also possible to produce some long-term prognoses. It is conceivable that this will change in the future, when the emerging markets presently characterized by such unusually high rates of saving "graduate" and become more like the advanced industrial countries. It is safe to assume that the graduation would be accompanied first by a rise in consumption by individuals, as the precautionary motive for saving in conditions of insecurity gradually diminishes. But secondly, it is also likely that the governments will be tempted to behave more like the advanced countries and increase their spending—on infrastructure in order to maintain the economic miracle, on social expenditures as these countries too face the issue of aging populations.

---

[29] Kotlikoff, Fehr, and Jokisch 2003; Kotlikoff and Ferguson 2003.
[30] IMF 2004, 218–19.

Most likely, however, is an increase in expenditure on technology items that have a military potential, and that can thus be viewed as likely to increase power.

A very long-term comparative perspective on past episodes of imperial rule holds some analogies. The ease with which the United States and other big countries can finance their deficits appears to be analogous to probably the most famous case of long-drawn-out imperial decline, that of Habsburg Spain.[31] Sometimes it appears in consequence that there is a "free lunch" for the hegemon. The equivalent to the inflows of funds to all the advanced countries in the last decades of the twentieth century was the story of New World silver, which initially appeared as a source of immense strategic power. It let Spain have something (mostly the services of enlisted and mercenary armies) apparently for nothing. The inflow of silver did not immediately lead to Spanish decline, but it did produce over an extended period of time a hollowing out of the Spanish economy and in the end also a loss of strategic preeminence. Such analogies suggest not an immediate collapse as a result of twenty-first century global imbalances, but the basis for a rather longer term shift of power and influence. In the course of that shift, the security advantages that currently constitute the major advantage of the United States (and the real source of the unique or exorbitant privilege of the dollar) are likely to fade.

Another way of making this point is to say that maintaining the dollar as a stable store of value will become a more costly option when foreigners as well as Americans see American stability in less rosy terms than they did at the end of the twentieth century and the beginning of the new millennium.

Of course, the world has been there before. States, especially hegemonic states, face a constant danger of overspending their capital and hence of ruin in the manner described by Adam Smith:

> The progress of the enormous debts which at present oppress, and will in the long-run probably ruin, all the great nations of Europe, has been pretty uniform. . . . When national debts have once been accumulated to a certain degree, there is scarce, I believe, a single instance of their having been fairly and completely paid. The liberation of the public revenue, if it has ever been brought about at all, has always been brought about by a bankruptcy; sometimes by an avowed one, but always by a real one, though frequently by a pretended payment.[32]

---

[31] See Elliot 2006.
[32] Smith 1976, 446, 447.

The U.S. dollar will be the major international currency as long as the United States remains the world's largest concentration of political and military might as well as of economic potential.[33] Economic and political power tend to go along with each other in a world that is insecure and at the same time places a high value on security and growth. Such concentrations of power can be self-sustaining when they attract the capital resources and the human resources (primarily through skilled immigration) that may allow exceptional productivity growth to continue. When and if they close themselves off to sources of innovation—as, for instance, Golden Age Spain did—the process of relative decline becomes much faster. Crises, such as the financial crash of 2008, tend to make politics more introspective and nationalistic. Since the isolationist impulse, in which mass politics attacks the elite view of international engagement, is one important part of the American political tradition, it is impossible to close off this possibility. At the time of writing, the isolationist answer does not appear to attract enough Americans to make this more than a very serious worry.

---

[33] In 1970, Robert Mundell reached a similar conclusion: see Swoboda 1971.

# 3

# U.S. CURRENT ACCOUNT DEFICITS AND THE DOLLAR STANDARD'S SUSTAINABILITY

## A Monetary Approach

Ronald McKinnon

Economists have failed rather dismally to construct convincing theoretical models of why the seemingly endless U.S. current account deficits are sustained by the seemingly endless willingness by the rest of the world to acquire dollar assets right through the U.S. financial crisis of 2007–08.[1] Reflecting this conceptual inadequacy, many see the continuation of such global "imbalances" as unsustainable because foreigners—both governments and their private sectors—will eventually cease buying dollar assets, which will trigger a collapse in the dollar's value in the foreign exchanges. Beginning with the infamous twin deficits of the Reagan presidency in the 1980s, such failed predictions have been commonplace for more than twenty years.

Throughout Asia, the Americas, and much of Africa, the dollar remains the dominant currency as a vehicle for clearing international payments between banks, as a unit of account for international trade in goods and services, and as a reserve cum intervention currency for governments. True, the euro has become by far the most important regional currency, spanning the smaller

Author's note: This chapter, written for this book, extends and revises my "The U.S. Current Account Deficits and the Dollar Standard's Sustainability: A Monetary Approach" *CES ifo Forum* 4 (2007).
[1] Further discussion of the financial crisis of 2008–09 is contained in the addendum to this chapter. But the reader should remember that the body of the paper was written in the fall of 2007.

economies immediately east of the euro zone. There is a "euro standard" in eastern Europe. But the euro is not yet important for transactions among non-European countries, whereas the dollar dominates transactions *not* involving the United States, for example, when China trades with Malaysia or Brazil or Angola.

This resilience of the world dollar standard makes the dollar the definitive international money. Alone among nations, the United States has a virtually unlimited line of credit with the rest of the world to sustain its current account deficits because, in extremis, it could create the necessary international means of payment to repay debts to foreigners. Consequently, the United States can borrow heavily in its own currency because creditors of the United States voluntarily build up dollar claims. This confounds the prognosticators of the dollar's imminent collapse because they have seen less highly indebted countries in Asia and Latin America ultimately being forced to repay in crisis circumstances associated with devaluations and default.

What makes the position of the U.S. dollar, and the borrowing capacity of the American economy, so different? Will the consequent large buildup of liquid dollar claims by foreigners eventually undermine the dollar standard, or can the world and the United States live with this dollar "overhang" indefinitely?

## The Monetary Anchor Approach

Rather than appealing to America's military or commercial or political hegemony—past or present—to explain the dollar's continued international predominance and increasing U.S. indebtedness, I shall take a more purely monetary approach. It has two main facets.

First is the need for one common international money, really a natural monopoly, to facilitate complex multilateral exchanges in goods and capital flows. It is directly analogous to having a single money—as a medium of exchange, unit of account, and store of value—to facilitate purely domestic transactions within a purely national domain. If the dollar was not playing this invaluable role in today's international economy, the markets would have chosen some other national money to be the world's key currency. In my previous work, I touch lightly on this literature, emphasizing the importance of inertia in preserving the dollar's domain in international exchange.[2] Once a

---

[2] McKinnon 2005c.

national money becomes predominant internationally, economies of scale and network effects make it hard to displace.

Second, going beyond the purely domestic monetary analogy, the dollar acts as a *monetary anchor*—sometimes called nominal anchor—for the macroeconomic policies and price levels of other countries. This anchoring role takes a strong form when countries opt to fix their exchange rates (typically within a narrow band) indefinitely against the dollar—as with many western European economies (as well as Japan) in the 1950s and 1960s under the old Bretton Woods regime, or China from 1995 to 2005, or many small island economies that have dollar-based currency boards such as Hong Kong's. If the fixed nominal exchange rate is maintained long enough, and impediments to trade are absent, inflation rates in the prices of tradable goods in such countries converge to those prevailing in the United States.

More widespread at the present time, however, is a somewhat "weaker" form of the dollar's international role as a monetary anchor. Because prices of tradable goods and services, virtually all primary products, and most manufactures (except for exports from industrial Europe) are set in dollars in international markets, central banks in emerging markets and less developed counties unofficially peg "softly" to the dollar—sometimes called Bretton Woods II—in order to better stabilize their own internal price levels. Although most developing countries no longer have official dollar parities, they intervene continually to smooth high frequency, that is, day-to-day or week-to-week, fluctuations in their dollar exchange rates—and stand ready (with high dollar reserves) to prevent major fluctuations.[3] This has the added advantage of providing an informal hedge for importers and exporters against exchange rate risk when domestic financial markets are insufficiently developed, or ringed by capital controls, to allow an active market in forward exchange. Occasionally, even more developed economies, which nominally are floaters, will intervene. From 2003 into early 2004, the Bank of Japan intervened massively to buy dollars in order to prevent a sharp appreciation of the yen.

Instead of borrowing in its own currency, a debtor country on the dollar's (or euro's) periphery can only borrow on reasonable terms in foreign exchange—largely dollars (or euros)—and so bears the exchange risk. Thus, it must worry about fluctuations in the value of its currency against the dollar. A devaluation will increase the servicing cost of its dollar-denominated debts, forcing internal bankruptcies in the short run and inflation in the longer run—as per Argentina's deep devaluation in 2002, or those of the five East

[3] Reinhart 2000; McKinnon 2005a, chap. 1.

Asian crisis economies in 1997–98. Once a peripheral debtor country builds up significant foreign currency debts, it becomes vulnerable to an attack with capital flight that leaves it with insufficient dollars with which to repay its (dollar) debts. The resulting debt defaults, loss of access to foreign capital, and deep devaluation can then force a painful cutback in domestic expenditures and can force the government to fall. The markets know this, so they limit how much any peripheral country can borrow in the first place—although perhaps not stringently enough.

However, in the new millennium, after more than twenty years of U.S. current account deficits, most U.S. trading partners have become dollar creditors—but creditors that also bear the foreign exchange risk because they cannot lend to the United States in their own currencies. Instead, they pile up dollar claims. Those with substantial holdings of dollar assets worry that a sharp appreciation of their currencies would lead to capital losses for the domestic holders of the dollar assets, as well as a decline in the mercantile competitiveness of their exporters. If prolonged, an appreciation would impose domestic deflation—for example, the experience of Japan in the 1980s and into the mid-'90s.

Consequently, in order to avoid currency appreciation and deflation, surplus-savings countries, in Asia, the Persian Gulf, and elsewhere, are now trapped into acquiring dollar assets from the savings-deficient United States. If purchases of dollar assets by their private sectors are insufficient to cover their current account surpluses, their central banks step in as residual buyers to prevent their currencies from appreciating. The upshot is the huge buildup of official exchange reserves, typically in U.S. Treasury bonds, by central banks in Asia, oil-producing countries, and emerging markets more generally. These *stocks* of official exchange reserves now far exceed any estimate of what is prudent or optimal. Instead, these "reserves" are largely the unwanted residue from their efforts at exchange rate stabilization in the face of ongoing *flow* imbalances—their current account surpluses.

The U.S. current account (trade) deficit is the mechanism by which real resources are transferred from the rest of the world: the counterpart of foreign net purchases of U.S. financial and other assets. From its central position in the world's financial system, the United States alone can borrow in its own currency, that is, issue dollar-denominated debt. Because the United States is never going to run out of dollars, it can always avoid outright defaults on its government's debts—if only because the U.S. Federal Reserve system can always step in to buy back U.S. Treasury bonds held by foreigners.

Although foreign creditors see no default risk in holding U.S. Treasury bonds, they would balk at a substantial loss in the dollar's real purchasing

power—as with general inflation in the United States, or substantial devaluations of the dollar against several other currencies that reduce the dollar's
purchasing power elsewhere. Then, foreign central banks would no longer be
so anxious to stop their currencies from appreciating against the dollar, and
would withdraw from being dominant buyers of U.S. Treasuries.

Consequently, the key to maintaining the dollar standard in its present
form—and with it America's indefinitely long line of credit from the rest of
the world—lies mainly with the U.S. Federal Reserve Board's control over
monetary policy, and not directly with the U.S. Treasury's control over fiscal
policy or the American saving rate more generally. *As long as the American
price level remains stable, there is no well-defined ex ante restraint on the
amount the United States can borrow internationally.* That is, as long the dollar's purchasing power over internationally tradable goods and services is stable, foreign central banks are loath to let their currencies appreciate against
the dollar for fear of losing mercantile competitiveness in the short run and
facing deflationary stagnation in the longer run.

Is the Fed up to the job? As the central bank for the "Nth" country under
the dollar standard, the U.S. Federal Reserve normally does not intervene in
the foreign exchanges and, in a dollar-based world, exchange rate changes do
not strongly affect the U.S. price level, that is, pass-through is low. More easily than other central banks, the Fed can conduct a national monetary policy
largely independent of events in the foreign exchange markets. Because of
highly developed capital markets in the United States, it can focus directly on
stabilizing the U.S. price level by open-market operations targeting the federal funds rate of interest, while more or less ignoring exchange rate fluctuations. Indeed, the proper role of the center country is to provide a stable price
level independently, which becomes the nominal anchor for the system as a
whole—one that is particularly valuable for emerging markets on the dollar's
periphery.

In contrast, other central banks cannot ignore how their exchange rates are
moving against the dollar, and have to adjust to what the Fed is doing. In principle, therefore, the Fed can more easily commit itself to a policy of low inflation—although it has yet to name a definite low inflation target in the
mode of the European Central Bank or the Bank of England. Nevertheless,
the United States is the country where the Taylor Rule was born—where my
colleague John Taylor estimated the rule econometrically as if the Fed was targeting the rate of inflation of about 2 percent in the U.S. consumer price index (CPI).[4]

---

[4] Taylor 1993.

Although providing a stable monetary anchor is all well and good in normal times, America's monetary hegemony could still be undermined by calamitous "nonmonetary" events. One is an outbreak of protectionism in the United States that forces other countries, such as China, to appreciate their currencies, that is, to depreciate the dollar, much like the Nixon shock in August 1971. The second is a downturn in the U.S. economy, such as the current spreading housing crisis and recession, that essentially forces the Fed to abandon its goal of price stability and flood the economy with liquidity. In either case, the large overhang of liquid dollar assets owned by foreigners makes the Fed's management of the ensuing crisis more difficult—and threatens the United States with the loss of international monetary hegemony.

## Protectionism in the United States

Having the United States become more protectionist is a major threat to the dollar's predominance as international money. Other than ever-present political populism in a globalizing world requiring continual industrial restructuring, is there a legitimate economic cause for concern that foreign competitive pressure on American industry is too great?

The large U.S. current account deficit funded by foreigners buying dollar assets is helpful in averting a credit crunch in the savings-deficient American economy. However, the transfer of Asian savings to the United States in real terms shrinks the size of the U.S. manufacturing sector, a shrinkage that is at the root of the protectionist upwelling in the American Midwest and East Coast—even though full employment in the country overall has been maintained by the offsetting expansion of service industries.

Why is U.S. manufacturing particularly impacted? The principal Asian creditors—Japan, China, Korea, Taiwan—and principal European creditor Germany only export manufactures and are themselves major importers of services and raw materials including oil. Thus, their trade (saving) surpluses with the rest of the world, and bilaterally with the United States, are embodied in a surplus of manufactured goods exported to the United States—forcing a contraction in U.S. manufacturing employment.[5] Notice that because of more rapid technical change in manufacturing compared to other sectors of the economy, employment in manufacturing has been falling in all of the mature industrial countries. But it is falling relatively faster in the United

[5] McKinnon 2005b.

States because the American saving deficiency necessitates net imports of manufactures from foreign industrial, or industrializing, countries.

Therefore, American protectionism for manufacturing is not purely gratuitous politically. Unfortunately, however, the protectionists see it as an exchange rate problem rather than as an international saving imbalance. Although this perception is false, it is no less of a threat to destabilizing the purchasing power of the dollar and igniting inflation in the United States.

The large trade and saving surpluses of the oil-producing countries, such as the Emirates in the Persian Gulf, don't generate a similar protectionist response in the United States. Although Americans don't like the high price of oil, they need the oil. Moreover, oil is homogenous and relatively anonymous as to which country it's from in its impact on American industries, and there is no "obvious" exchange rate or tariff measures that the United States could take to change the behavior of, say, Saudi Arabia.

## Conflicted Virtue

By threatening trade sanctions against manufactured imports from trade-surplus countries unless they appreciate their currencies, many politicians and economists in the United States hope to force widespread devaluations of the dollar against the yen, renminbi, and the currencies of other industrial countries with saving surpluses—much like the Nixon shock of August 1971.

These threatened American trade sanctions thrust the surplus-saving Asian countries, producing manufactures, onto the horns of a dilemma called *conflicted virtue*.[6] Trade surplus countries are "virtuous" in the sense of being high savers, but this naturally generates a collective current account surplus in trade with the saving-deficient United States. American politicians and many economists then misinterpret these foreign trade surpluses, often accompanied by large buildups of official dollar exchange reserves, as per se evidence of unfair currency manipulation to keep Asian currencies undervalued. Thus, American politicians apply pressure to have the Asian currencies appreciated.

However, any individual Asian government knows that a substantial appreciation of its currency against the dollar would create domestic macroeconomic turmoil: exports, domestic investment, and spending more generally would fall with slower economic growth. A sustained appreciation of its

---

[6] McKinnon 2005a.

nominal exchange rate would eventually lead to deflation—as in Japan in the 1980s and 1990s, after the yen had risen all the way from 360 to the dollar in August 1971 to touch 80 in April 1995. But if the exchange rate fails to appreciate, the United States would apply trade sanctions on its exports. Thus, the foreign creditor country becomes "conflicted"—whence conflicted virtue.

In the worst-case scenario, American political pressure takes a more general form. Beyond any individual foreign country, suppose most American trading partners were coerced into agreeing to appreciate. Most have trade surpluses of greater or lesser degrees as the counterpart of the huge U.S. trade deficit. William Cline is a leading advocate of a more general devaluation of the dollar against thirty or more leading U.S. trading partners.[7] From the monetary approach to exchange rate determination, however, a general nominal depreciation of the dollar could only be sustained if U.S. monetary policy becomes more expansionary relative to its trading partners, that is, with inflation at home and relative deflation abroad.

In sustaining such a general dollar devaluation, how the necessary monetary adjustment would be partitioned between inflation in the United States and deflation elsewhere is quite arbitrary. It depends on the particular historical circumstances associated with such an economically cataclysmic event. For several years after the Nixon shock of August 1971, which required the sharp appreciation of European currencies, the Japanese yen, and the Canadian and Australian dollars, high inflation in the United States (initially suppressed by wage-price controls) and more subdued inflation elsewhere was the mode of adjustment. For ten years after the Plaza Accord of 1985 when the major industrial countries agreed to have their currencies appreciate against the dollar, there was outright deflation in Japan (whose currency appreciated the most), suppressed deflation in Europe (then called "eurosclerosis"), and relatively modest inflation in the United States.

### The Exchange Rate and the Trade Balance: The Phillips Curve Déjà Vu?

The belief in the economics profession, and among fellow travelers, that countries with trade surpluses should appreciate their currencies to (help) reduce the surpluses is very widespread. It lends respectability to American, and even European, politicians who demand that the currencies of Asian creditor countries be appreciated. Although plausible (like the belief in the Phillips

---

[7] Cline 2005.

Curve trade-off between inflation and unemployment in the 1950s and 1960s), this belief in the desirability of exchange rate appreciation for trade surplus countries (or devaluation for deficit countries) is not generally valid for the highly open economies characteristic of today's era of globalization.

Starting as an undergraduate, the average "economist in the street" is taught the elasticities model of the balance of trade. It is basically a micro-economic model in which export and import functions are separable from the rest of the macroeconomy and from each other. With this separation, an appreciation should reduce a country's trade surplus by raising the price of domestic exports as seen by foreign importers in their currencies, while the domestic-currency prices of imports increase. Thus, if these agents are at all price responsive, that is, if their price elasticities of demand are only moder-ately high, exports should decline and imports rise so that the net trade sur-plus is reduced.

Although this elasticities model is myopic because it ignores more com-plex macroeconomic repercussions from exchange rate changes, it is so seem-ingly straightforward that it remains popular for teaching students about the relationship between the exchange rate and the trade balance. When ex-plained to journalists, politicians, or even political scientists, it remains beau-tifully intuitive: "Sure, if appreciating the renminbi makes Chinese goods more expensive, we will buy less of them; and if American goods sold in China become cheaper, they will buy more of ours." Hence its popularity.

What then are the macroeconomic repercussions that could invalidate the microeconomic myopia of the elasticities model? First, consider economies that are highly open to foreign trade *and* to capital flows (capital account transactions are not in the elasticities model). The location of investment by multinational firms, and even some more purely national ones, becomes quite sensitive to the real exchange rate. If the renminbi is sharply appreciated against the dollar, China suddenly looks like a much more expensive place in which to invest, while the United States becomes more attractive. As invest-ment slumps in China, so does aggregate demand, including the demand for imports. The converse is true in the United States where increased investment stimulates aggregate demand. Although China's export growth slows because of the higher renminbi, so too does its import growth—leaving the net effect on China's trade surplus indeterminate.[8]

But renminbi appreciation has a further macroeconomic repercussion in the form of a wealth effect. Under the dollar standard, Chinese hold large stocks of dollar assets from their past trade surpluses because they don't (and

---

[8] McKinnon and Ohno 1997, chaps. 6 and 7.

can't) lend to the United States in renminbi. When the renminbi appreciates, Chinese owners of dollar assets suddenly feel poorer because their dollar assets are worth less for spending in China. This negative wealth effect further reduces spending in China, including spending for imports, making it less likely that China's trade surplus will be reduced as exports slow.[9]

The earlier experience of Japan, under great American pressure to appreciate the yen, is instructive. The yen rose from 360 yen to the dollar in August 1971 to touch 80 yen to the dollar in April 1995—an incredibly large nominal appreciation. Japan's trade surplus did not decline but rose erratically from close to zero in the early 1970s to average about 3 percent of Japanese GDP in the 1980s and 1990s. With a slump in investment, the high yen caused deflation and a long period of economic stagnation from 1992 to 2002 (Japan's lost decade), but it did not succeed in its primary objective of reducing Japan's trade surplus. The stagnating economy reduced the demand for imports even as export growth slowed from the high yen. From the early 1970s through 2007, Japan's price level fell relative to that of the United States, thus causing its "real" exchange rate to depreciate back to where it was before the Nixon shock of forced dollar depreciation in 1971!

Sharp currency appreciations can be economically disastrous while failing to reduce a trade surplus. However, the mainstream of the economics profession continues to believe that the exchange rate should be assigned to adjusting trade imbalances, that is, the dollar should be devalued against Asian currencies in particular—a belief that could yet undermine the dollar standard.

The Phillips curve fallacy—that moving to a higher rate of inflation will permanently reduce unemployment—provides an uncomfortable parallel to the fallacy that the "real" exchange rate can be manipulated to control the trade balance. Both are rooted in microeconomic myopia that fails to take longer term macroeconomic repercussions into account.

In the case of the Phillips curve for a purely national economy, it seems obvious that increasing aggregate demand, although somewhat inflationary, will increase employment. During the Bretton Woods period, this belief lay behind America's refusal to disinflate from the mild inflation of the late 1960s, which was making U.S. industry less competitive under fixed exchange rates. Instead of disinflating the U.S. economy because of fear of increasing domestic unemployment, President Nixon opted to continue with an easy money policy and restore American competitiveness in August 1971 by forcing other industrial countries to appreciate their currencies against the dol-

[9] Qiao 2007.

lar. The result throughout the 1970s into the 1980s was high and variable inflation (particularly in the United States), economic stagnation with higher unemployment, and no systematic change in the increasingly erratic U.S. trade balance.

Thanks to Milton Friedman, the world is no longer threatened by the Phillips curve fallacy bringing on another bout of global inflation.[10] But the exchange rate fallacy, that devaluing the dollar will reduce the U.S. trade surplus, is alive and well and could yet undermine the anchoring role of the dollar standard, with highly inflationary consequences for the United States.

### The Transfer Problem in Reducing the U.S. Current Account Deficit

Rather than an exchange rate problem, correcting today's global trade imbalances is a form of the transfer problem: spending must be transferred from trade-deficit countries (mainly the United States) to trade-surplus countries in the rest of the world (ROW). Reducing the U.S. current account deficit requires that net saving be increased in the United States and reduced abroad—particularly in Asia.

Consider the accounting identity

$$Y - A = CA = -CA^* = A^* - Y^*$$

where A is U.S. domestic absorption (total spending), Y is output (GDP), CA is the current account surplus (negative in the U.S. case), and the starred variables are the counterparts in rest of the world (ROW).

Given full employment output at home and abroad, clearly CA can only improve if $\Delta A < 0$, $\Delta A^* > 0$, and $\Delta A = -\Delta A^*$. To correct a trade imbalance for a large country like the United States, *absorption adjustment must be symmetric* with *ROW*.

But contrary to most literature on the subject, exchange rates need not, and probably best not, be changed as part of the transfer process for improving the U.S. trade balance.[11] To show why this is so, I draw on the older literature on the transfer problem associated with paying war reparations—particularly that by Ronald Jones's "Presumption and the Transfer Problem."[12] Adjustment in absorption, that is, aggregate spending, is two-sided because the loser (the transferor) must raise taxes to pay an indemnity to the winner (the transferee), which then spends it. But there is no presumption that the terms

---

[10]  Friedman 1968.
[11]  McKinnon 2007b.
[12]  Jones 1975.

of trade must turn against the transferor. That is, the losing country, which is forced into running a trade surplus (or smaller deficit), need not depreciate its real exchange rate to effect the transfer.

The definition of the "real" exchange rate is important here. Unlike Jones's approach, in a more "standard" model each country produces just one good that is, however, differentiated from the one-good output of its trading partner. Then in each country some of its own one-good output is consumed at home and the rest exported. Surprisingly, large-scale macroeconomic models—such as the Sigma model used by the U.S. Federal Reserve—typically still use this analytical simplification whereby all the economy's diverse outputs are combined into a single aggregate. In effect, each country's production (and consumption) of nontradable goods and services is simply bundled (aggregated) with its production of exportables. With such aggregation, the terms of trade, the price of the home country's one good against that of the foreign country's, say $P_1/P_2$, is the only relative price that can change in response to a transfer of spending. It is usually defined as the "real" exchange rate.

In this oversimplified world of one-good economies, how do the terms of trade change in our hypothetical scenario when absorption falls in the United States but rises abroad? The increase in demand in ROW will be primarily for its own (export) good rather than imports, which are a relatively small share of its GDP. Similarly, the fall in absorption in the United States will be concentrated on its own (export) good rather than imports, which are also a small share of U.S. GDP. Thus, relatively more of the U.S. good enters world markets than the ROW is willing to absorb at unchanged prices, so $P_1/P_2$ falls. That is, the terms of trade turn against the United States as an endogenous consequence of the transfer of spending. In addition to its primary burden of having to reduce A relative to Y, the United States would face a secondary burden from the adverse change in its terms of trade in the context of these "one-good" per country model specifications. For example, Paul Krugman is one of many influential authors who (mis)use the one-good assumption to conclude that the U.S. real exchange rate must depreciate in the context of the necessary reduction in absorption.[13]

But there is a better theoretical approach that relies on more diversified production in each country. Ronald Jones, among many other authors studying the transfer problem, specifies that each country produces a large body of nontradable goods and services as well as exportables and import substitutes.[14] So when the fall in expenditures in the United States is paired with a

---

[13]  See Krugman 1991, 2007.
[14]  Jones 1975.

rise in expenditures in Asia and elsewhere, the relative price of tradables versus nontradables must increase in the United States and fall abroad. How much is anybody's guess. However, with the necessary expenditure adjustments being spread out over some months or years, and modern technology continually eroding the distinction between tradables and nontradables, this necessary relative price change could be surprisingly modest.

But in the Jones model there is no presumption as to which way the terms of trade need change—except that it may be a small second-order effect. That is, the fall in expenditures in the United States releases American exportables to world markets at about the same pace as the demand for them increases from the increased absorption in the ROW. Therefore, in the short run, with sticky nominal prices in each country's exportable sector, the safest strategy in the transition is to keep the nominal exchange rate stable so that there are no "false" changes in the real exchange rate, as defined by the terms of trade.

With no change in the dollar's nominal exchange rate so that the dollar prices of tradable goods worldwide remain unchanged on average, the dollar's anchoring role for price levels in peripheral emerging markets (as per the monetary approach) would be undisturbed even though the U.S. trade balance improved from the transfer of spending.

## Bretton Woods I and II: Mercantilism Unbound

Instead of the dollar's monetary anchoring role, Michael Dooley, David Folkerts-Landau, and Peter Garber—henceforth DFG—present a mercantilist interpretation of why so many emerging markets have been "softly" pegging to the dollar since the early 1990s.[15] DFG presume that emerging markets in general, but Asian countries in particular, are deliberately undervaluing their currencies to generate export surpluses, particularly to the United States. They see the trade surpluses of these emerging markets (including Japan?) to be sustainable because of compatible mutual interests. The United States needs external financial support to offset its low domestic saving and the emerging markets (including Japan apparently) want higher real growth through exports to promote development.

DFG are to be commended for coming up with a model that at least tries to come to grips with long-term global "imbalances" that is, why U.S. current account deficits have run on for such an unexpectedly long time. They are right to ridicule proponents of dollar devaluation as throwing red meat to the

---

[15] Dooley, Folkerts-Landau, and Garber 2003.

protectionists, and scathing toward those who use faulty intertemporal modeling of international capital flows to continually predict an imminent collapse of the dollar. However, my alternative monetary approach to explaining the willingness of Asian governments, and those in other emerging markets, to stabilize their dollar exchange rates differs from DFG's mercantilist approach in several dimensions.

In this overview, however, I focus just on the most essential difference: DFG's frequent and incorrect use of the word *undervaluation* to reflect the exchange rate policies of countries on the dollar's periphery. In effect, DFG still see the exchange rate as a control variable for the net trade balance in line with the elasticities model of the balance of trade. In contrast, I see the exchange rate itself to have little or no predictive power for the net trade balance, which is dominated by saving-investment imbalances in the United States compared to its periphery; but the dollar exchange rate is significant for price-level determination on the periphery.

In their original paper, DFG drew an intriguing parallel between Bretton Woods I from 1950 to 1971—where the principal high-growth peripheral countries were those of western Europe and Japan—and what we now call Bretton Woods II, where the high-growth peripheral countries are now in Asia with a scattering of emerging markets elsewhere.[16] In DFG's view of the 1950s and 1960s, the western European countries and Japan—under cover of the Bretton Woods parity arrangements—kept the dollar values of their currencies "undervalued" in order to promote more rapid export growth into the American market. The Americans tolerated this mercantilist behavior because, during the cold war, they were anxious to promote recovery in western Europe and Japan.

Under Bretton Woods II, from the 1990s to the present, a large fringe of emerging markets—particularly in East Asia—intervene heavily to keep their dollar exchange rates "undervalued," in order, according to DFG, to generate export surpluses to better promote their economic development. They are willing to treat the resulting huge buildup of official exchange reserves, largely invested in low-yield U.S Treasuries, as an opportunity cost of more rapid export growth. On the other hand, the United States has tolerated this mercantilist behavior of the Asian group because it needs cheap finance to cover its very low rate of saving. Because both sides benefit, DFG see the Bretton Woods II regime of high Asian trade surpluses and high U.S. trade deficits as sustainable— hence the appeal of their model in explaining ongoing global trade "imbalances."

---

[16] Ibid.

TABLE 3.1.
Rules of the game: Bretton Woods II, 1992–2008

**Emerging markets outside of Eastern Europe**
    I. Fix exchange rates, or smooth exchange rate fluctuations, against the U.S. dollar, with or
        without declaring official dollar parities.
    II. Hold official exchange reserves mainly in U.S. dollars.
    III. Adjust monetary policy to maintain dollar exchange rate as nominal anchor for domestic
        price level—as per the monetary approach of McKinnon.[a]
    IIIB. Alternative interpretation: keep dollar exchange rate undervalued to generate an export
        surplus to promote more efficient industrialization—as per the mercantilist approach
        of Dooley, Folkerts-Landau, and Garber.[b]
    IV. Free currency convertibility on current account, but use capital controls when necessary.

**Eurozone and other industrial countries except Japan**
    V. Float exchange rate freely but keep U.S. dollars as a small precautionary reserve.
    VI. Pursue an independent monetary policy to target domestic inflation directly—as per the
        Taylor Rule.
    VII. No exchange controls on current or capital account.

**Japan**
    VIII. Intervene to prevent sporadic upward ratchets of yen against the dollar and deflation.
    IX. No independent monetary policy in liquidity trap to stimulate domestic demand. Rely on
        export expansion
    X. Hold large dollar exchange reserves.
    XI. No exchange controls on current or capital account.

**United States**
    XII. Remain passive in the foreign exchange markets without a balance of payments or exchange
        rate target. Accept large current account deficits to compensate for shortfall in domestic
        saving (or saving glut abroad).
    XIII. Keep U.S. capital markets, including custodial accounts, open to foreigners.
    XIV. Pursue an independent monetary policy to target domestic inflation directly—as per the
        Taylor Rule—and provide a nominal anchor for emerging markets as well as Japan.
    XV. Temporarily suspend the Taylor Rule if deemed necessary to counter the domestic
        business cycle.

Under Bretton Woods II, the more mature industrial countries, particularly the euro bloc in Europe but also such countries as Canada and Australia, now simply float their currencies so that they are not consciously "undervalued." I summarize existing exchange rate arrangements worldwide in table 3.1. Under "Emerging Markets Outside of Eastern Europe," there are two alternative Rule IIIs for interpreting dollar pegging. The first, Rule IIIA, gives the monetary anchor motivation (the McKinnon rule), and the second—Rule IIIB—gives the mercantilist undervaluation motivation (the DFG rule). Japan, with its chronic deflation and sporadic, but sometimes quite massive, foreign exchange interventions against the dollar, is classified separately with its own four rules. The United States, as the normally passive center country, gets its own four operating rules.

Taking the monetary approach, when domestic capital markets are underdeveloped or in disarray for some other reason, the central bank in a country on the periphery of a more stable valued central currency finds it much easier to peg to it as an external monetary anchor in its quest for domestic price-level stability. Consider some historical examples.

After World War II, the capital markets in both western Europe and Japan were in great disarray, with open and repressed inflation, multiple exchange rates, and government controls over both interest rates and bank lending. In 1948, with the advent of the Marshall Plan, individual European countries were encouraged to consolidate their finances, eliminate multiple exchange rates and balance of payments restrictions for current account transactions, curb inflation, and then each peg to the dollar at a unified exchange rate. The culmination of this process was the setting up of the European Payments Union in 1950, backed by a U.S. line of credit, to begin clearing international payments multilaterally by central banks at fixed dollar exchange rates—not even with the 1 percent margins of variation in the Bretton Woods agreement itself. With some modifications, these central dollar parities for western European currencies held for the better part of twenty years (although the 1 percent margins of variation around these central rates became common after 1958).

Japan was similar. From 1945 through 1948, there was open and repressed inflation, multiple exchange rates, and all kinds of interest rate and balance-of-payments controls for allocating foreign exchange. Then in 1949, the Detroit banker Joseph Dodge was sent to Japan with an American line of credit and instructions to encourage the Japanese to consolidate fiscally and curb inflation, unify the exchange rate, and begin phasing out exchange controls on current account transactions. Because of the financial chaos before 1949, the Japanese had no idea (nor did the Americans) what an equilibrium number for the unified exchange rate should be that would end the inflation but keep the economy viable for exporting. So they just guessed. They picked 360 yen to the dollar to be the anchor, and then geared the Bank of Japan's monetary policy to maintaining this rate so that the economy would grow into it.

But they didn't guess quite right. Inflation continued for a year or two before being phased out—and this left the yen somewhat overvalued in the sense that, in the early 1950s, Japanese companies were having difficulty exporting. But rather than give up their hard-won nominal anchor of 360 yen per dollar, they chose to disinflate further rather than directly help tradable goods producers by devaluing. It worked. By the mid-1950s, Japan settled on a high export-led growth path (much like China's today) with the domestic rate of wholesale price index (WPI) inflation in tradable goods converging to

being virtually the same as that in the United States, the anchor country, until the Nixon shock of 1971.[17]

The main point is that, in both Japan and western Europe in the 1950s and
1960s, dollar exchange rates were set to anchor national price levels and stabilize domestic financial markets—as our monetary approach would have it.
Unlike what DFG suggest, these rates were *not* cunningly "undervalued" to
promote export surpluses and secure a mercantile advantage over the United
States. Indeed, the United States had an overall current account surplus during Bretton Woods I.

Since the early 1990s, under the looser dollar pegging called Bretton Woods
II, the search for a monetary anchor also describes the behavior of Asian
countries and emerging markets elsewhere better than DFG's alleged mercantilist plot to deliberately "undervalue" their currencies to generate export
surpluses.

There are too many of these countries to do a historical analysis of each
one. However, consider China. Before 1990, China's currency was inconvertible, with exchange controls and mandatory state trading companies for importing and exporting that (with the exception of special economic zones)
insulated the domestic structure of relative prices from the international one:
the so-called airlock system. In this early phase of China's liberalization of its
domestic markets, it would not have been possible to use the nominal exchange rate as a monetary anchor. Indeed, the official exchange rate was set
(beginning at one yuan per dollar in 1978) quite arbitrarily and made little
difference to actual economic decision making within the country. And China
did experience something of a roller-coaster ride in domestic rates of inflation and real growth rates into the early 1990s.[18]

From 1993 to 1995, China suffered a major bout of inflation, peaking out
at over 20 percent per year. In 1994, in a major move toward current account
convertibility to satisfy the International Monetary Fund, China decided to
unify its multiple "swap" exchange rates with the official exchange rate, including a net depreciation in the unified rate of about the same order of magnitude as the internal inflation. Of course, nobody knew precisely what the
new unified rate should be in "equilibrium," but by 1995 the rate was pegged
at 8.28 yuan per dollar and held there for ten years. The economy grew into
this new monetary anchor and inflation converged down to the U.S. level.

Indeed, in 1997–98 there was net deflationary pressure in China from the

---

[17]  McKinnon and Ohno 1997; McKinnon 2007a.
[18]  McKinnon 2007c.

Asian crisis when the surrounding smaller countries (and export competitors)—Korea, Indonesia, Malaysia, the Philippines, and Thailand—were
forced into depreciating. Fortunately, China ignored foreign advice to depreciate with them (which would have made the regional calamity much worse),
held on to its nominal anchor of 8.28 yuan/dollar, and engaged in a large internal fiscal expansion to overcome the deflationary pressure.

So the China story in Bretton Woods II is similar to that of Japan's and
western Europe's in Bretton Woods I. Before securely pegging to the dollar, all
of these countries had inflation, financial disorganization, and inconvertible
currencies. The most efficient way out was to peg to the more stable central
money, and then move toward greater currency convertibility so that the dollar peg became a more effective monetary anchor. What is clear, however, is
that the nominal exchange rate cum future monetary policy in each case was
chosen in a crisis situation to secure domestic financial stability. The dollar
exchange rate was not deliberately, or even accidentally, undervalued so as to
secure a mercantile advantage for exporting to the American market.

Using our monetary approach, the Bretton Woods II model, in which peripheral countries continue to peg (albeit loosely) to the dollar as an anchor,
is potentially more robust than DFG's mercantilist approach. The monetary
model could survive a major rebalancing of trade flows associated with a rise
in net saving in the United States accompanied by an equivalent fall in Asia—
all with nominal exchange rates remaining unchanged as under our previous
discussion of the transfer problem.

### The U.S. Housing Crisis, the Trade Balance, and the U.S. Treasury

The necessary decline in overall spending in the United States must fall
mainly on the household sector. The huge net spending deficit of American
households, including residential construction, on the order of 4 percent of
GDP in 2006 and earlier was without historical parallel. However, with the
subprime crisis in home mortgages, with new restraint on mortgage lending,
coupled with a fall in home prices, the American household spending deficit
could reverse fairly quickly and become a normal surplus.

Should we worry about a deficiency in global aggregate demand when
American households reduce their spending? In the longer run, the overdue
righting of the financial imbalance in American households is both oppor-
tune and necessary to reduce the huge American current account deficit. But,
in the near term, when American households are no longer "consumers of last

resort," how can this be accomplished without falling into a pit of deficient aggregate demand at the global level?

Instead of nattering about the dollar's exchange rate, which is the wrong variable to adjust, the U.S. secretary of the treasury should now approach his counterpart finance ministers in East Asian countries and possibly Germany to expand aggregate demand jointly. In China, for example, household consumption has been lagging behind the very rapid growth in GDP; and China's recent success—not fully anticipated—in collecting taxes could be generating an as yet unrecognized fiscal surplus. Similarly, Japan has actually been running public sector surpluses over the past four years. So these governments, and Germany's, can afford to be fiscally expansive over the next two years or so as part of a worldwide countercyclical policy. Apart from international altruism, each of these countries has an individual incentive to expand fiscally because their exports will decline as the American consumer is forced to retrench.

If foreign governments jointly become more expansionary, the United States can better avoid another unwise round of unduly easy monetary policy—like that following the collapse of the high-tech bubble in 2001. And further American fiscal expansion (government dissaving) is not desirable if the current account deficit is to be reduced. (This does not rule out a balanced-budget expansion such as a substantial increase in the federal gasoline tax to support a much-needed rebuilding of roads and bridges.)

But how can U.S. treasury secretary Henry Paulson orchestrate with incentives a collective fiscal expansion in Asia and Europe? In April 1995, his predecessor, Robert Rubin, announced a strong dollar policy and the end of two and a half unhappy decades of Japan bashing to get the yen up and the dollar down, which severely damaged the Japanese economy. Circumstances are not quite the same in 2008–09. But today's China bashing to get the renminbi up has been going on for more than four years, with legislation in Congress threatening high tariffs on Chinese goods unless the renminbi is sharply appreciated. Somewhat surprisingly, Japan bashing also returned earlier in 2007 when the incoming Democratic committee chairmen—Carl Levin, Charles Rangel, Barney Frank, and John Dingel—wrote to Secretary Paulson to criticize the weak yen and unduly low interest rates in Japan.[19]

At this critical juncture, with the fall in American consumer spending, the way forward is clear. Secretary Paulson or his successor should call a summit of Asian and European finance ministers to work out a joint program of fis-

[19] McKinnon 2007a.

cal expansion outside the United States. In return, he would reinstate Rubin's strong dollar policy by ending the bashing of China and Japan to appreciate their currencies. Ideally, he could even promise to urge Congress to reform the notoriously arbitrary U.S antidumping laws and other protectionist legislation. And the Fed would forgo further easing that would otherwise weaken the dollar.

At the beginning of his term as treasury secretary, Paulson announced his intention of getting the United States to engage China "constructively." He judged that a smooth economic and political relationship between the two economic giants was key to their mutual prosperity in the new millennium. He was right.

But suppose, instead of this constructive engagement, the doctrinal battle on the exchange rate is lost. At the behest of American protectionists and many economists, suppose the U.S. government moves toward a policy of forcing continual dollar devaluation on its trading partners until there is a substantial reduction in the U.S. trade deficit. But because the supposed link between the relative price effects of exchange rate changes and the trade deficit is not there, the U.S. trade deficit need not, and likely would not, fall. In denial, the U.S. government keeps pushing for further devaluation—as it did with continued forced appreciations of the yen in the 1970s through mid-1995.

Once foreigners see this happening on a worldwide scale, they will stop buying dollar assets, leaving the dollar in potential free fall and losing their monetary anchor. But the major damage would be in the United States itself. The cessation of foreign purchases of dollar assets and capital flight from the United States will shock the saving-deficient American economy with a sharp credit crunch and high interest rates. Domestic spending in general, and that for investment in particular, would fall sharply so as to compress imports and reduce the trade deficit. But such a reduction in the trade deficit would come primarily from the catastrophic fall in domestic absorption and not from the relative price effects of the dollar devaluation, unlike how the elasticities model would have it.

Thus, in depreciating the dollar and ending the dollar standard, be careful what you wish for!

### Addendum: The U.S. Banking Crisis and Credit Crunch of 2008–09

The body of this chapter was written in the late summer of 2007, before the tumultuous events of 2008 and 2009. Since 2007, panic has swept through the

U.S. financial markets: the interbank credit markets have seized up from counterparty risk, federal authorities have intervened several times to bail out failing banks (particularly investment banks) and insurance companies, and the U.S. stock market has cratered. Although this financial panic originated from the collapse of the bubble in American house prices, it has become a global panic as European interbank markets also seized up—and stock prices in most emerging markets have fallen even more sharply than in the industrial countries. Worldwide, numerous commodity bubbles are deflating with the price of oil falling particularly sharply.

Perhaps it is not surprising that that such an upheaval in the center country of the world dollar standard should be so contagious. What is surprising, however, is that dollar assets—particularly U.S. Treasury bonds—remain in such strong demand by the rest of the world. The "flight to quality," both in the private U.S. interbank market and by foreign central banks holding exchange reserves, is quite extraordinary. Treasury yields have been bid down close to zero for very short-term (overnight) maturities, just 1 percent for six-month maturities, and 1.6 percent for two-year bonds. In the months from July to November 2008, when the crisis was unfolding and seemingly at its worst, the dollar suddenly strengthened (albeit after prolonged weakness) in the foreign exchanges against most other currencies, rising about 25 percent against the euro. (The yen has been the only major currency to appreciate significantly against the dollar.)

Paradoxically, despite the financial chaos in the United States, with a huge upsurge in contingent claims on the U.S. Treasury from the prospect of having to bail out even more failing financial institutions, the demand for dollar assets—and Treasuries in particular—around the world has apparently increased. If the international dollar standard is indeed in its death throes, this robust demand for Treasuries is hard to explain. Either Treasuries are still treated as a safe haven in times of great uncertainty, or foreign central banks are loathe to let currencies appreciate against the world's still dominant money during a global downturn for fear that their exports would become less competitive—or both.

As amazingly robust as the dollar standard under stress seems to be, the United States has been gravely weakened in its ability to mount a counter-cyclical policy to offset the global recession. Could China, and possibly other surplus-saving countries, help?

Though China and the United States are an unlikely duo to mitigate the current economic crisis, they have good reasons to cooperate. Both have strong vested interests in curbing global inflation, relaxing the credit crunch that threatens an economic downturn, and in preserving the foreign exchange value of the dollar. Trade between them is huge, but extraordinarily unbalanced. China is the largest creditor of the United States, nervously holding huge stocks of dollar claims. The large U.S. trade deficit in manufactures with China (and East Asia more generally) has contracted the U.S. manufacturing base and led to an upwelling of protectionist sentiment that inflames American politics. A cooperative economic program that addresses the near-term global macro-crisis on the one hand, and the festering China-U.S. trade imbalance on the other, is feasible and highly desirable.

The collapse of the U.S. housing bubble in 2007–08 is the proximate reason for the worldwide spread of the credit crisis. Aggregate demand in the global economy is declining because of the retrenchment in U.S. household spending, which is necessary to reduce the U.S. trade deficit. Because the Federal Reserve overreacted by cutting interest rates too much, the flight of hot money from the dollar worsened the seizing up of credit markets in the United States. When counterparty risks are acute, the huge U.S. interbank markets are further impaired because of a shortage of prime collateral in the form of U.S. Treasury bonds. As foreign central banks, such as the People's Bank of China (PBC), intervene to buy dollars to prevent their currencies from ratcheting upward, they invest the proceeds disproportionately in U.S. Treasuries and so incidentally worsen their shortage in private U.S. financial markets.

But China also has domestic financial problems including a banking squeeze. Because of low U.S. interest rates and American "China bashing" to appreciate the renminbi, the deluge of hot money inflows into China up to July 2008 greatly complicated the PBC's monetary policy. There were virtually no private capital outflows from China to finance its huge trade surplus, which further tightened credit conditions in the United States. Because of China's uncontrolled buildup of official exchange reserves before July 2008, Chinese money growth had been excessive, leading to too much inflation, some of which leaked out into the rest of the world. In trying to sterilize the domestic monetary consequences of the rapid buildup of official exchange reserves, the PBC has had to impose high reserve requirements on its commercial banks. But having to hold renminbi reserves on deposit with the PBC impedes the commercial banks' lending to the private sector.

To deal with the global crisis, how should the U.S. and Chinese governments proceed?

First, the United States should stop China bashing and, instead, encourage the PBC to stabilize the yuan/dollar exchange rate at "today's" level both to lessen the inflationary overheating of China's economy and to protect the renminbi value of its huge dollar exchange reserves. There is a precedent for this:

in April 1995, Treasury Secretary Robert Rubin ended twenty-five years of bashing Japan to appreciate the yen—and announced a new strong dollar policy that stopped the ongoing appreciation in the yen. Since July 2008, when the dollar has strengthened against all major currencies, the PBC has (temporarily) halted appreciating the renminbi against the dollar. Indeed, the rate has been kept close to 6.85 yuan/dollar since then. So now is a good time to convince the Americans on the mutual advantages of returning to a fixed yuan/dollar rate.

Second, after the PBC regains monetary control and China's price level stabilizes, the Chinese government should then agree to take strong measures to get rid of the economy's net saving surplus, which is reflected in its large current account and trade surpluses. This would require some combination of tax cuts, increases in government expenditures, increased dividends from enterprises so as to increase household disposable income, and reduced reserve requirements on commercial banks. Then, as China's trade surplus in manufactures diminishes, pressure on the American manufacturing sector would be relaxed with a corresponding reduction in America's trade deficit. Worldwide, the increase in spending in China would offset the forced reduction in U.S. spending from the housing crash.

Again, there is an important historical precedent. In the great crisis of 1997–98, most East Asian countries depreciated their currencies—with Indonesia, Korea, Malaysia, the Philippines, and Thailand, whose currencies were attacked, suffering steep economic slumps. Fortunately, China alone kept its dollar exchange rate stable, but it did face a potential deflationary slowdown. However, in March 1998, Premier Zhu Rongji announced his famous multi-billion dollar fiscal expansion to be spread out over the next four years or so. This avoided an economic downturn in China by sustaining domestic aggregate demand, and East Asian neighbors recovered faster because they could more easily export to China.

Now China is a much bigger actor on the world stage. With the slump in spending in the United States and elsewhere, China should step in with a big new fiscal expansion, which it is well placed to do because of its huge trade surplus that should be reduced anyway. China's public finances are now very strong with the surge in tax revenues, and the old bad loan problem with its banks has been largely corrected as enterprises—both state owned and private—became more profitable.

In contrast, U.S. public finances are in a mess. The precrisis fiscal deficit is still with us. In addition, the government has taken on huge new contingent liabilities from bailouts of innumerable financial institutions that will hamstring the federal budget for years to come. Thus, any new U.S. fiscal "stimuli," or big new spending programs not covered by tax increases, would seem to be out of the question. Even if implemented, they would wind up increasing the trade deficit.

In summary, a "negotiated" fiscal expansion in China (and possibly in other trade-surplus countries such as Germany), with a formal end to China bashing as the quid pro quo, would seem to be the most promising way of mitigating a global slowdown.

# 4

# ENDURING TOP CURRENCY, FRAGILE NEGOTIATED CURRENCY

## Politics and the Dollar's International Role

Eric Helleiner

Over thirty years ago, Susan Strange was prompted to write her classic work *Sterling and British Policy* because discussions over sterling's future as an international currency were dominated by the market-oriented analyses of economists. What was needed, she argued, was a more "political theory of international currencies" that recognized the central role of states and politics in determining the future of an international currency.[1] In this chapter, I suggest that the theoretical framework she developed—particularly the distinction between a "Top" and "Negotiated" currency—should be revisited because it can provide some useful insights into how political analysis can contribute to our understanding of the dollar's future as an international currency today.

Using the categories outlined in the introductory chapter, a top currency is one whose international standing is derived from the kinds of economic factors relating to confidence, liquidity, and transactional networks that are identified by *market-based* analyses. I argue here, however, that those eco-

Author's note: Special thanks to two anonymous reviewers, Jerry Cohen, Jonathan Kirshner, Chris Way, Hubert Zimmerman, and all the other participants in the Cornell workshops on "The Future of the U.S. Dollar." For their research help and support, I thank Troy Lundblad and the Social Sciences and Humanities Research Council of Canada. Some parts of this chapter are drawn from Helleiner 2008.
[1] Strange 1971b, 3.

nomic factors, in turn, rest on some important political foundations, which in the dollar's case are likely to remain stronger for some time than those of any potential challenger currency. At the same time, I also suggest that the dollar is increasingly assuming the status of a negotiated currency in some contexts. In these circumstances, its international status relies on the more direct political support of foreign governments in the ways that *instrumental* and *geopolitical* approaches suggest. Challenges to the dollar's international position in the near future, I suggest, are more likely to come from the uncertain politics associated with its increasingly negotiated status in these contexts.

## Different Kinds of International Currencies

*Market-based* approaches to the study of the dollar's future have generated diverse predictions, but they are united by their assumption that market actors will be the key determinants of the international role of a currency. In some contexts, this assumption will be well justified. Strange highlighted, however, how the balance of power between states and markets in the international monetary order may be more tilted toward the former in other contexts. A currency may, for example, derive its international status from the fact that a dominant or imperial state has imposed its use on subordinate countries or colonies. Strange suggested that this kind of international currency be called a "master" currency to contrast it with "top" currencies, which achieve their international position because of their inherent economic attractiveness.

She also introduced a third category to describe situations in which a state may back a foreign currency's international position not because it is forced to but for voluntary reasons. Some of these reasons might be related to factors that market-based analyses identify; that is, public authorities may choose voluntarily to use a foreign currency as an intervention currency, as a reserve asset or as an anchor for pegging their national currency because of issues relating to confidence, liquidity, and/or transactional networks. In these instances, that foreign currency should still be classified as a "top" currency in Strange's typology. But support for an international currency might also be encouraged by inducements offered by the issuing state in the form of aid packages, promises of market access, or military protection. Strange suggested that this kind of currency be labeled a "negotiated" one.[2]

The label was not meant to suggest that foreign state support for the cur-

---

[2] Strange also introduced one further distinction—"Neutral" currencies—to describe a currency such as the Swiss franc, which, like a top currency, achieved its international standing because of its inherent economic attractiveness, but which was not issued by a dominant economic power.

rency always resulted from explicit diplomatic negotiations. It might, she noted, simply emerge from "an implicit understanding" among the relevant parties.[3] Inclusive of wider circumstances such as these, I employ the term here to refer to any context where a currency's international role is supported by foreign governments for reasons that do not stem from the currency's inherent economic attractiveness.[4]

Strange did not intend her categories of international currencies to be rigid ones.[5] Indeed, in her view, any international currency could assume different roles *simultaneously* in different contexts. Even during its heyday as an international currency, sterling was never solely a top currency. It assumed this status in many parts of the world where market actors and foreign governments recognized the economic attractiveness of sterling's international role. But within British colonies, Strange highlighted that sterling was a master currency whose status reflected the fact that British authorities during the late nineteenth and early twentieth centuries had systematically—and often with considerable coercion—replaced indigenous forms of money in their colonies with either sterling or new colonial currencies that were tied tightly to sterling. And by the interwar and early post-1945 years, sterling increasingly acted also as a negotiated currency among independent countries that were members of the sterling area. Many foreign governments in the sterling area came to see their enduring support for sterling's international role as linked to specific benefits they might derive from their relationship with the British state.

Economic analyses of international currencies with at least some master or negotiated status will be incomplete because they make one or both of the following assumptions. The first is that market actors, driven by profit-maximizing goals, play the central role in conferring international currency status. The second is that, when public authorities are significant, their policies are driven primarily by the kinds of economic considerations that influence market actors—that is, those relating to confidence, liquidity, and transactional networks. Although these assumptions hold true in a top currency context, they are much less useful for an analysis of currencies with some aspects of master and negotiated status. In these instances, political authorities play at least some direct role in determining the international standing of curren-

---

[3]  Strange 1971b, 5.

[4]  This definition of the term is perhaps a little wider than Strange herself intended, but I think it usefully includes a set of circumstances that do not otherwise fall easily into her categories. I am suggesting that a negotiated currency's international position relies on the *voluntary* support of foreign states, in contrast to a master currency, and that this support, in contrast to a top currency, stems from reasons beyond the inherent economic attractiveness of the currency.

[5]  See especially Strange 1971b, 6–7.

cies. And they are motivated at least in part by various goals beyond confidence, liquidity, and transactional networks. A much more political form of analysis is thus necessary in any effort to understand the future of master and negotiated currencies.

This is not to suggest that political analyses are not relevant for top currencies as well. After all, each of the economic determinants of a top currency is in turn influenced by political factors. Here, however, politics acts as an *indirect* determinant of international currency standing—that is, its influence operates through the economic variables identified by market-based approaches. In the case of a master or negotiated currency, politics determines international currency standing through a much more *direct* channel. When analyzing master currencies, the focus of a political analysis can be primarily on the issuing state because of its coercive power over subordinate territories. In the case of negotiated currencies, however, analysts must examine the political motivations of both the issuing state and the "followers" as well as the interplay between the two parties.

## The Political Foundations of Dollar's Top Currency Status

A political analysis of the dollar's future must begin by examining its top currency status. There is no question that the dollar today is a top currency according to Strange's criteria. It remains an economically attractive international currency to market actors and governments around the world for reasons relating to confidence, liquidity, and transactional networks. But will this continue? Economists who have examined this question find it difficult to reach a consensus. An exploration of the *indirect* influence of politics on the economic determinants of the dollar's international position strengthens the position of those who argue that the dollar's top currency will endure for some time.

Predictions of an erosion of the dollar's top currency status have been made as far back as the 1960s and they have resurfaced most prominently at moments when the dollar is depreciating —namely, the early 1970s, the late 1970s, the late 1980s, the mid-1990s, and during the last few years. The assumption underlying these predictions is often that there is a close correlation between the dollar's international status and confidence in its stable value. To be sure, there is no question that this kind of confidence played an important role in boosting the status of past global currencies from the Venetian ducat to sterling. It was also important to the dollar's international position after World War II. But it is less clear that confidence in the dollar's stable value has been the most important economic factor sustaining that position since the 1970s. After all, the dollar's value has fluctuated considerably over this period while the currency has retained its international position.

What, then, has been the more important economic determinant of the dollar's top currency role? Transactional networks have been significant, both with respect to the enormous size of the United States within the global economy and with respect to the inertia associated with network externalities. But in my view the central factor sustaining the dollar's top currency position has been the unique liquidity of U.S. financial markets, particularly in a context where finance became increasingly liberalized worldwide after the 1960s. Footloose global capital has been attracted to the unique openness, depth, and breadth of U.S. financial markets in ways that sustained and even boosted the dollar's international role, despite its unstable value since the breakdown of the Bretton Woods exchange rate system.[6]

Both Japan and Germany issued currencies whose value was in many ways more likely to inspire confidence since the 1970s, but neither came even remotely close to housing the kinds of attractive financial markets that the United States did. Both countries had distinctive political reasons for deliberately refraining from cultivating the kind of open and deep domestic financial markets that would have boosted the internationalization of their currencies. It was this limitation, above all, that inhibited the yen and the deutsche mark from challenging the dollar's central global role. Indeed, it is no coincidence that the two dominant world currencies in the last two hundred years—the sterling and the dollar—both had very liquid and open capital-market-based financial systems that were very attractive for foreigners to operate in. The bank-dominated, credit-based financial systems of potential challenging states such as Japan and Germany have held back their ability to cultivate an international currency.

If this analysis is correct, it sheds an interesting light on predictions of the dollar's decline as a top currency today. Many such predictions focus on the erosion of confidence in the dollar's value that may be triggered by the large current account and fiscal deficits as well as the external debts of the United States. This erosion, they suggest, is taking place at a time when the dollar has a new challenger—the euro—whose ability to command the confidence of market actors is much greater because of its conservative management, constitutionally protected by the Maastricht Treaty. But if the dollar's stable value has not been the central foundation of the dollar's international position since the 1970s, these predictions may miss the mark. To be sure, a dramatic

[6] Helleiner 1994.

collapse in the dollar's value would undermine its international position (I return to this point below). But, in the absence of such a major crisis, more important to the dollar's top currency position may be the question of whether the euro zone—or other potential challengers—can present a credible alternative to the preeminent position of U.S. financial markets within the global financial system.

Simply asking this question quickly reminds us of why a currency such as the Chinese renminbi is very unlikely to become a top currency any time soon. Not only are Chinese financial markets overregulated and underdeveloped, but the kinds of liquid domestic financial markets that help to boost the international standing of a currency are most likely to flourish in political contexts characterized by limited constitutional government and pro-creditor legal frameworks.[7] The yen has much better prospects in this respect for challenging the dollar over the medium term, particularly since Japanese policymakers have shown more interest in promoting the yen's international role through domestic financial reforms from the 1990s onward. But they still have a ways to go.

The more serious challenge to the dollar's top currency position in this area comes once again from the euro. Euro enthusiasts highlight how the increasingly integrated European financial markets increasingly match or surpass their U.S. counterparts in size. But this challenge should not be overstated. Without a single fiscal authority, Europe's lacks a central European equivalent of the uniquely liquid and deep U.S. Treasury bill market, which plays such an important role in sustaining the U.S. dollar's global position. European financial integration also remains a work in progress with more initiatives needed in areas such as the creation of more uniform financial regulations and consolidation of exchanges. Whether political support for this work remains strong is an issue of crucial importance to the euro's future international role.[8]

Equally important is the failure of the Maastricht Treaty to specify clear procedures for the prevention and resolution of euro-zone financial crises. The significance of this limitation in the political infrastructure of the euro zone became apparent during the international financial crisis of 2008. As European financial institutions faced insolvency, there was no pan-European fiscal authority for them to turn to for support. National governments remained the backstop. When some national governments initially responded unilaterally, financial analysts raised the prospect that European financial integration

---

[7] See, for example, Stasavage 2003; Walter 2006.
[8] See, for example, Walter 2006; Henning 2000, 23–24; McNamara 2008; Cohen 2004, 71–73.

could unravel and that euro-zone unity itself might be threatened.[9] Faced with this prospect, European governments moved toward a more cooperative solution. Still, the crisis has left investors with an important question: How much trust should they place in the euro and European financial markets when fiscal cooperation has failed to keep pace with financial and monetary integration?

The crisis was also important in a second way in highlighting the dollar's enduring top currency status. It demonstrated how the dollar, not the euro, remains the "safe haven" currency in a crisis. Despite the enormity of U.S. financial difficulties, the dollar strengthened as the crisis became more severe. A central reason was that the U.S. Treasury bill remained the investment of choice for investors in an international financial crisis. The U.S. T-bill's position reflects not just the unique liquidity of the T-bill market but also the perceived safety of this asset, a perception ultimately backed by the country's political stability and its global power. To be sure, the credibility of the safety and attractiveness of U.S. financial markets as a whole was dealt a blow by the crisis of 2008. But the crisis also revealed how the U.S. T-bill market remains the fulcrum of the global financial system in a way that no European financial market does.

The dollar's top currency status thus looks likely to endure for some time in the absence of a severe exchange rate crisis. The dollar's top currency position is likely to be sustained not just by the overall size and global reach of the U.S. economy and the inertia stemming from the dollar's network externalities, but especially by the unique liquidity of U.S. financial markets. The strength of the latter derives from political foundations that are more solid than those of potential challenger currencies.

## The Dollar as a Negotiated Currency

If the dollar is exclusively a top currency, it is essential that we explore the political foundations of the economic determinants of the dollar's international position. And to the extent that the dollar is a negotiated currency, political factors become even more paramount.[10] The dollar's future would then be increasingly dependent on the political choices of the U.S. state and of other states to directly support the dollar's international position. Political analyses

[9] See, for example, David Oakley and Gillian Tett, "Credit Markets Point to Strains in Rich Economies," *Financial Times*, October 8, 2008.

[10] The category of master currency is much less relevant for the dollar today than it was for sterling.

of these choices could make a significant contribution to our understanding
of the dollar's future.

As far back as the 1960s, the dollar's international standing was already
partly a negotiated one. When growing U.S. external deficits in that decade
undermined confidence in the dollar, support for the currency increasingly
came from foreign monetary authorities who were motivated to provide this
support at least partly by broader political objectives. In some cases, foreign
support for the dollar stemmed from an implicit understanding that this
would preserve access to the U.S. market. In other countries (such as West
Germany) dollar reserve holdings were linked explicitly to broader bilateral
security relations with the United States.[11]

After the United States suspended the dollar's convertibility into gold in
1971, many questioned the dollar's future as an international currency and
assumed that it could only be maintained with more explicit political support. U.S. officials did indeed seek to preserve the dollar's international role
through some diplomacy, such as with Saudi Arabia after the oil shock of
1973.[12] But the need for such diplomacy diminished as the growing globalization of financial markets in this period bolstered the U.S. dollar's economic
attractiveness because of the unique liquidity of U.S. financial markets. In this
way, the dollar's international standing shifted from a partly negotiated currency to a more predominantly top currency because of the unique structural
power held by the United States within the more market-based international
monetary order that was emerging in that era.[13] The significance of foreign
political support for the dollar's international status diminished further in the
wake of the Paul Volcker's dramatic boosting of U.S. interest rates in 1979,
which provided new economic incentives for market and official actors to
back the dollar's international status.

Over the past decade, however, questions about the role of foreign political support in sustaining the dollar's international position have grown once
again as a number of foreign monetary authorities have accumulated enormous dollar reserves. The size of reserve holdings in East Asia have been
particularly large, with China holding about $1.8 trillion in mainly dollar-de-
nominated foreign currency reserves in mid-2008 and Japan acquiring over
$970 billion.[14] Other significant official dollar holders have been Russia, Tai-
wan, South Korea, India, and many oil-exporting countries in the Middle

[11]  See, for example, Gavin 2004; Calleo 1982; Zimmermann 2002.
[12]  Spiro 1999.
[13]  Helleiner 1994; Strange 1986.
[14]  Peter Garnham, "Growth of Global FX Reserves Begins to Show Signs of Wilting," *Financial Times,* September 4, 2008.

East. The levels of official dollar reserve holdings abroad have reminded many scholars of the situation in the 1960s when the dollar became increasingly dependent on foreign political support. Should the dollar, then, be described as partially a negotiated currency once again?

The term only makes sense in this context if the official dollar holders have accumulated these reserves for motivations unrelated to the market-based considerations relating to confidence, liquidity, and transactional networks. The proponents of the *Bretton Woods II* and *geopolitical* approaches discussed in the introductory chapter suggest that this is indeed the case. It is certainly true that some of the key official support for the dollar in East Asia comes from countries—most notably China, Japan, and South Korea—whose structural position in the world has left them highly dependent on the United States as an external market for their products. In the case of Japan and South Korea, this economic dependence is compounded by their reliance on the United States for military protection.[15] The support for the dollar coming from key Middle Eastern oil-producing countries is reminiscent of the role they have played before, a role that was often linked to their broader geopolitical relationship with the United States.

If the negotiated currency label makes some sense in this context, does this necessarily imply that a more political analysis of the future of the dollar's international role as a whole is in order? Some question whether the narrow focus on official reserves can tell us very much about the dollar's overall international standing in an international monetary order that appears to be dominated by powerful global financial markets.[16] But a dramatic selling of dollar reserves could influence private market behavior, particularly if the dollar's international position is being sustained to a considerable degree by the inertia of incumbency.

Just as important, foreign governments are increasingly becoming major actors within global financial markets through the establishment of government-controlled "sovereign wealth funds." Such funds have been established especially by East Asian countries that are seeking to invest their ballooning foreign exchange reserves more actively and by governments in many oil-exporting countries. Altogether, sovereign wealth funds now control approximately $2.5 trillion in assets, a larger sum than that controlled by the global hedge fund industry.[17] In this context, the state/market balance in global finance is shifting toward the former (as de Cecco also argues in chapter 6).

[15] Murphy (2006) explicitly links Japan's dollar support in the current period to the country's broader geopolitical dependence on the United States.

[16] See, for example, Truman 2005a, 63n17.

[17] Tony Tassell and Joanna Chung, "The $2,500bn Question," *Financial Times*, May 25, 2007.

As sovereign wealth funds become major players in global financial markets, foreign governments have another tool through which they can influence the international role of the dollar.

In addition to their reserve policy and investment choices in global markets, foreign governments also can influence the dollar's international role in several other ways that deserve brief mention. Some suggest that OPEC member governments can influence the dollar's role as an international unit of account through their choice of currency for oil pricing (although others point out that pricing decisions in this area are increasingly market-driven[18]). The choice of whether to maintain a formal or informal dollar peg is also significant. Foreign governments can also play a role of encouraging or discouraging the domestic use of the U.S. dollar as a store of value and medium of exchange. In a case such as Russia, which became one of the most "dollarized" countries in the world in the post-Soviet era, this latter policy choice can be quite significant.[19]

## The Durability of Foreign Support for the Dollar?

With the state/market balance in global finance currently shifting back in the direction of the state, those interested in the future of the dollar's international role do need to explore the political durability of the direct support it receives from foreign governments. Some believe that this support is quite solid. With respect to the reserve role, for example, Dooley et al. argue that neither the United States nor the official dollar reserve holders abroad have reason to upset the existing Bretton Woods II arrangement given the mutual economic benefits it provides.[20] But there are important reasons to be more skeptical of the political longevity of the current official support for the dollar's international role.

### The Growing Costs of Bretton Woods II

To begin with, the balance of benefits and costs associated with Bretton Woods II is changing. One of the main benefits for foreign governments of supporting the Bretton Woods II arrangement has been the attractiveness of the United States as an export market. Its appeal to foreigners was bolstered by the strong rates of U.S. economic growth. But the U.S. economic down-

[18] Momani 2008.
[19] Johnson 2008.
[20] Dooley et al. 2003, 2005.

turn after 2007 has called into question the ability of the United States to continue to act as the "buyer of first resort." At the same time, the trade patterns of many of the key dollar-supporting countries in East Asia have already been reorienting away from dependence on the U.S. market toward both intraregional trade and European markets.[21]

At the same time that the benefits of supporting the dollar are diminishing, the costs of holding dollar reserves are rising. For countries holding very large dollar reserves, such as China and Japan, the size of financial losses have been enormous when the dollar has depreciated in value. According to one estimate, each 10 percent decline in the dollar has the effect of generating a loss equivalent to approximately 3 percent of China's gross domestic product.[22] The losses on China's foreign assets are increasingly becoming politicized within the country, with questions being raised about why such a large portion of Chinese savings are being transferred abroad instead of being invested domestically to boost China's standard of living.[23]

Until recently, the losses experienced by the Chinese government were partially offset by the fact that its reserves could be invested in U.S. Treasury bills that earned a higher rate of interest than the low rate it paid out on the local government bills issued to sterilize the dollar inflows. But with the sharp decline in U.S. interest rates in early 2008, combined with rising rates in China, sterilization of dollar inflows no longer was profitable in this way for Chinese monetary authorities and they began losing billions of dollars each month from sterilization activities.[24]

There is one further potential cost of the accumulation of dollar reserves for many countries. When U.S. allies accumulated dollar reserves to stem dollar depreciation in episodes such as the late 1960s, late 1970s, or the late 1980s, it often proved difficult to sterilize large-scale currency intervention, with the result that the dollar purchases were soon curtailed in an effort to prevent domestic inflation. Those who predict that Bretton Woods is sustainable have argued that the two largest dollar holders—China and Japan—are less concerned about the potentially inflationary consequences of holding such large reserves than dollar holders in the past. They argue that Japanese authorities have seen currency intervention as a way to help reverse the domestic *deflationary* pressures Japan has experienced for over a decade, while Chinese au-

---

[21] In the all-important case of China, for example, Goldstein and Lardy (2005, 4) note that the United States now takes just one third of Chinese exports, while Europe's share is roughly a quarter.

[22] Cohen 2008b, 462.

[23] For example, see Setser 2008.

[24] Richard McGregor, "Beijing Begins to Pay Price for Forex 'Sterilisation,'" *Financial Times*, February 1, 2008.

thorities are better able to contain inflationary pressure because of the heavily regulated nature of the Chinese financial system.[25]

But these arguments look less convincing as time goes on. Japan no longer is suffering from a severe deflationary risk. And the argument that the Chinese government can contain domestic inflationary pressures has been challenged by many in the past[26] and looks increasingly shaky as prices begin to climb in that country. The Chinese case is particularly important given how inflation has been strongly associated with social instability in China's history. China's support for Bretton Woods II is often explained on the grounds that the Chinese leadership seeks to preserve social stability by continuing to support employment growth in the export-oriented coastal regions. But if the cost of this support is social unrest arising from inflation, then the leadership may reconsider its position.[27]

Dollar support could also become increasingly associated with inflation in another way. The U.S. financial crisis of 2007–08 has prompted a radical shift in U.S. monetary policy that could undermine the "monetary anchor" rationale for foreign dollar support outlined by Ronald McKinnon in chapter 3. Because of the severity of the crisis, the Federal Reserve cut interest rates on a scale and with a speed that is unprecedented in several decades and which could call into question the anti-inflation commitment of the U.S. central bank. Some important countries with currencies pegged to the dollar had already been questioning the dollar's "monetary anchor" role as the greenback depreciated in value. These questions became even more intense in various countries, including the oil-rich Gulf Cooperation Council countries, which are increasingly dependent on imports from nondollar regions. As the costs of these imports have risen considerably with the dollar's depreciation since 2002, inflationary pressures—already growing in many of their economies because of the oil boom—have been building in their local economies, triggering widespread calls for an abandonment of the dollar pegs. Kuwait ended its dollar peg in May 2007, and more active discussions about the issue have arisen in other key states, such as Qatar, the United Arab Emirates, and even Saudi Arabia.[28]

---

[25]  Dooley and Garber 2005, 159.

[26]  See, for example, Goldstein and Lardy 2005; Eichengreen 2006; Roubini and Setser 2005.

[27]  Chin and Helleiner 2008.

[28]  Joanna Chung and Peter Garnham, "Plummeting Dollar a Big Headache for Pegged Currencies," *Financial Times*, March 14, 2008; Simeon Kerr, "Qatar Considers Dropping Dollar Peg in Response to Rising Inflation," *Financial Times*, January 31, 2008; James Drummond, "Call to Revalue Saudi Currency by 30%," *Financial Times*, July 16, 2008; James Drummond, "Abu Dhabi Ponders End of Dollar Peg," *Financial Times*, July 7, 2008.

## Geopolitical Uncertainty

Turning to the geopolitical basis of foreign dollar support, Kirshner notes in chapter 9 that one key difference from the 1960s is the fact that support for the dollar no longer comes exclusively from countries that are close military allies of the United States. Given the historical affinity between security and monetary ties, this fact may be significant. Put bluntly, the dollar's position may be less secure in a context in which the largest holder of dollar reserves—China—is considered by many as more of a geopolitical rival than an ally of the United States. Political scientists can certainly cite many historical examples when official reserves have been used as a weapon by their holders for geostrategic purposes, and some analysts worry that China could soon do the same.[29]

Such rivalry has not yet influenced Chinese policy toward the dollar.[30] To be sure, one member of a Chinese government economic research institute, Xia Bin, caused some controversy in the summer of 2007 with the speculation that China's reserves could be used as a "bargaining chip" with the United States. But an anonymous official at the People's Bank of China quickly clarified that U.S. dollar assets would remain an important component of its reserves because "the dollar enjoys a major position in the international monetary system, based on the large capacity and high liquidity of US financial markets."[31] Still, U.S. analysts worry about whether Chinese policy might change in the future, particularly in the context of a U.S.-China security dispute.[32]

There are signs that political tensions are influencing some other dollar-supporting countries. Juliet Johnson shows how resurgent nationalism in Russia has prompted Russian officials to take a number of measures to lessen their dependence on the dollar.[33] These have included initiatives not only to diversify the country's official foreign exchange reserves away from dollars but also to "de-dollarize" the domestic monetary system and eliminate the role of the dollar in domestic oil trading. In linking their challenge to the dollar with the push for greater political independence from the United States, Russian officials are following in de Gaulle's footsteps.

Dissatisfaction with dollar dependence may even be growing among coun-

---

[29] See, for example, the comments of Flynt Leverett in Daniel Dombey, "America Faces Diplomatic Penalty as Dollar Dwindles," *Financial Times*, December 28, 2007. For political science analysis, see Kirshner 1995.

[30] See Bowles and Wang 2008.

[31] Quoted in Richard McGregor, "China Affirms Dollar's Global Reserve Status," *Financial Times*, August 13, 2007.

[32] See, for example, Setser 2008; Liss 2008.

[33] Johnson 2008.

tries that have long been loyal supporters of the currency. Katada highlights how Japanese officials have increasingly promoted the yen's international role since the late 1990s through both direct and indirect means, and she suggests that a key motivation has been to reduce the dependence of Japan and East Asia on the United States, a dependence that was blamed partially for Japan's bubble economy of the 1980s and for the severity of the 1997–98 East Asian financial crisis.[34] This is not to suggest that Japan's initiatives have been successful. The legacy of Japanese colonial rule and the geopolitical rivalries among East Asian countries have made the yen's direct promotion difficult, and have led Japanese officials increasingly to back the idea of an Asian Currency Unit as the means to reduce dollar dependence in the region (an idea whose study was endorsed formally by East Asian governments in 2006).

Some scholars have also suggested that concerns about recent U.S. policy toward the Middle East could encourage some key countries in that region to reconsider their support for the dollar.[35] They certainly are being encouraged to do so by critics of U.S. foreign policy. In late 2007, two of the most outspoken critics, Iran and Venezuela, pressed OPEC members to shift oil pricing away from dollars to a basket of currencies. Iran's president, Mahmoud Ahmadinejad, called the dollar "a worthless piece of paper" while Venezuela's president Hugo Chávez predicted "the collapse of the dollar empire."[36] But Saudi Arabia remained loyal to the dollar, resisting the appeal, and the initiative failed. Benjamin Cohen argues (chapter 7), however, that Middle Eastern countries might be more willing to shift away from the dollar if the EU chose to promote the euro's role more actively in the region.

Will European authorities take on promoting the international role of the euro in a direct fashion? Since the euro's creation, European monetary authorities have stated that they have little interest in actively promoting the euro's international role. Even with the accession of new countries to the European Union, European policymakers have not gone out of their way to encourage new members to adopt the euro.[37] At the same time, the euro's creation was certainly driven, at least in part, by the strategic goal of boosting Europe's role in the world and challenging U.S. power in the international monetary realm.[38] The possibility of a more active promotion of the euro in

[34] Katada 2008.
[35] See, for example, Eichengreen 2004, 8. For an excellent review of this issue, see Momani (2008) who is more skeptical of change in the region.
[36] Quoted in Najmeh Bozorgmehr, "AhmadiNejad and Chávez Delight in 'Empire's Collapse,'" *Financial Times*, November 20, 2007.
[37] See, for example, Pascha 2007.
[38] Henning 1998, 2006.

regions such as the Middle East, driven by strategic goals, can thus not be ruled out in the future.

If foreign support for the dollar may be less solid than in the past for these various reasons, the possibility of an unstable future for the dollar's negotiated status could grow in another way. Under Bretton Woods I, "free riding" behavior and "bandwagon" dynamics vis-à-vis reserve holdings were partially kept in check by the binding agent of a military alliance and various international policy networks among Western officials in the financial and monetary realm.[39] Under Bretton Woods II, this glue is much less present. The risk of defections generating a herdlike momentum away from a depreciating dollar may thus be higher, particularly given that there is now a more serious alternative to the dollar in the form of the euro.[40] We have today, in other words, a more fragile political equilibrium among dollar-supporting states in which a sudden change in expectations could perhaps generate quite rapid change.

### What Role Will the United States Play?

If there were to be a serious run on the dollar, the dollar's fate as an international currency would be influenced by U.S. policy choices. A Volcker-like reaction could help to restore confidence and the dollar's status as more of an exclusively top currency. But Volcker's "hard money" policy was only possible politically because of the strength of an anti-inflationary domestic political coalition within the United States at the time. Could such a coalition be mobilized again? Given the high levels of personal and public debt within the United States, one would normally be skeptical. However, Herman Schwartz (chapter 5) suggests that the normal inflation preferences of debtors may be reversed in the short term in the current context. Many cash-strapped Americans are presently very vulnerable not only to spikes in food and fuel prices but also to nominal interest rate increases, which both influence mortgage interest rate resets and depress housing prices (thereby undermining home equity). This creates a rather large constituency that is very hostile to inflation in the short term.

Another strategy to defend the dollar's international position would be to strike more explicit bargains with other states to sustain the dollar's international role—that is, to defend the dollar's global standing by transforming it into more of a negotiated currency. This was the strategy that Britain pursued for much of the twentieth century, and it is an important reason—likely more

---

[39] Even in this context, Eichengreen (2006) notes that collective action problems eventually undermined cooperation among dollar supporters.

[40] Eichengreen 2004, 2006; Goldstein and Lardy 2005, 9.

important than market-based explanations about "inertia"—for why sterling's life as an international currency lasted so long.[41] Is it likely that the U.S. government would follow in the British government's footsteps? The political context is obviously quite different. Many members of the sterling area were British colonies, forced to embrace and support sterling by their subordinate status. By contrast, members of the informal U.S. "dollar area" today have more autonomy to make their own choices to support the greenback and might require significant inducements to encourage them to continue to back the greenback's international position.

The possibility of the United States offering such inducements was in fact raised at the time of the euro's inauguration. In 1999–2000, there was a brief debate within the United States about promoting formal dollarization abroad more actively, particularly in the Americas, through U.S. promises to share seigniorage or lender-of-last-resort support with dollarizing countries. Although the debate reflected a renewed interest in explicit "negotiation" as a tool to sustain the dollar's international position, it also highlighted that U.S. policymakers were not willing to bear the formal costs—even quite small ones—that might be associated with maintaining a negotiated international currency. The proposals failed to win much support, even from internationally oriented domestic economic groups, and they were shelved.[42]

Domestic support for the dollar's international role appears to be much less strong than was the backing within the British political system for sterling during its decline from global preeminence. In the latter case, the British policy was strongly influenced by a powerful and enduring "Treasury–Bank of England–City of London" axis that was strongly committed to sterling's international role from the nineteenth century onward, even when this jeopardized British policy autonomy.[43] American policymakers have been much more strongly and consistently committed to prioritizing the defense of U.S. policy autonomy.[44] For much of the postwar period, there was in fact little conflict between U.S. policy autonomy and the dollar's international role. Indeed, the dollar's global preeminence buttressed U.S. power and policy autonomy within the global system. As David Calleo notes, it helped loosen the financial constraints that U.S. policymakers encountered in pursuing various domestic and foreign policy goals.[45]

But if the dollar's international role begins to erode and requires special support, U.S. policymakers may be forced to a choice. The dollar's interna-

---

[41] Eichengreen 2006; de Cecco 1974.
[42] Cohen 2004; Helleiner 2003a, 2006b.
[43] Ingham 1984.
[44] See, for example, Gowa 1984a.
[45] Calleo 1982.

tional role would suddenly become more of a burden and something that U.S. power, economic resources, and diplomatic influence must be mobilized to defend. Given the sheer scope of these capabilities, the U.S. state could certainly defend the dollar's international role effectively if it chooses to do so. Historical experience suggests that the easiest deals to strike would be with states within what Peter Katzenstein calls the "American imperium."[46] But whether American policymakers will be willing to embrace this option in the coming years is less clear.

If the past is any guide, U.S. policymakers might even want to reduce the dollar's international role in such circumstances as a way of minimizing the policy-constraining risks of a "dollar overhang." At the time of the severe dollar crisis in 1978–79, for this very reason, U.S. policymakers strongly supported international negotiations among the G5 to develop a mechanism that enabled foreign governments to diversify their reserves away from dollars without generating a major dollar crisis.[47] Under this proposal, foreign governments would have been allowed to deposit dollars in a special "substitution account" at the IMF and be credited in certificates denominated in the IMF's currency: Special Drawing Rights, or SDRs (whose value is made up of a weighted basket of the world's leading currencies). Because this exchange was off-market, foreign governments would have been able to diversify their assets without undermining the value of the U.S. dollar.

Of course, there would have been some costs. Although SDRs could be used by foreign governments to pay for future balance of payments deficits or transfers to other governments, assets denominated in this currency would be less liquid than those in dollars. The account also risked losing money if the dollar fell since its liabilities were denominated in SDRs whereas its assets were dollar-denominated U.S. Treasury bills. U.S. efforts to shift this exchange rate risk to the IMF—by asking the Fund to back the account with its gold holdings—ultimately complicated the negotiations. When the dollar rose sharply after U.S. monetary policy tightened dramatically in 1979, the idea left the global public policy agenda.

Proposals for a substitution account have been raised again in the current era. Prominent U.S. economists such as Fred Bergsten (who was involved in the 1978–80 discussions) have suggested it and Robert Mundell has suggested that "the Chinese are thinking in terms of this."[48] Given the lack of enthusi-

---

[46] Katzenstein 2005.

[47] See Gowa 1984b.

[48] Mundell quoted in Reuters, "Dollar Crisis Looms, Says Nobel Laureate Mundell," Reuters News Agency, June 3, 2008. Fred Bergsten, "How to Solve the Problem of the Dollar," *Financial Times*, December 11, 2007.

asm for the IMF among many dollar-holding governments today, a less ambitious version might stand a better chance of being implemented at this moment. Peter Kenen has suggested that the European Central Bank (ECB) could
create a special facility that bought dollars from other central banks in exchange for newly issued, off-market, *euro* instruments. This proposal would
enable the ECB to minimize the risk of a dollar sell off generating a further
appreciation of the euro. U.S. and European officials could share the exchange
rate risk involved through the Europeans exchanging some portion of the U.S.
Treasury bills they purchase for special euro-denominated U.S. T-bills.[49]


## What Future for the Dollar?

What is the future of the dollar as an international currency? In this chapter,
I have suggested that Strange's typology of different kinds of international
currencies—particularly her distinction between top and negotiated currencies—provides a useful framework for exploring how *political* analyses might
help to answer this question. The dollar's international role partly reflects its
top currency status, which is sustained by the kinds of economic factors identified in *market-based* analyses relating to liquidity, confidence, and transactional networks. I have suggested that the unique liquidity of U.S. financial
markets has been the most important of these and that it rests, in turn, on political foundations that are very likely to remain stronger than those of potential challenger currencies for some time.

Although the dollar remains a top currency, it also has increasingly assumed some of the characteristics of a negotiated currency—that is, a currency whose international status is supported voluntarily by foreign states for
reasons beyond the economic factors identified by *market-based* approaches.
This political support, I have suggested, is increasingly fragile. From the
standpoint of many supporting states, the benefits of the Bretton Woods II
arrangement are diminishing while the costs of dollar support are growing.
The *geopolitical* basis of foreign official support for the dollar is also looking
less firm. Moreover, as foreign support becomes more fragile, it is not clear
that the United States will show the same kind of willingness to defend its currency's international role through negotiations that Britain did when sterling
was in decline. Indeed, U.S. policymakers may even see some merit in negotiated reductions of the dollar's role.

If there is a threat to the dollar's international position in the near future,

---

[49] Kenen 2005.

then it is likely to stem from the uncertain politics of its negotiated status. To what extent would the erosion of official support for its negotiated status undermine its broader international role? If the erosion was sudden and provoked a major exchange rate crisis for the United States, it could be quite significant. But what may be most significant in the coming years is the evolving balance between states and markets in global financial system. If the balance swings toward the former, the politics associated with the dollar's negotiated status will likely become more significant. On the other hand, those politics will have less impact on the dollar's overall international role if we remain in a more market-oriented global financial system. In that scenario, the more important political developments will be those that affect the economic determinants of the dollar's top currency status. In either situation, however, there is a common lesson. If we want to understand the future of the dollar, we must continue to heed Strange's call to move beyond economic analyses to examine the *political* foundations of international currencies.

# 5

# HOUSING FINANCE, GROWTH, AND THE U.S. DOLLAR'S SURPRISING DURABILITY

Herman Schwartz

Nothing seems more distant from a discussion of the future of the dollar as *the* international reserve currency—a universal, abstract, delocalized metric for and store of value—than housing, which appears irredeemably local, material, and specific. Yet the two were inextricably bound together during the growth cycle of the past twenty years.[1] America's housing finance system gave the United States above Organisation for Economic Cooperation and Development (OECD)-average growth from 1991 to 2005, and this in turn shifted the dollar from a negotiated currency to a top currency during those years.[2] Housing, or, more properly, housing finance systems and mortgage backed securities (MBS), are not intrinsically the pivot of the international financial system.[3] But over the past two decades, contingent forces made housing finance of considerable importance—so much so that defaults on subprime mortgages packaged into MBS forced central banks and the U.S.

---

Author's note: I thank Gerard Alexander, Eric Helleiner, Jonathan Kirshner, and Gregory Nowell for comments and criticism; errors will be packaged into a CDO and sold to unwitting Norwegian municipalities.

[1]   And it is worth remembering that British foreign investment and American housing were tightly connected in the nineteenth century; see Brinley 1973 and Kuznets 1967.

[2]   See Eric Helleiner (chapter 4) for an elaboration of the concepts of "top" and "negotiated" currency.

[3]   Mortgage-backed securities (MBS) and securitization will be explained later.

Treasury into unprecedented and escalating efforts to rescue illiquid credit markets.

What then is the relationship between the global housing boom, capital flows through the United States, and the long-run trajectory of the U.S. dollar? The usual answers—though not those in this book—display three weaknesses. They reify the dollar, treating its global preeminence as an independent source of economic power, rather than as a manifestation of broader U.S. economic power. They typically consider dollar politics from an interstate or international point of view, rather than looking at how capital flows percolate in different ways through different domestic financial systems. Finally, they also typically use aggregate data to assess the U.S. "balance sheet," obscuring how the effects of specific capital flows and financial channels do not net out. All three weaknesses conceal important underlying conditions that affect states' and international market actors' degree of support for the dollar.

I argue that in the long 1990s U.S. housing finance markets helped make the dollar what Susan Strange called a top currency, one with a natural, market-based attraction for investors. Put simply, U.S. housing finance markets translated falling nominal interest rates into extra aggregate demand and thus above OECD-average levels of GDP and employment growth in the United States. By contrast, the more repressed housing finance markets in Japan and most continental European countries impeded the translation of falling interest rates into increased aggregate demand, producing below average rates of GDP and employment growth. Housing turbocharged the U.S. economy and in turn bolstered the dollar's position. Differential rates of growth made the dollar attractive to private actors in OECD economies on a purely economic basis, that is, as a top currency. Housing-led growth also led to more imports of Asian sourced goods, making the dollar attractive to political actors in developing Asia as a negotiated currency. Both factors reinforced inflows into dollar-denominated securities that further reduced borrowing costs in the U.S. economy, creating a self-sustaining housing-led growth cycle that lasted until 2005. Above average growth was a significant supplement to the usual factors—primarily deep, liquid capital markets—that induce actors to use the dollar as a reserve currency.

Housing-led growth rested on the availability of specific resources with finite supply: continued disinflation and a supply of new buyers at the bottom of the U.S. housing market. By 2005, both were exhausted, shifting the U.S. dollar from a top to a negotiated currency as the *relative* growth advantage of the United States over Europe and Japan shrank. On the one side, U.S. economic dynamism helped power Chinese economic growth to the point where China began exporting inflation rather than deflation. On the other side, the pool of new creditworthy borrowers evaporated as imports helped slow wage growth in the bottom 60 percent of the U.S. income distribution. The United States became a less obvious place to invest, weakening foreigners' attachment to dollar-denominated assets and shifting the dollar back into a negotiated currency.

Nonetheless, the shrinking growth differential does not mean that the euro, the dollar's only plausible rival, will displace the dollar in the medium run. The same housing-finance-market factors that supported the dollar's top currency status in the long 1990s condition its negotiated status after 2006. This has both economic and political aspects. On the economic side, the housing finance and collective bargaining systems in the countries at the heart of the euro zone continue to suppress aggregate demand there. This caused their below average growth in the long 1990s, and in turn led private actors to underinvest in their own economies while buying U.S. and other foreign assets. The euro zone, and particularly Germany, thus relied on external demand for growth. The same is true for Japan, though the yen is a distant alternative to the dollar these days. Changing housing finance and collective bargaining systems in ways that might spark more domestic demand and thus growth would require wrenching and probably politically unacceptable changes in euro-zone pension systems and industrial finance.

Intra-European differences in housing finance markets create an addition political barrier for the euro. The countries that opted out from the euro or various EU treaties—Britain, Denmark, and Sweden—have housing finance markets more like that of the United States than of continental Europe, as does the Netherlands and Norway. Like the United States, these countries enjoyed above average GDP and employment growth in the 1990s. These countries were also disproportionately invested in the United States during the long 1990s. Thus, they were double winners, inclining them to continued *political* support for the dollar and a U.S.-centered international financial system. This split breaks up a potential coalition of European countries around a project to propel the euro from a regional to a global reserve currency.

The dollar's primacy rests on both market-based and Bretton Woods II foundations. I foresee a gradual weakening of the dollar's role, with the extent of decline conditioned by the degree to which economic growth in the core countries in the euro zone catches up with U.S. growth. On the market-based side, private investors will continue to buy dollar assets so long as the United States grows, or is perceived to grow *relatively* faster than euro-zone countries and Japan. Asian central banks and oil exporter sovereign wealth funds have motivations closer to those elucidated in the Bretton Woods II argument. Their ability to increase their relative holdings of euros is a function of European growth and European receptivity to their exports, because the counterpart to increased developing country holdings of euro-denominated assets is increased European trade deficits. Europe's trade deficit with China jumped from €128 billion in 2006 to €160 billion in 2007, but at the cost of considerable political friction. The 2008 financial crisis and the subsequent global economic slowdown inevitably will limit European receptivity to widening deficits with Asia.

Neither the relative openness of the U.S. economy as compared to continental European economies nor *relatively* faster U.S. growth is likely to change. This implies that export-oriented developing economies will continue to at least hold dollar assets or maintain a stable proportion of dollars in their accumulation of new assets. And here, too, European countries with housing finance systems similar to the United States are also more accepting of Chinese goods, reinforcing the fault line inside the EU over the euro's role. I am thus much less "declinist" than the pessimistic authors in this book, because my analysis offers an explanation for *cycling* in the dollar's position as the growth differential between the United States and its peer rich country competitors expands and contracts. The next few years most likely will resemble that of the 1980s, when U.S. growth and thus the dollar's position as a reserve currency slipped relative to Japan and Germany and thus relative to the yen and the deutsche mark. Renewed U.S. growth in the 1990s restored the dollar's position, just as a renewal of the relative growth gap will probably keep the dollar central to international capital flows in the near future.

Differential growth upheld the dollar, and U.S. global financial arbitrage animated differential growth. The United States operated a system of financial arbitrage at the global level: all debt is not created equal. The United States systematically borrowed short term at low interest rates from the rest of the world and then invested back into the rest of the world long-term for a higher return. The inflows in this system of arbitrage depressed benchmark interest rates for mortgages, while capital outflows from the United States went into instruments that do not affect benchmark rates. This arbitrage generated not only outsized international investment returns for the United States, but also outsized domestic growth from 1991 to 2005.

This system of arbitrage connected *differentially* to OECD housing finance markets and thus produced heterogeneous outcomes with respect to employment and GDP gains in the OECD over the past twenty years.[4] Just as all debt is not created equal, America's creditors and rivals are not all the same.

---

[4] See Nitzan 1998 on differential accumulation.

Falling global *nominal* interest rates after 1990 potentially could have reflated all OECD economies. Differences in the institutional structure of housing finance markets instead caused uneven employment and GDP gains that favored the United States and countries with similar housing financial markets. Housing-led differential growth restored the U.S. dollar's top currency status after its decline in the 1980s.

The U.S. housing boom, bust, and financial crisis could produce a new style of state economic regulation that is potentially conservatizing. The effort to unwind the current subprime mortgage debacle has already produced unprecedented government intervention in financial markets, but its fiscal cost is likely to limit new government initiatives. Additionally, homeowners facing mortgage interest rate resets should be hostile to inflation in the short term, because interest rate resets threaten them with foreclosure. This hostility to inflation and higher nominal interest rates in the United States is an equilibrating factor for the dollar. All things being equal, low nominal interest rates produce more growth in the United States than elsewhere.

Above OECD-average U.S. growth was central to the dollar's top currency position, but the symbiotic relationship between global capital flows and U.S. differential growth is not a perpetual motion machine. Housing will not drive future U.S. growth, raising the same uncertainties about how growth will return that characterized the end of the 1980s. Equally so, the financial collapse portends a reorganization of the financial sector. Neither of these imply a permanent end to renewed and above OECD-average U.S. growth.

### U.S. Arbitrage in Global Financial Markets

All politics is local; real estate is even more local. Nevertheless, local housing markets interacted with global capital markets in ways that affected the dollar. The usual literature sees the dollar's position as a source of seigniorage, and fears that a weakening dollar could create a *constraint* on government policy and spending that might shelter people from the market. Other versions argue that an overly strong dollar has been a *constraint* on the "real" economy and particularly manufacturing, which then secondarily affects average people through the kind of employment they can obtain. By contrast, I will argue that the specific form global financial flows took in the 1990s and 2000s created *opportunities* for growth that materialized through the housing sector.

My starting point is a well-known paradox: the United States has been both a large net foreign debtor and the recipient of net positive international investment income since the early 1990s. A smart or lucky individual might have net positive investment income despite net debt. But it is implausible that at an economy-wide or global level all Americans are systematically better investors than all foreigners.[5] Instead, the United States operated a global system of financial arbitrage that produced net income. Arbitrage occurs when an intermediary exploits price differences between similar commodities in two different markets, buying and selling that commodity at the same time. I characterize this process as *arbitrage* rather than *intermediation* because the U.S. economy benefited from differences in prices for financial goods created by differences in growth rates and regulatory systems.[6] The United States in the aggregate was not simply accommodating natural foreign preferences for short-term assets.

Differences in political, regulatory, and housing market finance structures produced these price differences. At the macroeconomic level, the United States systematically borrowed short term at low interest rates from the rest of the world, and then turned around and invested back in the rest of the world in longer term, higher risk, higher return, active investment vehicles. The depth and sophistication of U.S. markets enabled these flows, but did not determine the shape they took. At the microeconomic level U.S. financial institutions transformed cheap short-term foreign borrowing into a huge variety of higher yield, longer term mortgage backed securities and collateralized debt obligations (CDOs). Physically, U.S. arbitrage transformed cheap overseas credit into outsized domestic investment and in particular into (literally) outsized housing. This produced relatively faster U.S. growth, reinforcing the flow into dollar-denominated assets. No single actor or institution operated this system of arbitrage. Rather, it emerged from the behavior of discrete market actors, particularly the large financial firms that created financial housing-based derivatives and China's central bank.

Space constraints prevent a detailed analysis of U.S. global arbitrage.[7] But a simple breakdown of inward and outward foreign investment stocks presents the essentials needed here. Table 5.1 shows that approximately three-fifths of U.S. assets took the form of foreign direct investment and holdings of equities at year-end 2006. By contrast, three-fifths of foreign investment in the United States occurred as passive holdings of bonds and loans. Thus, at a macroeconomic level, the world subsidized the global expansion of U.S. firms and financial intermediaries and the U.S. economy. Ronald McKinnon (chap-

---

[5] Gourinchas and Rey 2005.

[6] See Despres, Kindleberger, and Salant 1970 for the original "intermediation" argument about the U.S. trade deficit.

[7] See Schwartz 2009.

TABLE 5.1.
Relative share of FDI, portfolio equities, portfolio debt, and loans in international holdings,
year-end 2007

|  | FDI[a] | Portfolio equities | Portfolio debt[b] | Loans | Total |
|---|---|---|---|---|---|
| $ Billion |  |  |  |  |  |
| United States | 5,148 | 5,171 | 1,478 | 5,002 | 18,615 |
| Rest of world | 3,524 | 2,833 | 6,965 | 5,387 | 19,810 |
| Of which, central banks |  |  | 2,931 | 406 | 3,307 |
| Shares (%) |  |  |  |  |  |
| United States | 27.7 | 27.8 | 7.9 | 26.9 | 100.0 |
| Rest of world | 17.8 | 14.3 | 35.2 | 27.2 | 100.0 |
| Of which, central banks |  |  | 88.6 | 12.3 | 16.7 |

Source: Bureau of Economic Analysis, *International Investment Position*, http://www.bea.gov/international/index.htm#iip.
[a]Market valuation.
[b]Omits trivial U.S. holdings of currency and foreign holdings of U.S. currency totaling $279 billion, as well as derivatives, which largely net out.

ter 3) presents a comprehensive analysis of the U.S.-Asia negotiated currency connection via Bretton Woods II, allowing me to concentrate on the connections to mortgage markets that made the dollar a top currency.

The key point is that foreign purchases of U.S. Treasury debt and debt and MBS issued by Fannie Mae and Freddie Mac helped to drive down interest rates on U.S. mortgages during the long 1990s. By December 2006, foreign investors held 52 percent of marketable U.S. Treasury securities and 16.8 percent of outstanding agency debt.[8] Nearly all U.S. mortgages are referenced against the interest rate on the ten-year Treasury bond.[9] Lower T-bond interest rates thus flow through immediately to new mortgage originations and less quickly to adjustable rate mortgage resets. Recycling of Asian trade surpluses—the Bretton Woods II phenomenon—during the late 1990s and early 2000s depressed yields on ten-year U.S. Treasury debt by about ninety basis points, or almost 1 percentage point, and as much as 150 basis points in 2005.[10] European and oil exporter acquisitions of dollar-denominated portfolio assets should have had much the same effect in the early to mid-1990s, when those groups primarily funded the U.S. trade deficit.

Foreign purchases of "agency" debt have an equally direct effect on hous-

[8]  Department of the Treasury 2007, 3, 5.
[9]  The majority of U.S. mortgages have a thirty-year maturity. But refinancing, trading up in housing, and long-distance moves mean that few American families actually hold a mortgage to that maturity.
[10]  Warnock and Warnock 2006.

ing and thus U.S. growth. Agency debt comprises MBS originated by Fannie Mae (Federal National Mortgage Agency) and Freddie Mac (Federal Home Loan Mortgage Corporation), as well as direct loans funding their operations. The U.S. federal government created Fannie Mae in 1938 to make housing more affordable by creating a national market for mortgage funding. Fannie Mae was privatized in 1968–70 and then effectively renationalized in the 2008 crisis.[11] Savings and loan banks (i.e., the U.S. version of *sparkassen* or building societies) got Freddie Mac, their own version of Fannie Mae, in 1970; it was fully privatized in 1989 and renationalized in 2008.

Fannie Mae essentially invented the modern MBS market in 1981 and pioneered the overseas sale of MBS. Freddie Mac invented the collateralized mortgage obligation (CMO), a derivative that slices up principal and interest payments so that investors can buy bonds with maturities and returns that vary from the underlying individual mortgages.[12] Securitization allows banks to move mortgage loans off their books by selling those mortgages to the capital market and thus replenishing their capital. This allows banks to originate yet more loans while earning the bulk of their income from fees. Before securitization, banks held mortgages to maturity and made money off the interest-rate spread between deposits and loans. By 2007, agency MBS and borrowing accounted for nearly half of the outstanding U.S. residential mortgage debt of $11.1 trillion. A further quarter of outstanding mortgage debt was privately securitized, leaving only 25 percent in the traditional, illiquid bank-held format.[13]

Fannie and Freddie's securitization of mortgages enabled overseas sales of these assets to a wide range of customers, including central banks. Absent securitization, foreign funds could enter the U.S. market only if foreign banks established a presence in the market or if U.S. banks accepted exchange rate risks and borrowed offshore. In 2001, foreign holdings of agency MBS amounted to $133 billion. By 2007 foreign holdings exceeded $1 trillion, with foreign official institutions—that is, Asian central banks—holding the majority.[14] Without a standardized product and liquid markets, foreigners would have been less willing to buy mortgage assets from the United States,

---

[11] This privatization spun out the unsubsidized portions of FMNA as FMNA, leaving behind the third government sponsored enterprise (GSE) giant "Ginnie Mae," the Government National Mortgage Agency, to provide subsidized lending for public housing projects. See Seabrooke 2006 for a comprehensive study of the relationship between the GSEs and U.S. state power.

[12] The CDO (collateralized debt obligation) is a generic version of the CMO, produced by bundling different debts into a synthetic product, to create a specific set of maturities, risks, and returns through the use of derivatives.

[13] Credit Suisse 2007; Federal National Mortgage Agency 2006; Federal Home Loan Mortgage Corporation 2006; Federal Reserve 2008.

[14] Department of the Treasury 2007, 11.

making it harder for the United States to fund its trade deficit. Non-agency MBS did not become important until 2004–07.

While the foreign share of securitized agency and private label debt is *relatively* lower than its share of Treasury debt, the *absolute* amounts are not as disparate because in mid-2007 total agency debt amounted to nearly twice the marketable Treasury debt. Indeed, until the explosion of federal deficit spending after 2007, agency debt typically constituted a third of all marketable U.S. debt securities, public and private, and thus was central to the deep, liquid American financial markets of which analysts speak. Consequently, foreign purchases of U.S. MBS energized a giant circle: foreign purchases of Treasuries depressed the reference rate for mortgage interest rates, causing the issue of new mortgages through refinancing or purchase; the new mortgages were then bundled into MBS and sold to foreigners; their eager purchases further depressed mortgage rates, enabling banks to fund yet more mortgage debt.

As McKinnon notes, virtuous Asians provided much of this cash. Japan and China accounted for 46 percent of foreign agency MBS holdings—plus more private MBS—and 51 percent of foreign Treasury holdings in mid-2007. Conventional wisdom sees this accumulation of foreign debt as a problem for the dollar. The reverse was true from 1991 to 2005. Disinflation and access to cheap foreign loans strengthened the dollar as a top currency by enabling above-average rates of growth for the United States in relation to OECD countries. Housing was central to that growth process in ways that would have been difficult for other, smaller sectors.

## Differential Effects of Housing Market Financial Structures

Though now a dim memory, 1989 saw serious speculation that the yen or European currencies might replace the dollar.[15] While the dollar comprised nearly 75 percent of official reserves in 1978, by 1989 it had fallen below 50 percent as central banks diversified into deutsche marks and yen.[16] Various European currencies peaked at 40 percent of holdings in 1990, and the yen at 10 percent. Yet by 2001 the dollar was back to 70 percent of official holdings, and the euro was down to 25 percent. Private attraction to the dollar—the real measure of a top currency—traced the same pattern as measured by the strength of the dollar relative to other currencies. Why?

[15] Bergsten 1991.
[16] Wooldridge 2006.

The 1990s saw profound disinflation. Long-term *nominal* interest rates fell everywhere in the OECD, and especially in Europe. Euro zone long-term interest rates fell from 11.2 percent in 1990 to 3.5 percent by 2005. U.S. long-term rates declined less, from 8.7 percent to 4.0 percent from 1990 to 2003.[17] The lower nominal cost of borrowing should have stimulated growth everywhere. And indeed, the United States and its OECD competitors all experienced positive effects from the supply chain revolution, the emergence of the Internet, and mobile communications. But the structure of housing finance in the United States and similar countries was more likely to translate disinflation into increased aggregate demand and thus increased growth than was the case in the core euro-zone countries. Housing finance markets thus account for above OECD-average U.S. growth in the long 1990s. (Note: the argument here is not that the housing market accounts for all U.S. growth, but rather the *difference* between the United States and the core euro-zone countries.) Disinflation and U.S. arbitrage in global capital markets stimulated the domestic housing market by providing relatively low interest rates to existing homeowners wishing to refinance their mortgages and to new homebuyers willing and able to bid up home prices. Relatively faster U.S. growth revalidated the U.S. dollar's position as a top currency for OECD countries.

It could be argued that a strong U.S. dollar merely shifted activity into the nontraded sector, raising returns to the nontraded sector and thus driving up housing prices. Yet Scandinavian currencies and perforce the Dutch all followed the euro in weakening versus the dollar. Logically this should have led to weak housing prices, as in Germany, Austria, and Italy. Instead, as we will see, the similarity between Dutch, Scandinavian, and American housing market financial institutions produced the same sort of boom in all of them.

Housing market institutions like those in the United States translated 1990s disinflation into increased demand and rising employment through the normal Keynesian multiplier mechanisms. Countries with housing finance market institutions least like those in the United States, and which in addition stifled growth of aggregate demand through wage restraint, experienced less growth. In a disinflationary environment, financial repression hindered growth, rather than accelerating it. Four key features characterize U.S. housing finance markets:

1. relatively high levels of private, individual homeownership
2. relatively high levels of mortgage debt in relation to GDP

[17] *OECD Factbook, 2005,* http://www.sourceOECD.org.

3. easy and relatively cheap refinance of mortgages as well as "cash out" of home equity
4. high levels of securitization of mortgages

These features, with occasional help from tax subsidies for mortgage interest, enabled a relatively straightforward process of Keynesian demand stimulus to operate in the U.S. economy in the 1990s and even more so in the 2000s. As nominal interest rates fell, homeowners refinanced mortgages, shifting considerable purchasing power away from rentier interests and toward individuals with a higher propensity to consume goods, services, and housing. This consumption in turn generated new employment through standard Keynesian multiplier effects. This new employment sustained the expansion by helping shift the federal budget into surplus, thus enabling the Federal Reserve to continue lowering interest rates. Much the same happened in equity markets, but for the average person the housing market was a more important source of new consumption power, because more people own houses than own equities, the average person has more housing equity than stocks, and the propensity to consume housing wealth is higher. Retrospective analyses confirm that the release of home equity mattered much more than rising share markets for the net increase in real personal consumption in the OECD from 1996 to 2006.[18] Again, though, without any easy way to tap that equity, the latent additional purchasing power in home equity remained exactly that: latent. This is why countries needed to combine all four features to get economic leverage from disinflation.

Widespread ownership without mortgage debt, as in Italy, meant consumers could not lower their housing costs and free up purchasing power. Widespread homeownership with costly and difficult refinance, as in France, meant that homeowners could not translate falling nominal interest rates into a smaller interest burden. Shallow homeownership and difficult refinance meant rentier interests prevailed over debtor consumption, as in Germany, where housing prices fell despite lower interest rates. As of 2004, all forms of securitized mortgage debt amounted to less than 20 percent of GDP for most European countries.[19]

Falling interest rates also ramified through liquid housing markets to create fictitious capital that also generated employment and growth. Nominal interest rates matter for asset valuation. Falling nominal interest rates meant that the same nominal dollar income could service larger mortgages. People

[18] Federal Reserve Bulletin, *Recent Changes in U.S. Family Finances*, 2006, A8; Ludwig and Slok 2002; Bank for International Settlements 2003, 130; Borio 1995; Case, Quigley, and Shiller 2001.
[19] European Commission 2005, 125–26; European Mortgage Federation 2005, 116.

entering the housing market thus bid up housing prices because they could enjoy more "housing" at the same monthly mortgage price. Alternately, incumbents could refinance their mortgages at a lower interest rate, enjoy lower monthly payments, and consume the savings. The nominal value of all U.S. residential real estate increased from roughly $6.5 trillion in 1991 to over $20.5 trillion in 2005.[20] Securitization of mortgages accelerated this process by allowing banks to validate, price, and liberate the fictitious capital in housing. Consumers tapped their increased home equity through mortgage equity withdrawal (MEW), and MEW contributed to outsized levels of consumption and aggregate demand. Repackaged as MBS, MEW and new mortgages flowed overseas as the counterpart to the growing U.S. trade deficit.

The U.S. Fed estimates that 80 percent of the increase in U.S. mortgage debt in the 1990s can be accounted for by MEW, and that MEW ran at roughly $0.3 trillion annually from 1991 to 2000 and then at roughly $1 trillion annually from 2001 to 2005.[21] MEW flowed through three different channels. Roughly one third of home equity was used to pay down higher interest rate consumer debt, freeing up cash for future consumption. One third was used for home improvements, which typically are very labor intense and thus have immediate employment effects. And one fourth flowed directly into consumption.[22]

All this mattered for support of the U.S. dollar. Support for a top currency is a matter of *relative* performance, not absolute performance, because market participants always want to outperform the average.[23] Money disproportionately flows into assets that are performing better than the average. Dollar-denominated assets appeared to perform at above-average levels in the long 1990s because the housing-driven U.S. economy performed at above OECD-average levels in those years. Figure 5.1 graphs the *relative* growth in absolute employment and GDP per capita from 1991 to 2005 for seventeen OECD economies (although the underlying analysis includes nineteen rich OECD economies).[24] It shows the degree, in percentage terms, by which a given country either *outperformed or underperformed* the average level of GDP and employment performance for the indicated OECD countries.[25]

---

[20] Greenspan and Kennedy 2007, 26.

[21] Ibid., 9, 17.

[22] Ibid., 8.

[23] Nitzan 1998. Faster growth drew in more immigrants, which in turn helped push up housing market prices—another positive reinforcement.

[24] Ireland is excluded from figure 5.1 as an extreme outlier—GDP and employment rose at four times the average rate; Spain and Portugal are excluded because truly comparable data are not available.

[25] I divided the difference between the percentage change in absolute employment or GDP for a specific country by the average percentage change for the OECD reference group, and then divided

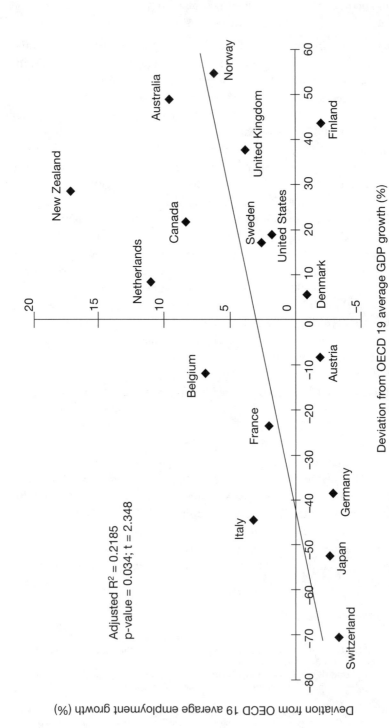

**Figure 5.1.** Deviation from weighted average level of GDP and employment growth, 1991–2005, seventeen OECD nations, in percentages

GDP growth captures the increase in output and the potential for increased profit volume. Employment growth, measured as the number of new jobs, captures the creation of new purchasing power as well as the potential for increased fiscal revenue and decreased welfare-related expenditure. More people at work means fewer people on the dole.

Figure 5.1 is constructed by taking the weighted average of OECD GDP growth rates and the average growth in the actual number of employed people for these OECD countries, adjusting for the change in population, and then measuring the percentage deviation from that average for individual countries. I adjust for population to control for the very different rates of population growth across these countries, since rising population alone could account for increased employment numbers or GDP. Actual employment uses the head count of people in employment (not the unemployment rate) to capture job creation. And I assess these against the weighted growth rate because it more accurately captures the distribution of gains and losses across the OECD. Figure 5.1 shows an unsurprising but nonetheless significant correlation ($R^2$ = .2185, p = .034) between employment and GDP performance. The data from figure 5.1 are used in table 5.2 to construct a reverse misery or "unmisery" index combining the degree of deviation from the average evolution of population-adjusted employment and GDP gains for the period 1991–2005. Figure 5.1 raises two questions. Did housing-led growth crowd out manufacturing growth, as some critics argue? And was growth really connected to housing finance markets?

Tables 5.2 and 5.3 provide data that help answer these questions. The data in table 5.2 dispel the myth that the U.S. boom was only about Harold James's gas-guzzling SUVs and McMansions. The United States and other "winner" economies typically had above average growth in economy-wide gross value added, in manufacturing gross value added, in gross fixed capital formation (GFCF), and in metals and manufacturing GFCF, compared to the stagnant economies. GDP and employment gains were not solely about housing construction. In almost all of the winners the change in the absolute level of GFCF in housing was smaller than the overall growth of GFCF. Moreover in most of the winners, the share of housing and all construction in GFCF fell; in the United States, for example, it fell from roughly 65 percent of GFCF in 1991 to 48 percent in 2005. Although U.S. housing investment shot up in 2006 and 2007 this hardly explains the prior fifteen years. On the contrary, the "hollowed out" U.S. economy experienced a doubling of investment in metals and

---

that by the average percentage change for the OECD reference group, yielding the degree of under- or overperformance relative to the reference group. Negative values in the chart could thus correspond to *actual* gains during the 1991–2005 period. The point is to show *relative* gains, however.

TABLE 5.2.

Relative economic performance in select OECD economies, 1991–2005, adjusted for changes in population, and ordered by "unmisery" index

| Relative change in real: | Australia | UK | Canada | USA | Netherlands | France | Italy | FRG | Japan |
|---|---|---|---|---|---|---|---|---|---|
| Gross value added (%) | 52 | 49 | 19 | 21 | 5 | −23 | −46 | −30 | −48 |
| Manufacturing GVA (%) | −68 | −79 | 24 | 71 | −35 | −35 | −99 | −79 | −47 |
| Gross fixed capital formation (%) | 119 | 33 | 18 | 66 | −32 | −52 | −70 | −94 | −128 |
| Metals and machinery GFCF (%) | 297 | −28 | 4 | 60 | −5 | −62 | −86 | −81 | −77 |
| Housing GFCF (%) | −9 | 1 | −3 | 90 | −32 | −69 | −90 | −96 | −159 |
| Number of employed (%)[a] | 10 | 4 | 8 | 2 | 11 | 2 | 3 | −3 | −3 |
| GDP (%) | 49 | 38 | 22 | 19 | 8 | −24 | −44 | −38 | −53 |
| Unmisery index[b] | 5.9 | 4.1 | 3.0 | 2.1 | 1.9 | −2.2 | −4.1 | −4.1 | −5.5 |

Source: Author's elaboration from www.sourceOECD.org data.

Notes:

[a] Percentage change in absolute number of people employed in 2005 versus 1991, as compared to the average change for all rich OECD countries. Performance is judged against all twenty rich OECD economies.

[b] Unmisery index = 10* (ΔEmployed + ΔGDP), i.e., ten times the relative change in number of employed plus relative change in GDP, adjusted for population changes, in order to construct a normalized −10 to 10 index.

Interpretation: 0% = perfectly average performance; < 0 below average; > 0 above average. Thus the increase in Australian economy-wide gross value added was 52% greater than the OECD average, after adjusting for population changes; Japan's increase was 48%, lower than the average.

TABLE 5.3.
Comparative housing finance market characteristics, select OECD countries, ordered by synthetic housing index

| | UK | Australia | USA | Canada | Americanized rich average[a] | Average all 20 | Repressed rich average[b] | Japan | FRG | Italy | France |
|---|---|---|---|---|---|---|---|---|---|---|---|
| Relative transaction costs for property acquisition, as % of total cost | 4.8 | 3.8 | 0.6 | 2.8 | 3.3 | 0.0 | -4.1 | 1.2 | -1.9 | -7.7 | -6.9 |
| Is mortgage securitization possible? (10 = yes and common; 0 = no or rare) | 10.0 | 10.0 | 10.0 | 10.0 | 6.0 | 4.4 | 0.7 | 0.0 | 4.0 | 0.0 | 0.0 |
| Home equity withdrawal 1990–2002 (as % of GDP *10) | 7.0 | 7.0 | 5.0 | 2.0 | 4.7 | 3.2 | 0.3 | 1.0 | 0.0 | 1.0 | 0.0 |
| Mortgage debt as % of GDP, 1992 | 64.3 | 50.8 | 58.0 | 43.1 | 53.4 | 44.7 | 32.2 | 36.8 | 54.0 | 11.4 | 22.8 |
| Owner-occupied housing, 2002 (%) | 68.0 | 70.0 | 69.0 | 66.0 | 64.7 | 64.6 | 63.9 | 60.0 | 42.0 | 80.0 | 55.0 |
| **Synthetic housing index[c]** | **7.00** | **6.59** | **5.65** | **5.13** | **4.9** | **3.2** | **0.9** | **2.37** | **2.34** | **0.49** | **0.17** |

*Sources:* Row 1: "Global Property Guide, Housing Transaction Costs in the OECD," http://www.globalpropertyguide.com/articleread.php?article_id=95&cid= Row 2: Pietro Catte, Nathalie Girouard, Robert Price, and Christophe André, "The Contribution of Housing Markets to Cyclical Resilience," *OECD Economic Studies* #38, 2004/1, pp. 125–56. Row 3: OECD National Accounts at www.sourceOECD.org; Kostas Tsatsaronis and Haibin Zhu, "What Drives Housing Price Dynamics: Cross-Country Evidence," *BIS Quarterly Review* (March 2004), pp. 65–78 at pp. 69–70, pp. Massimo Giuliodori, "The Role of House Prices in the Monetary Transmission Mechanism across European Countries," *Scottish Journal of Political Economy* 52, no. 4 (September 2005), pp. 519–43, at pp. 523–24. Row 4: Catte, et al., p. 138; Swedish National Board of Housing, Building and Planning (Boverket), "Housing Statistics in the European Union 2004," Falun, Sweden: Intellecta Strålins, 2005; data supplied by European Mortgage Foundation. Row 5: Data supplied by European Mortgage Foundation.

[a]Britain, Denmark, Sweden, Netherlands, Australia, New Zealand, Norway

[b]Japan, Germany, Austria, France, Belgium, Italy, Spain

[c]SHI calculated by normalizing all data to 1–10 range, adding all five indicators and then averaging.

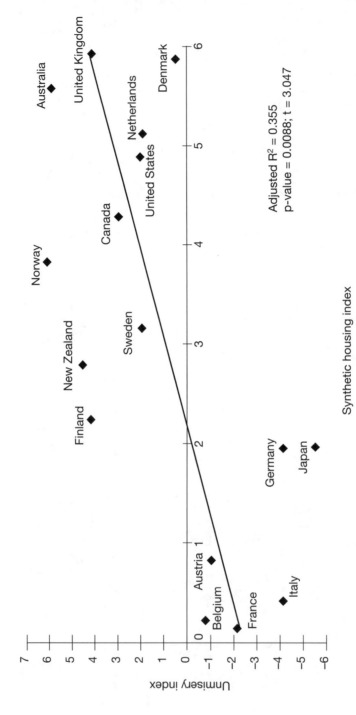

**Figure 5.2.** Synthetic housing index versus "unmisery" index. Interpretation: The chart assesses the connection between housing finance market arrangements and *relative* growth. Excluded data: Ireland is excluded as an outlier (its "unmisery" index is 35, housing index 3.5), but its position confirms the general logic here; Spain, Switzerland, and Portugal are omitted because of missing data.

machinery manufacturing investment, while "manufacturing powerhouses" Germany and Japan each saw only a one-fifth increase in this investment over the whole fifteen-year period.

What about the connection between housing finance markets and growth? Table 5.3 displays data for the important housing market financial market characteristics noted above.[26] I use this data to create a synthetic housing index that tries to capture the degree to which a given housing finance market facilitates the translation of falling nominal interest rates into additional purchasing power. This index combines the rate of homeownership, the ratio of mortgage debt to GDP, the availability of home equity withdrawal, the level of transaction costs involved in mortgage refinance, and whether or not securitization of mortgages is possible.

Figure 5.2 then correlates the "unmisery" data and the housing index data from tables 5.2 and 5.3 to show how housing market characteristics relate to relative employment and GDP gains. Figure 5.2 shows a significant relationship between U.S.-style housing finance systems and above-average employment and GDP growth ($R^2 = .355$, significant at $p = 0.0088$). During the long 1990s, then, a virtuous (but not perpetual) cycle of rising home prices, rising consumption, rising income and employment, and rising profitability drew foreign capital into U.S. dollar-denominated securities. Much of this investment flowed into Treasury and agency securities, reducing interest rates and providing a further boost to aggregate demand and housing prices. And this in turn reinforced investment flows from relatively slowly growing OECD economies toward economies with housing booms, particularly the United States. All this made dollar-denominated securities attractive in the market, strengthening the dollar's value and restoring its position as a top currency after the turbulent 1980s. By 2000 private inflows accounted for over 80 percent of America's overseas borrowing.[27]

Housing thus helped the U.S. dollar regain its position as a top currency. Had U.S. growth merely been average, or below average, market actors would have continued the 1980s' drift toward other currencies. But we still have not shown how this intersects with the interests and politics of individuals. Does the interaction of housing and the U.S. dollar create a microlevel politics that enhances the dollar's position as a top or negotiated currency?

---

[26] Table 5.3 reflects the situation prevailing in the mid- to late 1990s. Some countries partially liberalized their mortgage markets and introduced mortgage securitization at the end of the 1990s. MBS volumes remained relatively small, however.

[27] U.S. Treasury Department 2008, 13.

## The Politics of Homeownership in Relation to the 2008 Crisis and Beyond

The U.S. housing boom, housing bust, and current more-than-just-housing financial crisis have created two counterpoised political pressures over inflation and liquidity as actors fight over who bears the losses from the crisis.[28] The potential losses are very big: the subprime and Alt-A mortgages at the heart of the crisis nominally amounted to $1.56 trillion in early 2007.[29] And by depressing housing prices they also threaten the much larger pool of jumbo and prime mortgages. By early 2009 more prime mortgages than subprime mortgages were in foreclosure.[30] These pressures bear directly on the dollar's position in two ways. First, they have created an unusual reversal of typical creditor-debtor interests around inflation, as well as creating hostility to higher nominal interest rates and higher taxes. Second, in a clear demonstration of what a "negotiated currency" actually means, threats to dollar-denominated securities gave America's foreign creditors substantial influence in triggering policy responses to the ever expanding financial crisis in summer 2008.

The classic arguments about housing suggested that private homeownership created a politics inimical to a universal welfare state because mortgages crowded out taxes early in a household's life cycle. Jim Kemeny and Francis Castles both argued that the need to accumulate a down payment and then to service a mortgage would incline homeowners against higher taxes for public services.[31] The classic arguments largely address the early post–World War II period. We must thus supplement the classic arguments with one salient fact reflecting current realities: there is a lot of wealth and money to be lost if housing prices fall. Outstanding U.S. mortgage debt totaled $11.1 trillion at the end of 2007, and market prices at that time implied that homeowners had about $11 trillion of nominal equity in their houses.[32] The fear of foreclosure and equity evaporation is what creates the tension around interest rates and inflation. Lower interest rates would help maintain housing prices, validating creditors' assets, by allowing subprime buyers who cannot make payments to sell their house to buyers with better credit. But if central

---

[28] See Schwartz and Seabrooke 2009.

[29] Credit Suisse, *Mortgage Liquidity du Jour*, March 12, 2007, 28.

[30] Dina ElBoghdady and Sarah Cohen, "The Growing Foreclosure Crisis," *Washington Post* January 17, 2009.

[31] Kemeny 1980; Castles 1998; Kemeny 2005. A recent study of Australian public opinion suggests that homeowners with mortgages are 50% more likely to express tax resistance than free and clear homeowners or renters: Wilson 2006, 530.

[32] Greenspan and Kennedy 2007, 26; Freddie Mac, *2005 Annual Report*, 2; FRB data at http://www.federalreserve.gov/pubs/oss/oss2/2004/bulletin.tables.int.xls. For comparison, home equity represented 40% of British household wealth: Aoki, Proudman, and Vlieghe 2004, 415. The country case chapters in Schwartz and Seabrooke 2009 suggest patterns similar to those in the United States.

banks supply the liquidity needed to keep interest rates low they risk driving up long-term inflation. Let's look at homeowners' interests first.

Why have debtors' short-run interests around inflation reversed? Put simply, many households at all income levels had shoehorned themselves into crippling mortgages homes at boom-era prices. This left them with little cash flow to handle the sudden jump in food and fuel prices. These jumps dramatically increased their personal risk of foreclosure. Inflation particularly threatened buyers who used adjustable rate mortgages (ARMs, i.e., variable rate mortgages) with rising interest rates once their mortgage rate reset. Nearly $1 trillion in subprime and Alt-A ARMs were scheduled for resets in 2007–08.[33] And the cascade of foreclosures that would result from interest rate resets also affected older, incumbent borrowers through their variable rate home equity loans.

Consider typical subprime households. Subprime borrowers typically had bad credit scores and low income relative to their debt. These families were in their early thirties, had approximately $37,000 in disposable income after taxes, and accounted for much of the 5 percentage point rise in the home-ownership rate in the United States that occurred from 1994 to 2005.[34] As late housing market entrants, these families on average paid a high price relative to their incomes—borrowing $200,000 on average—because housing prices rose well ahead of incomes. This high debt-to-income ratio meant that most of these mortgages were done as ARMs. ARMs accounted for about 20 percent of mortgages in the 1990s. But during the housing bubble the share of subprime and Alt-A mortgage originations jumped from 2 percent in 2002 to 20 percent in 2006, and 92 percent of these were ARMs. The typical Alt-A buyer, with good credit and an excessively large loan in relation to income, was in much the same position, as 68 percent of these loans were ARMs. The typical subprime ARM in 2007 was resetting from about a 7 or 8 percent annual interest rate to something closer to 10–10.5 percent.[35]

Even older, incumbent borrowers were vulnerable to interest rate resets. At around $50,000 or $55,000, average post-tax incomes for households aged 45–54 in the fourth income quintile are about one-third higher than for households aged 25–34. These families typically had some equity in their house, and generally had a fixed rate loan. But this is precisely the group that

[33]  Data from Calculated Risk website at http://calculatedrisk.blogspot.com.

[34]  Bureau of Labor Statistics, *Consumer Expenditure Survey 2004*, 9; Chambers, Garriga, and Schlagenhauf 2007. More recent BLS data is unfortunately not available yet. This introduces a *conservative* bias into the analysis because housing prices rose substantially faster than incomes from 2004 to 2007.

[35]  Credit Suisse, *Mortgage Liquidity du Jour*, March 12, 2007, 4–5, 19, 21, 26; see also Freddie Mac, *2005 Annual Report*, 12.

used mortgage equity withdrawal to extract cash through home equity lines of credit (HELOC) or closed equity loans.[36] HELOCs are effectively a second mortgage secured on the owner's existing equity and most often used to remodel the house, purchase durable goods, or repay more expensive credit card debt. Approximately one-fourth of U.S. homeowners have a HELOC or similar housing-related debt, amounting to just over $1 trillion, or a bit over 10 percent of total mortgage debt. HELOCs and other forms of mortgage equity withdrawal accounted for about 6 percent of disposable income from 2001 to 2007, up from the 2 percent level prevailing before 2001, and thus were a major contributor to excess U.S. consumption and the trade deficit.[37]

Rising inflation and taxes are a triple threat to these debtor families. Although inflation erodes the real long-term cost of their mortgage, this only helps if these families can hang on to their house in the long run. In the short run, inflation almost immediately increases mortgage payments as the nominal interest rate resets on ARMs. As of 2006—before food and fuel prices really shot up—20 percent of homeowners (homeowners, not households) in the bottom half of the income distribution were already spending more than half their income on housing. A further 19 percent were spending between 30 percent and 50 percent of their income on housing. Altogether, *homeowners* at all income levels spending more than 30 percent of their income on housing constitute 30 percent of all homeowners and 20 percent of all U.S. households, including renters.[38]

Inflation also indirectly reduces homeowners' equity as interest rates rise. Rising nominal interest rates depress housing prices. This threatens new homeowners with negative equity—owning more on the house that the market says it is worth. Rising interest rates depress the market price of houses because potential buyers confront higher monthly payments at any given price point. By June 2008, housing prices had already fallen 18 percent from their peak, leaving an estimated thirteen million homeowners with negative equity, and obliterating the typical equity in 2005 and 2006 vintage subprime and Alt-A mortgages. The 30–35 percent decline from 2006 levels that is needed to bring housing prices back into line with traditional price-to-income ratios or price-to-rental ratios would leave nearly 30 percent of U.S. homeowners, or twenty-three million households, with negative equity.[39]

[36] Bureau of Labor Statistics, *Consumer Expenditure Survey 2004*. A closed loan has a fixed term; a HELOC is permanently available to be drawn on.

[37] Greenspan and Kennedy 2007, 11, 43.

[38] Harvard University Joint Center on Housing Studies 2008; Credit Suisse, *Mortgage Liquidity du Jour*, March 12, 2007, 26.

[39] Calculated Risk, "Homeowners with Negative Equity," September 30, 2008, http://calculated risk.blogspot.com/2008/09/homeowners-with-negative-equity.html.

Declining home equity matters not only because households with negative equity are more likely to be foreclosed. Declining home equity also threatens the balance sheet of the average household. Home equity accounts for one third of the average American household's assets. But in the bottom six income deciles, median net worth is only $38,000, and is almost exclusively home equity. These deciles own only 6 percent of all U.S. stock holdings, while deciles seven and eight hold only 11 percent. By contrast, the top 10 percent by income owned 58 percent of stocks in 2006.[40] Put differently, the bottom six income deciles had $1 trillion in net worth in 2006, but falling home prices have almost certainly taken away the entire $1 trillion.

Finally, the run up in housing prices has probably made all of our groups hostile toward and vulnerable to rising taxes. Higher housing prices mean higher property taxes (i.e., "rates"), which squeezes other revenue sources. In the United States, property taxes are fundamentally a local revenue source that pays for education, policing, and some social services. They account for roughly 70 percent of local government revenues and 10 percent of total revenue at all levels, and their dollar volume increased at twice the rate of all taxes from 2000 through 2005.[41] From 2001 to 2004, the average property tax bill rose 21 percent in the United States. By 2007, property taxes took 3.4 percent of total personal income.[42] Because rising housing prices have fed into higher property taxes through rising assessments, it has become harder to increase other tax burdens for national purposes such as broad social programs. Citizen protests in 2006 and 2007 forced changes to and in some cases caps on both the level of and rate of increase for property taxes in twenty U.S. states.[43]

These dynamics reverse the usual debtor preference for inflation. Housing market incumbents in the 1960s and 1970s generally preferred inflation, which rapidly and unambiguously reduced their real debt burden while inflating the nominal value of homes. But homebuyers in the 1960s and 1970s typically used *fixed rate,* long amortization (thirty-year) mortgages and did not have HELOCs. And they typically had reasonably secure jobs with the expectation of a long tenure and inflation adjustments to their wages. These conditions made inflation a one way bet favoring debtors. Consider a typical

---

[40] Calculated from Federal Reserve Bank, *Survey of Consumer Finance,* 2001 and 2004, based on online data at http://www.federalreserve.gov/pubs/oss/oss2/2004/bulletin.tables.int.xls; Federal Reserve Bulletin, 2006, *Recent Changes in U.S. Family Finances,* A8.

[41] OECD revenue database at http://www.sourceOECD.org.

[42] Tax Foundation at http://www.taxfoundation.org/taxdata/show/1775.html, and http://www.taxfoundation.org/taxdata/show/1913.html.

[43] Patrick Jonsson, "High Property Taxes Driving a New Revolt," *Christian Science Monitor,* March 28, 2006, and Ron Scherer, "States Try to Ease Property Tax Rise," *Christian Science Monitor,* June 5, 2005.

Californian buying a $20,000 tract house in 1960 using a 1.75 percent Veterans Housing Authority fixed-rate loan. And even today we might imagine that long incumbent homeowners who refinanced into fixed low interest rate mortgages after the Asian financial crisis or 9/11 might prefer a bit of inflation, *if their incomes keep pace*. But that is a large if, given that many high-income jobs in the financial and real estate sectors evaporated during 2008, and that most incomes are no longer inflation adjusted. If incomes failed to rise in the relatively benign economic environment of the 2000s, why will they rise in the post-bust era?

To summarize, the large number of debtors with ARMs or with tight budgets should exhibit a preference for low inflation in the short run. The current conjuncture only directly shifts the preferences of those most vulnerable to rising interest rates and declines in home equity. But a shift in the preferences of only 5–10 percent of voters can be electorally decisive. And subprime and Alt-A mortgages are geographically concentrated in electorally important states such as California, Virginia, Florida, and Texas, the first three of which also have relatively expensive metropolitan housing. It could be argued that a targeted bailout might relieve indebted homeowners. But the scale of such a bailout would still be quite inflationary given the scale of the problem even before the October 2008 financial meltdown.

On the other side of the inflation equation, the financial community, as well as America's creditors, have an interest in *more liquidity* even at the risk of *higher* short-term inflation. Both commercial and investment banks had huge stakes in CDOs built on MBS, and on credit default swaps insuring those CDOs. Moody's estimated in 2007 that global exposure by various "special investment vehicles"—off-balance-sheet entities created by banks to escape Basel II capital adequacy regulation—ran at around $1.2 trillion, a number that seems too low in light of the cascading bank failures in mid-2008.[44] Either way, falling home prices and rising delinquencies posed a huge problem for financial firms. If financial firms marked these devaluing assets to market, they would obliterate their capital and go into overt or covert bankruptcy, like Lehman Brothers, Bear Stearns, Wachovia, and American International Group (AIG). If they didn't mark them to market and wrote them off, no one would lend to them. They thus sought massive injections of cash from the Federal Reserve and the Treasury in order to stabilize asset prices and their capital bases. The bailouts—$1.6 trillion by September 2008—constituted huge increases in the money supply. Financial institutions hoped that in-

---

[44] Peter Thal Larsen and Paul J. Davies, "Trouble Off Balance Sheet Raises Concerns," *Financial Times*, August 23, 2007.

creased liquidity would keep them solvent long enough for higher inflation to bring nominal incomes and nominal house prices back in line, allowing them to mark their dodgy debt to market at something closer to its par value. When this failed to resolve the crisis, the U.S. state partially nationalized nine core financial firms by buying $125 billion worth of preferred shares in October 2008 and guaranteeing $1.5 trillion in bank debt.

In the 1980s and 1990s, the financial community and elite income groups constituted the social base for very low inflation and a global push for independent central banks, often at the expense of employment levels. Finance pursued a parallel politics of market deregulation and fiscal restraint. Meanwhile, individual financial firms developed adjustable rate mortgages and aggressively securitized loans to move interest rate risk off their books. But in the current conjuncture they now need a few years of 4–5 percent inflation to bring nominal housing prices back to something close to the nominal value of the mortgages secured by those houses. This would validate the bad mortgages on their books, bringing their balance sheets back into balance with fewer write-offs or less new capital.

In a clear demonstration of what it means to be a negotiated currency, foreign creditors clearly influenced the timing and choice of bailout targets. The increasing concentration of foreign holdings of U.S. dollar securities in fewer countries and public authorities in those countries gave increasing market power to those countries, particularly to the Chinese. By 2008, China probably accounted for more than one-eighth of all portfolio holdings of U.S. securities. The Chinese state's refusal to absorb more agency MBS in summer 2008 was the proximate cause for the renationalization of Fannie Mae and Freddie Mac. Up until July 2008, foreign official investors were absorbing about $20 billion per month in agency debt. But in July and August, China actually shed $4.6 billion in agencies, while other foreigners sold $10.1 billion. Fears that foreigners would sit out a $200 billion refinancing for Freddie and Fannie in September 2008 prompted the Treasury to impose its conservatorship on the two agencies. Nonetheless, foreign creditors had no place to go with their dollars. They dumped agencies, only to buy $71 billion in Treasuries instead.[45] Similarly, AIG's $300 billion in credit default swaps (i.e., insurance on bond defaults) benefiting European banks apparently forced the Treasury to nationalize AIG. AIG's holdings of bankrupt Lehman Brothers bonds and its $25 billion in payouts on bad MBS depleted its capital base. An uncontrolled AIG bankruptcy would have seriously damaged major Euro-

---

[45] Saskia Scholtes and James Politi, "Bank of China Flees Fannie-Freddie," *Financial Times*, August 28, 2008, http://www.ft.com/cms/s/0/74c5cf58–7535–11dd-ab30–0000779fd18c.html.

pean banks by forcing them to increase their regulatory capital or to call in loans.[46]

Both a low inflation–low interest rate regime and a direct bailout affect the U.S. dollar's global position. The low interest rate regime will deter investors from shifting additional cash to the United States, unless the United States continues to maintain a growth differential with the rest of the developed world. And low interest rates in general tend to stimulate the U.S. economy more than Japan or the euro zone. But it is hard to see how large masses of consumers trying to build up a big enough equity position in their homes to be able to refinance into lower interest rate fixed-rate mortgages will be able to contribute anything to a growth differential that ultimately derives from increased spending rather than increased saving. Furthermore, bailouts exacerbate the fiscal deficit. This too is likely to have adverse consequences for investment flows into the United States and U.S. dollar-denominated securities. In the short run the unwinding of the housing bubble is unambiguously negative for the dollar. Over the long term, though, broader resistance to inflation helps secure the dollar's position.

## The Housing Finance Crisis and the Future of the U.S. Dollar

In this chapter I argued that housing financial systems played an important role in making the U.S. dollar a top currency for OECD countries and a negotiated currency for developing Asia from 1991 to 2005. Deep and liquid U.S. financial markets certainly exerted their own influence on actors' choice of reserve currency. Yet these markets were not independent of the U.S. housing finance system, which supplied one third of the "depth" in the form of highly liquid mortgage backed securities from Fannie Mae and Freddie Mac. The American housing finance system also generated differential growth versus Japan and the euro zone. Fiscal restraint, falling prices on imports from Asia, and large volumes of short-term, low-interest lending to the U.S. market depressed nominal interest rates on U.S. mortgages. Falling interest rates created increased aggregate demand because the structure of U.S. housing markets permitted easy and cheap mortgage refinance and home purchasing. This housing-led Keynesian demand stimulus gave the United States and similar countries above-average OECD levels of GDP and employment growth, inducing self-sustaining capital inflows. Above average growth secured the

---

[46] Daniel Gros and Stefano Micossi, "The Beginning of the End Game . . . ," September 20, 2008, http://www.voxeu.org/index.php?q=node/1669.

capital flows that made the U.S. dollar a top currency. Capital flowed out of rich OECD economies that could not translate disinflation into increased aggregate demand and into the United States on a portfolio basis. Above average growth also reinforced the position of the U.S. dollar as a negotiated currency, because above average growth made the United States a large and growing market for exports from developing Asia.

It is important to note that this process was conjunctural, in that disinflation fueled the U.S. growth motor, and that housing price bubbles, like any asset bubble, cannot continue indefinitely. Thus, I am not arguing that at all times and under all circumstances U.S.-style housing markets are more likely to lead to above average growth. Indeed, the reverse is obviously true: *inflation* probably percolated through U.S.-style housing markets in differentially detrimental ways for the dollar in the 1970s and 1980s, and clearly helped push many borrowers into foreclosure during the 2006–08 period, precipitating a global financial crisis. My analysis suggests why U.S.-style housing institutions are deleterious in an inflationary environment. Inflation leads to *rising* nominal interest rates on mortgages, which sucks demand out of the economy more rapidly when mortgage debt is high relative to GDP and homeownership is widespread. During the 1970s and parts of the 1980s the United States had higher inflation and thus higher nominal interest rates than Japan and the core euro-zone countries. This caused the GDP and employment motors to run in reverse. Japan and corporatist Europe had superior employment and sometimes GDP performance from the late 1970s until 1990–92.[47] And as noted above, the dollar's attractiveness as a reserve currency faded in the 1980s, until the 1990s disinflation reversed this relationship.

It is also important to note that U.S.-style housing finance institutions are not a perpetual motion machine. The financial flows that drove U.S. growth contained two internal contradictions that ultimately choked off this cycle of growth. First, the positive feedback loop between U.S. and Asian/Chinese growth required deflation/disinflation to continuously free up more purchasing power in the United States. From 1991 through July 2007, prices for developing Asia's exports to the United States fell 27 percent, enhancing U.S. consumers' purchasing power and Asian trade surpluses.[48] And swelling Asian trade surpluses were of course recycled into U.S. Treasuries and agencies, depressing interest rates. But China's export successes also implied rapid Chinese growth, and thus increasing Chinese calls on global raw materials

[47] Kenworthy 2002.
[48] U.S. Bureau of Labor Statistics website, http://data.bls.gov/PDQ/outside.jsp?survey=ei.

and China's own supplies of semiskilled labor. Raw materials prices started rising in 2004, and Chinese wages began rising in 2007. China thus began exporting inflation rather than deflation. This forced U.S. interest rates up, breaking the disinflationary dynamic that was powering U.S. growth.

The second limit on perpetual housing growth was exhaustion of the pool of potential new entrants or upgraders in the housing market. This pool dried up as lending markets chased less and less creditworthy buyers and home-ownership rose 5 percentage points above historical levels. Absent a large increase in incomes at the bottom of the market, this last tranche of new homeowners would necessarily find themselves stretched when it came to affording even an average house after a decade of rapid increases in housing prices. And without new entrants at the bottom, those in the middle would have no one to sell to and thus no realized equity to finance their own movement up the property ladder. But because the 1990s disinflationary growth model relied on increasing volumes of imported Asian goods, workers at the bottom of the income distribution eventually faced downward pressure on wages. Increasingly expensive houses could not be bought by increasingly impoverished workers, unless buyers and lenders were willing to engage in varieties of fraud in order to repackage subprime mortgages into "toxic waste" CDOs and then sell them to investors—which they did until this market collapsed in 2007. Efforts to restore the U.S. growth differential versus the euro zone and Japan and thus restore the U.S. dollar's top currency position necessarily involve some improvement of income at the bottom.

The exhaustion of deflationary pressures and creditworthy buyers by 2005 put the U.S. dollar's position as a top currency back in play just as it was during the 1970s and '80s. Then, higher than OECD-average inflation in the United States led to lower than OECD average growth. Fear of higher U.S. inflation and the reality of slower U.S. growth going forward from 2008 are likely to make the dollar more of a negotiated reserve currency for the foreseeable future. The dollar will rely on the forbearance of Asian and oil exporting states, for whom Bretton Woods II and geopolitical considerations respectively loom largest. Whether the dollar can once more attract support on a market-based basis and thus regain its position as a top currency remains to be seen. Whether housing finance will play the same key role in this financial balance of terror around renewal of the U.S. dollar is unclear. But it certainly cannot fail to play some role, because of its sheer size in terms of outstanding assets and because of its huge macroeconomic effects.

The central issue for the dollar in the medium term is thus whether Europe, Japan, and developing Asia can decouple from the U.S. economy. If these areas can attain risk-adjusted growth rates above that of the U.S. economy, the dollar will be in considerable trouble. This is particularly true if growth in core Europe approaches or exceeds U.S. levels. Some current analyses suggest that unwinding the U.S. housing bubble will shave at least two and possibly as many as four percentage points off U.S. growth over the next few years.[49] This clearly puts the United States at a disadvantage relative to the euro zone, because the latter figure implies a serious recession.

Against this, though I wouldn't bet my house on it, my sense is that the dollar will muddle through for two reasons. First, the political changes needed to attain *consistent* above OECD-average growth in the euro zone's core states are so painful that the euro will not rise above its current regional status. The euro zone is unlikely to escape unscathed from America's housing finance crisis. Far from decoupling, European and Japanese growth decelerated even more rapidly than U.S. growth in 2008 and 2009. Europe's banks also faced their own difficulties, prompting the same sort of extraordinary interventions and nationalizations that occurred in the United States during 2008. In winter 2008–09, governments fully or partially nationalized banks in Belgium, Britain, France, Germany, the Netherlands, and Switzerland.[50] Although the *relative* gap in growth rates between the United States and Europe will be narrower than that which emerged in the long 1990s, it will persist, which favors the dollar.

Second, the time required for adjustment means that foreigners either must accumulate more U.S. assets or step up purchases of U.S. goods. In particular, given what the United States can export, China and the other Asian exporters will have to scale back domestic industrial promotion programs. In the medium run, the dollar is thus likely to be more of a negotiated currency than a top currency, with central banks and sovereign wealth funds having more influence than private investors. The terms of the negotiation will be set by foreigners' relative appetite for U.S. goods as compared to U.S. assets, and by well-to-do Americans' willingness to curb their appetite for imported goods.

[49] Reinhardt and Rogoff 2008.
[50] Stephen Castle and Katrin Bennhold, "European Officials Debate Need for a Bailout Package," *New York Times*, October 2, 2008; http://www.nytimes.com/2008/10/02/business/worldbusiness/02regulate.html.

# 6

# FROM MONOPOLY TO OLIGOPOLY
## Lessons from the Pre-1914 Experience

Marcello de Cecco

Are we at a turning point in world economic and monetary history? Will it be an abrupt, nonlinear turning point? In what direction will world monetary and financial events turn? Will the turn be dictated, as Eric Helleiner suggests in this book, by political forces, as certainly was the case in 1914? Can we escape a comparably grim outcome?

My essay is a nonformalized, literary attempt at comparative system dynamics. The international currency experience of recent decades certainly has some features in common with that of the fifteen years preceding 1914: a declining economic superpower at the center, Great Britain in those years, the United States today, challenged by large newcomers, then Germany and especially the United States, now the so-called BRIC (Brazil, Russia, India, and China) countries, which have been growing at very high rates. The declining superpower issued the international currency, but its role was challenged by another currency. In our time this seems to be the euro; in the pre-1914 period it was gold, which threatened to become the sole basis of the international gold standard and gradually to relegate sterling to a declining role, to be played mainly within the borders of the British Empire.

But why not stress the similarity of the present system with that of other periods, for instance the interwar one when a multiple-currency international system really came into existence (see Benjamin Cohen, chapter 7)? Because the private part of the international financial system of the 1920s and 1930s became much smaller and much more constrained by government regulations, which increasingly restrained national financial intermediaries in their international transactions. Wartime controls never faded away and were reintroduced with a vengeance, almost everywhere, in the 1930s. Central banks strictly implemented government policies during the war and never went back to the effective independence some of them had enjoyed before 1914. Relations between state and market, in other words, leaned toward the state in the two interwar decades. On the contrary, developments in monetary and financial relations since the early 1980s show a trend away from the state and toward the market that more closely resembles the gold standard years. Although the state was ascendant in the decade before 1914, the private international financial market was developing so fast, at least until the 1907 crisis, that power relations tilted toward the state only with the outbreak of the Great War and the adoption of the command economy at least in the strategically relevant economic sectors in the belligerent countries. Neither in the pre-1914 period nor today is there the obsessive subservience of finance to politics that pervaded the interwar years. Power relations between state and market are much more balanced, and embedded in the economic globalization that characterizes both the international gold standard period and the last two decades. However, it is worrisome that the mercantilist-protectionist turn the world took in the fifteen years before 1914 bears a strong resemblance to what is happening today.

In addition, international monetary pluralism seems in our days different from the one ruling in the interwar years, when no currency appeared on the scene that was not strictly the expression of national sovereignty. Today, although the new star on the horizon of the world economy is certainly China, which has the largest trade surpluses and accumulates reserves faster than any other country, the rising star on the international monetary horizon is not the Chinese renminbi, at least not for some time yet. Nor are the currencies of Brazil, Russia, and India rising stars. It is the euro, a strange supranational currency whose central bank, like the Federal Reserve, does not accumulate reserves by intervention but lets the market freely set exchange rates. Is the euro more similar to gold than to a national currency? Like gold, it is not the expression of national sovereignty. Its market value is freely determined by demand and supply. Like gold and unlike national currencies, it has no fiscal role, as it cannot be used to back the public debt of the member countries. Unlike gold, the euro has no intrinsic value. Unlike gold, it is issued by a central bank, although the European Central Bank is a constitutionally relevant institution of the European Union, on the same level as the European Parliament, and is completely independent of political power, national or otherwise (although it is accountable to the European Parliament).

We have the impression that the euro will coexist with the dollar for a long time. Perhaps the dollar will slowly come to play the role that silver played for many centuries, its users being more and more interested in its means of exchange and transactions functions and less in its store of value functions. Those last may become the defining prerogatives of the euro. If the euro acquires some of the features that for two thousand years were associated with gold, it will be used, as gold was, to denominate savings instruments and capital transactions, like house and land sales and perhaps even international commodity transactions. Are we going into a long phase similar to bimetallism? Unlike some modern economists, who think that there can only be a single monetary standard, Leon Walras gave a satisfactory theoretical proof that gold and silver can coexist as complementary monetary metals, if their relative prices are allowed to adjust and are not kept unreasonably fixed.

But, first, we must wait to see whether dollar depreciation continues and if it becomes much greater than it has historically been, and, second, how euro countries react to a dollar depreciation that makes them lose market shares in world trade in favor of those countries whose currencies fluctuate with the dollar. A related question: How long will dollar depreciation proceed before it becomes a rout, as happened to silver in the last decades of the nineteenth century, when its use as a monetary metal to make full-bodied coins was altogether abandoned by all developed countries and relegated to very poor countries such as China and India? How can the huge U.S. financial sector keep doing business using a fast-depreciating currency? It was, after all, the British financial community that dictated that sterling maintain a high international value, even if it meant sacrificing a good part of the British industrial structure (see Kirshner, chapter 9, and McKinnon, chapter 3). Are U.S. financial leaders going to be able to do the same about the dollar? After all, the pound, which in 1965 still represented about 20 percent of world monetary reserves, had been reduced to insignificance ten years later. Thirty years later, however, we see its return as a reserve currency, having replaced the yen, which performed that function in the '70s and '80s (the long siege on the yen in the 1970s and '80s, to compel it to revalue, is mentioned and underlined in McKinnon, chapter 3).

## The Euro as a Reserve Currency

The euro is a very peculiar currency. It is not a national currency, and by de-sign the countries that have given the European System of Central Banks the task of issuing it have renounced monetary sovereignty, by severing the link between public debt and money creation. The ECB is by law forbidden to buy the national debt of any of the Economic and Monetary Union (EMU) mem-ber countries or any other public debt on the primary market. Fiscal policy is thus separated from monetary policy. What the ECB calls "open market op-erations" are therefore swaps between the ECB and commercial banks, as was shown in August 2007. As a late triumph of monetarism, further enhanced by the explicit task assigned, in price stabilization, to money supply control, the ECB was given the exclusive role of assuring price stability in the EMU. Of late, however, the ECB seemed to bow to the rational expectations school by tacitly adopting inflation targeting. It also quietly demoted money supply as a prime policy instrument in favor of interest rate control.

As a result of all this, the euro appears as a very good candidate for a re-serve currency, its future value being assured by the conservative policy the ECB, by statute, must follow. There was, however, for the deutsche mark and there is for the euro a structural reason working against a stable international role. The German economy has been, since 1870, an export economy, pro-ducing investment goods for the whole world. It has a built-in tendency to ac-cumulate reserves, rather than to create them for the whole world. Because of its extra large investment-goods-producing sector, it is incapable by itself of generating the rate of growth in demand that it needs to achieve full em-ployment. This mercantilist bias was temporarily weakened by reunification, which for almost a decade upset fiscal balance in Germany, raised German public debt, and generated demand for the whole European economy, as Ger-many modernized the eastern lands it had acquired in 1989. German indus-try, however, went through a severe restructuring immediately after that, as firms relocated cheap product and parts and components lines to eastern Europe, while keeping only the high-value-added ones, plus research and de-velopment and company governance in Germany. This created massive un-employment (with high unemployment payments) in Germany, pressure on wages was reduced and internal demand was compressed, after the early stages of infrastructure modernization were completed in the former East Germany and fiscal balance was slowly regained. Through this strategy, Ger-many reacquired its export capacity, which it also did because it re-created, by relocation and investment, an integrated productive system in central Eu-rope like the one it had established there before 1914 (when Central Europe was known as Mitteleuropa). It was thus ready to supply the Asian and other emerging economies (China in particular) with sophisticated investment goods when they started booming in the early years of the new century. Europe is not yet self-contained from the macroeconomic point of view: it still has to import demand from outside to achieve a full employment rate of growth. The problem may have become even larger, given the production integration that now exists between Germany and Mitteleuropa.

In the years since the EMU got going, the task of providing enough demand for the world economy has thus been performed by the United States, which absorbs 15 percent of world imports, while it ships only 7 percent of world exports. As a result of trade and payments imbalances but also because a momentous financial revolution was unleashed in the United States that drastically reduced American financial institutions' credit supply constraints, the U.S. monetary system has therefore generated the liquidity that fueled the world boom. The euro was, on the contrary, managed much more conservatively. China's share of world imports has also risen very impressively in the same years, but it has constantly shown an export surplus toward the rest of the world, in particular toward the United States. (Here, my analysis completely agrees with that of Calleo in chapter 8.)

The euro went through an initial phase, at the end of the 1990s, when the dollar was very high, the Fed having to battle against the latest phase of the information, communication, and technology (ICT) bubble, and the new single European currency, after a very strong start, became and remained below parity with it. The ICT bubble finally exploded and the U.S. economy fell into serious recession, compelling the Fed to retrace its steps and bring interest rates down to extremely low levels that had not been seen for decades. Foreign policy and increased military expenditure also required monetary accommodation. Monetary conditions have been, as a result, extremely permissive in the United States, even after the Fed started raising rates, because the dollar began to weaken, but also because monetary conditions are determined, in the present U.S. financial system, by private financial institutions' competitive behavior as much as by the central bank.

In this new phase of U.S. monetary conditions, the euro began to appreciate and to gain credibility as a reserve currency. Recent estimates by Deutsche Bank economists have set the present share of the euro in industrial countries' reserves at more than 50 percent of the total, if one excludes those held by Japan, which are still predominantly in dollars. That means that the euro reserves are now larger than the dollar reserves of those countries.

In recent years, total world currency reserves have grown very fast, and the dollar accounts for two thirds of the total, while the euro is still less than a third, and sterling has mustered an unexpected resurrection, with 5 percent of world reserves now held in pounds. This means that after a brief initial uncertainty the euro has been welcomed in the reserves of central banks, because its share of total reserves is equal to what legacy currencies used to have in spite of the fast rate of increase in dollar reserves.

In recent years, reserves have been accumulated by emerging market countries, especially by those in Asia, signally by China, while after the oil price increases, oil producers, including Russia and of course Middle Eastern countries, have also piled up reserves. Russia now predominantly holds euros, while Middle Eastern oil producers still favor the dollar.

The case of China is the most important, since China alone now holds more than one trillion dollars in reserves. After 2002, when the dollar began to fall, the Chinese diversified their reserves in favor of the euro, but starting in 2004 they have kept a stable portfolio, as far as currencies go, and it is predominantly composed of dollars. More than they have switched out of short-term dollar assets, the Chinese and other large reserve holders have used some of their forex resources to invest in real foreign assets. This poses delicate sovereignty problems to host countries, which will become clearer if the phenomenon grows.

It would be strange if things were otherwise. Emerging market countries' reserves, signally those held by China but also by others in the same group, are mainly accumulated as a result of currency interventions made to prevent those countries' currencies from appreciating vis-à-vis the dollar. Rapid accumulation of dollar reserves by emerging market countries has led some economists to speak of a new Bretton Woods, a direct reference to the policy of dollar reserve accumulation by countries such as Germany and Japan in the 1950s and '60s. Those countries wanted to export to the United States to bolster their pace of development; in order to allow the United States to keep buying their exports without devaluing the dollar, they accumulated dollars. Now it is the turn of countries such as China, India, Brazil, South Korea, and the ever-present Japan to do the same. They are trading off the availability of an open market for their wares in the United States and of competitive exchange rates for their currencies against gigantic purchases of dollars.

Accordingly, this view assigns low probability to the rise of the euro in the near future as a currency capable of replacing the dollar as the U.S. market will still be the crucial market for emerging countries. The propounders of the new Bretton Woods theory also believe that it is impossible for the world trade and payments system to be on a multiple currency standard. They think that, because of network externalities, there can only be one world currency standard at a time. The currency that provides the standard may change, as in the past the pound sterling was replaced by the dollar. But polarization of the system is inevitable. There cannot be, according to this view, more than one currency as the standard at any one time.

In my view, the present situation is not comparable to that of the "Trente glorieuses," the golden age of the Bretton Woods system. Above all, this is because there is now no strategic trade-off for very large reserve owners such as China as there was for such countries as Germany and Japan in the Bretton Woods decades. The Soviet threat has dissolved, or at most become the Russian threat, the world is not polarized, and an oligopoly of power is rapidly coming about, one that is more like that which existed before 1914. Oligopolies—that is the trouble with them—can be collusive or competitive. So far we have seen the collusive phase. More precisely, perhaps, we could classify the post-Soviet world set-up as a Stackelberg model, with the United States leading.[1] With the rise of China and the growth of the euro, we may now be moving to a competitive oligopoly, a much more dangerous state (see the chapters by Helleiner and Calleo). Countries started again to move as units, not as members of a polarized world, with the two halves kept together by mutually exclusive ideologies, as was the case until the demise of the Soviet Union and before the rise of China and the euro. Bretton Woods had at its roots the concepts of superpower and of limited sovereignty. All other historical examples of gold exchange standards, as Bretton Woods was, involved colonial countries that held the mother countries' currency as reserves. As soon as John Maynard Keynes analyzed the concept of the gold exchange standard in "Indian Currency and Finance," this was noted by, among others, Gustavo del Vecchio, an eminent Italian economist who reviewed the book. It was also noted by other contemporary economists, who wrote that a sovereign country had to keep its reserves in gold, a neutral reserve instrument and also the only one that would remain liquid in case of war.[2]

## A More Appropriate Historical Comparison

Several features exhibited by the international economy in the decades that preceded World War I strongly remind us of those of the present day. One stands out, first and foremost: the sensationally rapid growth of the United States, a country that went from being a relatively secondary player in the world economy to becoming one of its protagonists. It was a new arrival on

[1] In game theory within economics, a Stackelberg model is one where there is a firm that acts as a market leader to which other firms respond.
[2] See, for example, von Lumm 1912.

the scene, as it acquired, through mass immigration, a population that put it near the top of the world league, and after late territorial conquest (mainly at Mexico's expense) it became as big as a continent. The real revolutionary feature of the U.S. ascent was, however, the growth of its productive capacity, in modern agriculture as well as modern industry. In a way, the U.S. ascent was even more revolutionary than that of China has been in our time. Compared to Old World countries, the United States had almost no industrial or agricultural infancy, and its industrial growth did not go through a long "primitive accumulation" phase based on the exploitation of impoverished masses of workers (slavery involved only the Southern economy, while industrialization took place mainly in the Northeast), although it certainly was shielded by heavy protection and for a while the quality of its products was low compared to that of European ones. Its wages were always higher than those prevailing in Europe. It had no serious technological gap to fill. In the United States both agriculture and, a little later, industry were at the cutting edge of (especially labor-saving) technology. After the end of the Civil War, the United States just exploded on the world scene, sucking in the largest part of capital exports and of emigrants from the Old World to build its infrastructure and industrial and agricultural structure.

In the same decades, another country, this time in Europe, grew to world eminence. This was, as is known, Germany, which developed in a couple of decades into the investment goods industry powerhouse of the world that it remains to this day. It was potentially no challenge to the United States, as it did not have the geographical size the United States possessed. But it succeeded in organizing a productive system by which it supplied investment goods to all the developing countries of continental Europe, including Austria-Hungary and the rest of Mitteleuropa, Italy, and Russia, and absorbed their industrial and agricultural products and their raw materials. This was known as the original "Mitteleuropa System."[3]

Meanwhile, in the Far East, a third industrial star was beginning to shine, that of Japan, a country whose pace of modernization was even more sensational, bringing it in only a few decades to the status of great power, after two military victories, against China and, much more remarkably, against Russia, showed the mettle of the Japanese leadership and the capability of the newly built Japanese industry.

---

[3] For an excellent study of Mitteleuropa, see Bresciani Turroni 1909. Bresciani, against the German "Geschlossen-Staat" theories popular at the time, identified the area's structural foreign trade bias, which even today characterizes the whole of the European Union.

## Emerging Powers, Britain, and the Gold Standard

With the ascent of the United States and Germany, the resurrection of Italy and Japan, the rapid modernization of Russia, and the return on the scene of France after its defeat in the Franco-Prussian War, the world preeminence of Great Britain was seriously challenged. Not only the political but especially the economic map of the world was dramatically redrawn in those decades. British relative industrial and agricultural decline in these decades is well known. Much less known is the challenge that the adoption of the gold standard by most advanced and developing countries represented for Great Britain. Although it is considered by most monetary historians as a positive step toward world monetary equilibrium, was it really positive for the world and for Great Britain? It may have been a mixed blessing for both.

In earlier decades, British financial entrepreneurs and bureaucrats had, especially though the unintended consequences of Peel's Act, invented the centralized gold reserve, entrusted to the Bank of England, and developed the largest and most powerful deposit banking system in the world. This gave their financial system a remarkable elasticity, but it also exposed it to sudden and damaging confidence crises. A massive inverted pyramid of potentially unstable credit relations was built on a very scant reserve and a very inflexible paper currency.

As long as Britain kept a virtual monopoly over the gold standard—with most other countries sticking to the silver standard and a few of them to bimetallism—the Bank of England, which kept the only gold reserves of the huge British financial system, would be able to stem gold outflows by raising its interest rate, attracting gold from the rest of the world in the process. In France, gold circulated as coin together with silver. When the Bank of England's rate went up, gold was shipped mainly from France (although it stemmed the outflow of British short-term funds from the City and even attracted gold from dozens of other countries). The Paris—London connection relied on the House of Rothschild's control of the silver and gold trade in both countries. But it also crucially depended on the City's ability to finance the largest part of international trade, especially that in raw materials and primary commodities. London, moreover, financed a big share of long-term investment in the whole world. The proceeds of long-term loans were redeposited by foreign debtors at short term with the same London banks that had floated the loans. Finally, it was London firms that operated the largest market where new gold flowed directly from the mines to be auctioned or sold privately, while a good part of the proceeds were kept as short-term deposits with London intermediaries. For these reasons, an increase of the Bank of England's rate induced largely British financial operators to keep their deposits in London to earn the bigger interest and the Bank's gold reserves stopped bleeding. It was a purely commercial decision on the part of the operators, solely inspired by profit maximization.

This simple mechanism was put to a very tough test when more and more countries decided to adopt the gold standard and created central banks to manage the new monetary regime. These banks could not rely on a deep and resilient money market to help them avoid the more deflationary features of the new regime. They could not borrow gold from the market as easily as the Bank of England did, just by raising their interest rates. When they did, gold did not flow in, as their countries were net debtors rather than net creditors vis-à-vis the international financial market. New gold standard countries, as a consequence, tended to take a very dim view of any outflow of gold from their reserves. They knew they had no valid instrument like a bank rate to attract gold. They had to pile up the metal to abide by the convertibility rules. At the same time, fearful of free gold movements, they invented, with the help of their governments, ways to restrict gold outflows, in order to minimize their influence on the real economy.[4]

As country after country, having adopted the gold standard, began to put serious obstacles in the way of gold exports, the Bank of England found to its chagrin that when it raised the bank rate gold did not flow in as easily it had done when only England and France had important central banks. France preferred losing gold to raising interest rates, having very large gold reserves and an enormous gold coin circulation to use as a giant buffer stock to protect interest rate stability. The double act between Britain and France worked well while it lasted. Britain worked with a slender centralized gold reserve. This increased the cost efficiency of its own financial system, which more and more frequently had to pay the price of increased interest rates. France, where traditional agriculture still provided over 40 percent of total employment, could not develop a deposit banking system that was as efficient as that of the British. It decentralized the gold reserve among its citizenry, letting French and British arbitrageurs get hold of some of it and ship it to London when a bank rate increase made it convenient to remit gold. As I already noted, the presence in Paris and London of the two main branches of the House of Rothschild made arbitrage operations smoother and cheaper. France remained, until the 1880s, on a bimetallic standard, so that when gold was summoned to London, silver took its place in circulation and in the payments of the

---

[4] See again von Lumm 1912.

Banque de France.[5] It also helped that Rothschild family members were on the directorates of both the Bank of England and the Banque de France.

This precarious but effective mechanism began to falter when central banks were created in more and more countries and did not take the French central bank's Olympian attitude when they lost gold, but worked to insulate the gold in their vaults from the free market. The Bank of England's discount rate had to go much higher than it previously did, before gold stopped going out of London or began to flow back there. Its effects on the economy became substantial, and they were noticed by the public and by the financial and the political class.

Things were not helped by the consolidation movement that occurred in British deposit banking at the same time. It was so intense that at the turn of the century Britain found itself with a handful of giant deposit banks, by far the largest in the world. In order to raise profits the new giant banks started raiding the traditional preserves of the City of London's specialized intermediaries, some of whose owners also sat in the court of directors of the Bank of England and thus made British monetary policy. The City had traditionally worked on borrowed funds, which its specialized intermediaries transformed into instruments of international trade and finance. Some of the funds came from abroad, but most came from the deposit banks, which traditionally had been based in the English counties. The banking giants that emerged from amalgamation had London headquarters and very large networks of branches (up to seven hundred each), which took deposits in every corner of Britain and used them to perform the tasks hitherto performed by other intermediaries—for instance, financing the stock exchange and even international trade. Bank rate raises thus stopped attracting funds as easily as they previously did, not only from abroad but also from the rest of Britain.[6]

Traditional British financial circuits therefore became increasingly jammed because the rest of the British and the world financial systems were organized in a way they had not been before. The German, American, Austro—Hungarian, and Italian financial systems were organized along different lines, with so-called universal banks playing most of the roles that specialist institutions played in Britain. Everywhere, large deposit banks kept very scant gold reserves, calling on the central bank when they needed gold. But, unlike the Banque de France, with its mammoth gold holdings, which were justified by its size, the German Reichsbank was also dwarfed in size by the growth of German large banks and could not keep a reserve adequate to the size of the Ger-

---

[5] On this, Flandreau (2004) has written extensively and authoritatively.
[6] On this subject, see de Cecco 1974 and the literature it quotes.

man banking system. The United States had no central bank. The sixty-five hundred national banks could issue banknotes, but the law required that they keep federal bonds as reserves against the notes. When they had to issue notes, they had to buy Treasury bonds, mostly from the Treasury, giving gold in exchange for them. The Treasury kept that gold in its vaults and, as many contemporaries observed, only gave it back to the market during domestic or international financial crises.[7]

U.S., German, Russian, and Italian banks were much more involved in long-term financing of national industry than British banks were, often buying and holding industrial shares. Moreover, although their assets had low liquidity, their liabilities had a much higher liquidity, making the financial systems of those countries structurally fragile and requiring continuing and substantial intervention by central banks to maintain stability. Until 1913, there was no such institution in the United States, while in Germany the Reichsbank discovered in the course of several crises between 1907 and 1912 that it did not have sufficient gold to stem outflows and maintain monetary and financial stability.

The rise of organized finance in the rest of the modernized world thus enlarged but also reduced Britain's capacity to "conduct the international orchestra" as it was supposed to do—precisely in those years when such an orchestra was supposed to have played at its best. With the rest of the world developing their financial systems to provide active assistance to fast industrialization, British financial intermediaries would often be working in a not very hospitable environment. The countries where they still had an easy life were, predictably, those of the formal British Empire and of the Dominions, whose financial systems were organized to be ancillary to that of the mother country. Their activities in the United States were very profitable, but could cause serious policy problems to British monetary authorities.

## Disequilibrating Forces

U.S. financial affairs remained very peculiarly organized until the outbreak of World War I. Until 1913 the United States did not have a central bank. It had a gold reserve kept by the federal Treasury, which, because the growth of national income swelled fiscal revenues, and because of bond purchases from the national banks to back their note issues, became a gigantic mountain of gold in the fifteen years before the war. The U.S. Treasury was neither able nor

---

[7] See Foxwell 1912 and Nogaro 1912, and also many articles in the *Economist* and in the *Bankers' Magazine*.

willing to recycle gold to the financial system as often and as flexibly as a central bank would have done. After the country adopted the gold standard at the end of the 1870s, it was not only the federal Treasury that hoarded gold. The large U.S. farming population in the Plains and Western states absorbed gold on a very large scale indeed. They sold their crops in summer, were paid in gold coins, and kept them at home, not trusting banks very much (they had very good reasons not to), until the time came, in the following months, to buy seeds, agricultural machinery, and consumer goods. Then the coins flowed back to the Eastern seaboard, where the most modern part of the U.S. banking system was located.[8]

When farmers absorbed gold, it became scarce in the East, interest rates in New York went up, and gold flowed from the only place where there was a free gold market, the City of London. In turn, the Bank of England raised its rate to stem the outflow and gold sometimes flowed to London. There were awkward times, like the famous Black Week at the start of the Boer War, when the bank rate went up and no gold arrived.[9] Similar occurrences became more frequent as the importance of transatlantic agricultural trade increased, especially after Britain, starting in the mid-1890s, became utterly dependent on agricultural imports because of the final decline of British agriculture, defeated by bad weather and cheap grain from the Americas.

British financial institutions were thus enriched by American business, which they secured because of the peculiar structure of the U.S. financial system, where banks could not legally own out-of-state branches and mostly remained unit banks, even if some of them grew very large. They had to invent a huge interbank deposit network to establish links to one another, and it was a very fragile setup, easily dislocated by lapses in confidence. Like those in London, banks in the United States made short-term loans to New York stock exchange brokers and considered them as cash reserves. When there was a credit squeeze in New York, the absence of either bank networks or a central bank induced short-term rates to rise to remarkable heights, and London finance houses had to come to the rescue, lending short-term funds at a very good profit.

But the Bank of England and the British Treasury, to which it fell to manage the international gold standard, were not helped at all by U.S. gold accumulation or by the peculiar structure of the U.S. financial system. The United States was indebted to the British financial system, relying on it for the supply of short- and long-term capital. American funds were placed in London

[8] See Sprague 1908 for an excellent description of this process.
[9] See Clapham 1944, vol. 2.

when they were not needed at home, but were recalled without notice when need arose, as it did every autumn, to move crops to export points. This, the famous "autumn drain," caused short-term interest rates to rise to stupendous heights in New York, so that money flowed from London, depleting the Bank of England's gold reserve, and inducing it to raise the bank rate, thus transmitting disturbances first to the British financial system and then to other financial systems that were connected to London. Up to 1914, there was not enough arbitrage money disposed to close the annual autumn drain of gold.

The move to adopt the gold standard by more and more countries as the century drew to a close was thus very reserve-intensive just when the British financial system was becoming highly leveraged and came to own as little cash as possible, finding it more convenient to borrow cash when there was a sudden need for it from an international market that was ever less ready to supply it. This is another remarkable similarity with today's banking systems, where reserves are largely borrowed from the market.

Countries such as Germany, Italy, and Russia went on the gold standard but soon found that they could not abide by the rules of the game of a truly convertible currency. Their universal banks created deposits by loans to industry, which were often used to finance fixed investments. Illiquidity was thus a frequent state for these banking systems and central banks had to come to the rescue, knowing that their banks did not have deep and resilient money markets to turn to.

All this caused recurrent difficulties for the British unofficial managers of the international gold standard, and only by lucky coincidence could some countervailing forces be used by the Treasury and the Bank of England to balance international accounts in order to keep sterling freely convertible. The discovery of large deposits of gold in South Africa was one of these countervailing forces. It soon turned into a very large inflow of gold into London, where it was sold and the proceeds were "pro tempore" deposited in British banks. The world stock of gold doubled in the two decades before 1914.

The organization of the Indian economy to suit British needs was another of these forces, perhaps the most important, even if its crucial role was for a long time largely overlooked even by specialists. The Indian financial system was geared to the British one by technical arrangements that have since then gone under the name "gold exchange standard." For a long time, India was not allowed to have a gold currency; it was kept on a silver standard, long after silver had been discarded by most modernized countries and its price had fallen precipitously. The low value of the Indian rupee made Indian raw material exports boom in the late 1890s and in the first decade of the new century. India thus acquired a very positive trade balance, and was formally put on the gold standard. But it was compelled to keep the reserves it accumulated as a result of its export boom in the form of British government paper and deposits with London financial institutions. This system was imitated by other colonial powers in their monetary relations with their colonies. Because of its size, however, it was only the Indian economy that played a crucial role in balancing the accounts of the international gold standard, which would have tilted more toward disequilibrium by reserve accumulation in the gold standard countries, and in particular by the drain on the world gold stock caused by the senseless accumulation of a giant gold pile by the U.S. Treasury and by the seasonal drain of gold to the U.S. farming states.

It is commonly said that the pre-1914 gold standard was really a sterling standard. Although true, this should not be considered as a positive or stable state of affairs. Sterling had no credible challengers as an international currency until World War I. There was, however, increasing reason to doubt that sterling could have remained on the gold standard; that is, that the pound could have kept its gold value had the mentioned lucky coincidence of South African gold discoveries and the cynical use of Indian economic and financial resources by the Raj and by the India Office not helped to manage Britain's international accounts.

### International Financial Crises in the Pre-1914 Era

In the last fifteen years before World War I, several international financial crises occurred at short intervals. The Boer War started the series. When the Transvaal, under President Paul Kruger, declared war on England in October 1899 all gold shipments to London stopped, as the Boer authorities placed an embargo on the mines. At the time, the Transvaal produced 25 percent of all the world's gold, and it was all sold in London, the proceeds being, temporarily at least, deposited with English banks. The Bank of England had an unofficial right of first refusal of that gold and refilled its meager stock as it found fit to do so. From April 1900 to April 1901, no gold was mined in the Transvaal. Central banks began to bid for gold. In December 1899, the bank rate was at 6 percent in London, a height it had not reached since the Baring Panic of 1890. The Reichsbank's rate was at 7 percent, the highest in its history. The Boer War also showed how fragile the U.S. banking system was. On December 18, 1899, Wall Street call money rates climbed to 186 percent. Although no gold came from South Africa, London was able to get reorganized, importing gold from elsewhere and out of the Indian gold standard reserve, which was in British government bonds. The bank rate was thus lowered and remained low as long as the war lasted, allowing the British government to borrow at a reasonable cost.

Yet, the Boer War showed how powerful the United States had become in world finance. Exports of agricultural products had grown enormously, and a huge trade surplus had accumulated. U.S. investors used part of it to buy a sizable share of British public debt issues. They also bought large chunks of German public debt. In addition to that, in European financial circles it was believed that American investors kept about $200 million invested at short term in the money markets of Europe. America had thus become a financial giant, which began to flex its muscles well before World War I. The yawning gap that existed between its financial power and its domestic monetary institutions, which would be closed only shortly before the outbreak of the world war, became the most dangerous threat to world financial and monetary stability, undermining the Bank of England's efforts to "conduct the international orchestra."

This became glaringly evident in the 1907 crisis, which started in the United States at the end of a huge industrial and financial bubble, which had spread to most of the world's real and financial markets. At the epicenter of it, as also would happen in London in the summer of 1914, was the stock exchange. This was because both in the United States and in England, and in the many peripheral countries where crises broke out, stock exchange speculation was financed through short-term loans from the domestic and foreign commercial banks, which considered, dangerous as it was, such loans as liquidity, a sizable part of the reserves they kept against deposits or banknotes that had been issued.

It is useful to recall the sequence of crises that broke out in 1907.[10] The 1907 episodes were preceded, in the second half of 1906, by turbulence that involved the world markets, including London. U.S. stock exchange speculation threatened to collapse for lack of fresh financial resources. U.S. bankers found new resources in London to stoke the fire, as investments by London banks and no less than $35 million worth of gold (the equivalent of £7 million) left the Bank of England for the United States, reducing the Old Lady's stock of gold to a level as low as she had had in 1893. The Old Lady's furious reaction, threatening to raise the bank rate to hitherto unattained heights, put

---

[10] What follows owes a lot to Noyes (1909), which, in turn, is built on information mostly gleaned from a careful perusal of the *Economist*, as I was able to check by repeating the operation. Noyes's book has the great merit of looking at the 1907 international financial crisis as a world phenomenon, involving peripheral markets as well as those of the center. Clapham 1944, vol. 2, also notes most of the peripheral crises, but in his usual clipped and allusive style, which makes his books a pleasure to read, but only for those who already know the subject. A good account of the crisis is also provided by Foxwell 1912.

a stop to London bankers' enthusiasm for Wall Street. This would prove beneficial one year later, when gold was summoned again from London to stop the hoarding panic that had broken out in New York and spread to the whole of the United States.

The autumn 1906 money market crisis reverberated slowly but inexorably through the financial markets of the world's periphery, which had followed New York in a raw materials boom fueled by foreign money. In New York, a great part was also played by railway shares speculation following the railway wars of the U.S. financial magnates. It was the collapse of railway shares in the spring of 1907 that induced a general stock exchange crisis on Wall Street. (Some contemporaries thought the stock exchange crisis was induced by the passing of antitrust legislation introduced by President Theodore Roosevelt.)

As foreign finance hastily withdrew from peripheral markets, possibly as a consequence of the Wall Street crash, panics developed in many of them. The first market to collapse, in April 1907, was the Egyptian, which had been pumped up by British and local money, thus suffering when the English bankers tried to bring their funds home. Gold had then to be sent to the National Bank of Egypt from London, but the collapse continued well into the summer, with bank runs, currency hoarding, and general business disruption. At the same time, panic struck the stock exchange in Japan, where the victorious conclusion of the Russo-Japanese War had brought financial euphoria. After a summer lull, the turbulence resumed. On October 17, 1907, a panic broke out in Hamburg, a financial center historically linked to the London market. Interest rates climbed to 10 percent and brought down many banks, with the crisis spreading to other cities in Germany. It was declared the worst crisis to have affected Hamburg since 1857.

Similar convulsions occurred in the Danish and Dutch financial markets, also closely tied to London, in the same months. The Portuguese market was also affected by the reverberations of the U.S. crisis, which added to local political problems. South America could not, of course, be spared by the withdrawals of European funds. Chile was the worst affected. There, an exchange rate depreciation was followed by a deep and widespread banking crisis, with bank runs stemmed only by the issue of short-term treasury bills to banks.

The collapse of Wall Street's financial and real bubble made other panics pale into insignificance. It invented the most innovative financial institutions of the time, the famous "trusts." Very much like hedge funds and private equity have done in recent years, they exploited regulatory holes that allowed them to roam freely in all dimensions of finance. They had thus taken business from both investment and commercial banks, mixing deposit taking and venture capitalism, with frequent and large forays into company mergers and acquisitions, market cornering and cartel formation. It was an explosive mix that the whole world had watched in awe, without, however, refraining from joining in, as it grew ever greater in size and fragility. The Bank of England, as we have already said, had managed to bring the most important British banks home early in the feast, but their withdrawal probably precipitated the stock exchange collapse in April. In October 1907, the seasonal drain to the U.S. grain-producing states was added to the foreign drain, and the monetary and banking crisis broke out, bringing in its wake interest rates at incredible heights, bank runs, and currency hoarding. None of the trappings of financial crisis was absent. The Bank of England's bank rate then had to be raised to crisis level. It did draw gold to London, from two dozen countries. South Africa and India were especially crucial on that occasion.

The most telling episode of prewar international instability came, however, with the international political crisis of early summer 1914.[11] Even before Britain declared war, the international financial system collapsed. The British had enormous short-term credits in New York, while London was a net long-term creditor but a short-term debtor to the rest of the world. The trouble started in the Continental stock exchanges on July 24 and spread to London the next day, which was a settlement day for the stock exchange. London houses called back loans from New York and they got them. But the giant English commercial banks kept calling back their loans from the London discount market and the stock exchange, inducing a dangerous state of illiquidity. Money was recalled from the New York Stock Exchange and at first U.S. stock brokers obliged the calls of London lenders. As demand for short-term funds increased and war loomed nearer, however, New York financial institutions decided to call off the game, and declared a moratorium. After they had done that, London could only choose to follow suit. The gold standard thus ended before war broke out, with a decision to postpone payments that was equivalent to a suspension of convertibility, even if the latter was never officially declared.

It is clear that it was the giant British commercial banks that precipitated the crisis. They had a huge amount of deposits but a substantial part of their reserves was invested at very short term in the London Stock Exchange and in loans to the accepting houses, which used them to finance the international commodity trade. The London giant banks knew that very large funds were placed in the London money market by German universal banks and that those funds were likely to be withdrawn as soon as possible. This would have

---

[11] On this episode, see the literature quoted in de Cecco 1974 and also the account given by Clapham 1944, which, rather peculiarly, came out not in his book on the Bank of England but as an appendix to Sayers's later work (1976) on the history of the British central bank.

created a state of illiquidity in which the principle of "first come, first served" would be the only functioning one. The English commercial banks therefore decided to preempt everybody else by withdrawing their loans to the money market.

They thought this pessimistic view could be justified by some recent international episodes.[12] In the Moroccan crisis of 1911, the French had withdrawn their funds from Berlin and outflows from Berlin occurred also on the occasion of the Balkan War of 1912. German banks had thus decided to strengthen their gold reserves, and bought gold in London in the last two years before the outbreak of the world war. London big banks extrapolated from those episodes and were the first to the trough in the summer of 1914. By their behavior they precipitated the crisis, but their defense was that war was coming anyway and that peacetime behavior on their part would not have been enough to keep the London market open.

This was not a small point. French behavior in the Agadir incident had been chastised in international banking circles, and British financial elites thought they had to respect creditors' rights to their funds even if they were citizens of an enemy country. This was the basis of the credibility of the London financial market. It had allowed the British to finance their wars by borrowing from foreigners. The British public debt was considered as a prime strategic weapon by British and foreign observers alike, such as David Hume and Immanuel Kant. It allowed the British to wage war with borrowed money, while other states had to keep a physical war chest that was unutilized except in times of war. The British used the borrowed funds to subsidize allied armies on the Continent, sparing them the cost of a standing army. Thus they could maintain and increase a huge fleet to blockade the Continent and defend the empire, including the enforcement of the Monroe Doctrine on behalf of the United States, which for a long time had a very small fleet.

World War I put an end to that strategy. The Allies decided to fight it as a war of civilization against the barbarians, and nice concepts such as the sanctity of private property and savers' rights were thrown out of the window. British big banks obviously believed all this was going to happen, and acted accordingly to protect their interests, thus wrecking the peacetime financial system and forcing the adoption of wartime finance.

In *The Great Illusion,* a little book that came out in 1913 and ran into many editions and translations, a British publicist called Norman Angell acquired instant fame by maintaining that, because of the extent to which the world economy and finance had become integrated, war and territorial conquest

---

[12]  See G. Paish's letter to Lloyd George reproduced in de Cecco 1974.

had become useless for economic advantage. International finance would collapse at the first signs of a European war and the peacetime world economy would grind to a halt. On the evidence of German behavior in the 1911 Agadir confrontation between the French and German armies and navies, when the Germans had to come back from the brink because of the collapse of their own stock exchange and the revolt of their own great bankers,[13] Angell inferred that the economic cost of a great war had become too large for a trading nation such as Germany, which invested more than it saved and depended on British and French capital to generate enough world demand for its exports. He hoped that his book would convince the German political class of the futility of territorial conquest and armaments races in the age of globalization, when other factors made countries rich and powerful.

The author was right about the collapse of world finance even before war was declared. What happened in the summer of 1914 proved it *ad abundantiam*. His skepticism about reserves accumulation and naval construction races was less well founded. Other liberal writers, such as John Clapham, also ask themselves why the Continental powers ran a gold accumulation race, like they ran the naval construction race, in the ten years before 1914, and especially after 1907.[14] Gold stocks were puny compared to the import needs of large powers. Perhaps a rationalization of this behavior, if it can be attempted, ought to take into account the German success with the blitzkrieg in 1870. A short attack war, made possible by railways and mobile troops, could be waged by running down previously accumulated stocks of gold, arms, and munitions, and victory achieved before they were depleted. Moreover, saturation bombing, which destroyed enemy industrial capacity and infrastructure such as roads and railways, was not yet available.

### Politics and International Monetary Relations

Does this prove the new Bretton Woods theoreticians right? Superficially it does, because the gold standard was formally destroyed by the outbreak of a world political and military crisis. If a counterfactual is allowed, we may ask how long it would have taken the British to exhaust the possibilities offered them by India's trade and financial resources and by South Africa's gold being marketed through London. Those were, a moment's reflection will suffice, solutions that had very little to do with free trade and with laissez-faire economics. In fact, the whole setup of the world economy in the years of the first

---

[13] A very good contemporary account of the Agadir financial crisis was given a year later by Lescure 1912.

[14] Clapham 1944.

globalization was a very nationalistic-mercantilistic one: central banks were created to retard rather than enhance the functioning of the free gold market, to "put sand in the wheels" of the international gold standard, to stabilize domestic interest rates and credit conditions. The British imperial bureaucracy was often mobilized to find resources sufficient to allow London to continue running the gold standard. A free market for gold existed only in London, and there it functioned only because South African and Australian gold, whose production increased enormously in this period, was shipped to London to be sold and the proceeds of the sales were temporarily deposited in British banks. In other financial centers, gold was not sold freely. Governments and central banks interfered with gold flows, in order to stabilize the local currency and maintain its gold convertibility.[15]

In the last fifteen years before war broke out, there was a veritable scramble for gold, which did not become more noticeable only because South Africa and Australia provided an abundant supply of it. Governments and central banks were amassing gold for strategic reasons. Gold movements—except those between London and Paris—became one way only. Gold became, in the words of Baron Ansiaux, a Belgian financier and economist, a veritable "prisoner of war." Once it got in the coffers of a central bank, everything would be done to keep it there, whatever interest rates might prevail on world financial markets.

Many central banks, moreover, erected a thick barrier of foreign exchange reserves around gold reserves, and if world interest rates went up or if there was a payments imbalance, they would draw on them to preserve gold stocks. Once foreign exchange was in the hands of governments or in those of government-dominated central banks it was too easy to see its political dimension and use it as an instrument of foreign policy. Foreign exchange sometimes was deposited in foreign banks to achieve straightforward foreign policy objectives. This was certainly the case when the Japanese government, in 1905, signed an alliance treaty with Great Britain against Russia, and deposited, through the Yokohama Specie Bank, a very large amount in the Bank of England. But forex reserves could also be used not only to deprive the local central bank of its hard-earned gold but to prevent credit restrictions that brought deflation and recession. In one of his annual reports to shareholders, the governor of the Dutch central bank prided himself on having prevented an outflow of capital solely by using his portfolio of bills on London, keeping the gold reserve intact.[16]

---

[15] On this, see von Lumm 1912.
[16] See Foxwell 1912. But also, on the more general phenomenon, see Clapham 1944.

A mercantilist, protectionist model of international economic and financial relations, which was the clear forerunner of the one that prevailed after the war-economy experience in most developed countries, thus started operating in the fifteen years before 1914, a time dubbed the "Heyday of the Gold Standard," when most modern countries adopted it, the so-called rules of the game were supposed to work, and Britain was said to conduct the international financial orchestra through bank rate changes. International financial cooperation, especially among central banks, was not common practice, if we exclude relations between the Bank of England and the Banque de France and sporadic mutual help between other central banks (on this issue, see Nogaro 1912). The gold standard was supposed to be managed by independent central bankers, but it became less and less so as foreign reserves were suddenly withdrawn by the monetary authorities of one country from the financial center of another country when a political crisis broke out. It sometimes also depended to some extent on the character of individual central bankers.

## Back to the Present

The pre-1914 international currency experience certainly has some features in common with the present one, with a declining economic superpower at the center that is being challenged by large, rapidly growing newcomers. Nowadays, the newcomers are China and other large emerging countries. Then, they were Germany and especially the United States. Their impact on the world economy in the last two decades before the World War I should be properly emphasized.

The declining superpower issued the international currency, but its role was challenged by another currency. In our time this seems to be the euro; in the pre-1914 era it was gold, which threatened to become the sole basis of the international gold standard. No national currency thus seemed destined to replace sterling at the center of the international monetary and financial system in the short run. The French franc, the German mark, and the U.S. dollar all grew in importance during this period, but it was gold that replaced sterling to an increasing extent, as the world became increasingly turbulent, several local wars broke out, and the threat of a great war loomed. London remained the center of the international payments system, but managing the huge financial network that came to span the world became ever more difficult for the British financial elite and more and more disequilibrating for the British economy. Thirty-five of the world's major commercial banks established a branch in London and they used it to get cash when they needed it and deposit spare cash with the stock exchange or in the money market at very short term. The most active, and the most unsettling for British authorities, were the German and American banks, which had a difficult relationship with the world prime financial center as long-term debtors and short-term creditors. As the great powers prepared for the war economy, gold became the economic interface of armaments. It was considered as the international means of payments of a world economy in times of war, as private and public debt and paper currency replaced its use for domestic circulation.

Undoubtedly, the present globalization process is occurring on a very mercantilist and nationalist mode. BRIC, the countries that are expected to be the final winners in this race, all adopted frankly dirigiste-mercantilist growth and trade policies decades ago, when they started their modernization policies, and they are taking part in globalization very much on their own terms. An armaments race has also started again: President Bush renounced the Anti-Ballistic Missile Treaty and has been recently followed by President Putin. China, Russia, Japan, India, Pakistan, and Brazil are all strengthening their conventional military assets and entering the military space and nuclear sectors. The United States wants to erect an anti-missile missile network in countries near Russia. These new developments, however, do not resemble the cold war bipolar military balance. They remind us more of the pre-1914 arms race, as the new arms race is conducted on a purely nationalistic basis, without much ideology on display.

Open wars have, in the last decade, been fought again in Europe, in the Balkans, in addition to the conflicts that have broken out in more traditional trouble spots, such as the Middle East and Africa. If we remember the fast succession of wars in the last fifteen years before 1914, similarities between the two globalization processes abound. The Spanish-American War, the Boer War, the Russo-Japanese War, the two Balkan wars, the Italo-Turkish War, plus Fashoda, Agadir, and other incidents all occurred in the heyday of the first period of globalization and of the triumph of the gold standard. The rise of protectionism and nationalism in Europe coincided with that globalization process. The same has characterized the years after the breakdown of the Soviet informal empire. The European enlargement process has included countries, such as Poland and the Baltic countries, where nationalism had been suppressed for fifty years and obviously nurtured a pent-up demand for it. With all the dramatic political events taking place after 1989, it is not strange if we find striking similarities between the financial crises these events sparked, and those which, as often, riddled the international financial system between 1898 and 1914.

The fast pace of financial innovation that has characterized the current globalization process is too well known to need detailed analysis here. What is again striking is that fast and deep financial innovation also occurred in the two decades before World War I. Apart from technical innovations, such as the transatlantic telephone cable and the radio (both of which were used by international finance as soon as they became available), financial innovation of the greatest import also took place. This included the rise of universal banking in Europe, and in a peculiar version in the United States, and the amalgamation movement in British banking, which produced the largest banks in the world. Giant stock exchanges also came to life, in London, New York, Paris, and Berlin, where huge new issues were floated for an international clientele and secondary markets became wide, deep, and efficient. Forward and future contracts were commonly used, especially in primary commodity transactions but also in financial ones, especially when transactions between nonconvertible currencies such as the Russian ruble and the Austrian crown were involved. The international acceptance market also became enormous. It was dominated by the British, but the French, the German, and, in particular, the American finance houses showed aspirations to swing their weight in that field, too. Thirty-five branches of foreign large banks were active in London in the last decade before 1914, helping but also hindering the British authorities' control of their own financial market.

In the last couple of decades, international financial disturbances have originated in large emerging countries. Sometimes they were the result of foreign financial investors' reactions to local government measures or to local private financial difficulties. International contagion has often been extremely fast. In the pre-1914 financial globalization, contagion from one center to another was also very rapid. Similarly, center country monetary policies have reverberated through the whole international financial system in both periods.

But what happened in one of the new financial centers of the polycentric environment that prevailed in the years before the Great War, and has again been occurring in the last two decades, is as important as what goes on in the formerly hegemonic financial system. Events occurring there are perfectly able to dislocate the center countries' financial systems and to diminish their ability to manage events. The Agadir episode, for instance, proved that the Reichsbank did not have enough reserves to face the withdrawal of short-term funds from Berlin. This was more dangerous than the alleged political motivation of French withdrawals. On that occasion, the Reichsbank was helped by the large U.S. banks, which bought German state bonds and other private short-term paper and so replaced the withdrawing French banks. After that scare, the Reichsbank hastily embarked on a policy of gold accumulation, also motivated by strategic preoccupations. And this seriously worried the Bank of England and the British giant banks, because they felt the consequences of German gold imports on the London gold market. U.S. large banks had also previously demonstrated their power by acquiring gold directly from South Africa, bypassing the London market. And they publicly boasted about it. There were other occasions when Paris and New York flexed their financial muscles.

There have been, in the last two decades, many similar episodes, showing the disequilibrating features of an international financial system that is changing from a monopoly into an oligopoly and where a huge private market has grown powerful enough to dwarf the public agencies, such as central banks and treasuries, and the international financial institutions that are meant to control it. Any largish country or private financial institution, by its misdemeanors or just by its difficulties, can transmit serious volatility to the whole international financial system, because of world financial connectedness. That is another point of similarity between the pre-1914 era and the current globalization process. A huge market has come about, but very large actors, both public and private, operate in it, their movements causing ripples that can turn into large waves and unsettle the whole sea.

Will the dollar come out unscathed from the great financial crisis that finally broke out in 2007, confounding all the Panglosses in the economics profession? Probably not, but official dollar holders around the world have so much at stake that they will try to resist a sharp and rapid decline in the dollar exchange rate with all their might. Foreign holders of U.S. securities have no less that $9.4 trillion worth of them in their hands, as much as the whole public debt of the United States, and about 37 percent of the 2007 U.S. GNP. Major central banks have been mounting massive defense operations to keep the dollar afloat throughout 2007 and 2008. Let us also note that, on September 11, 2008, the greenback was at the same level, vis-à-vis the euro, as it had been exactly one year before—1.38.

The exchange market was the last to be affected by the crisis, because financial institutions in the United States tried to get hold of as much cash as they could as sources of short-term liquidity dried up. They did so by abandoning all the bets they had made in the various financial markets of the world. In so doing they contributed to keeping the dollar afloat. In September 2008, the dollar was worth 0.68 euros, while it was worth the equivalent of 1.60 euros in 1985. The equivalent numbers vis-à-vis the yen are about 100 (2008) versus 250 yen (1985). There is no way of believing this long-term downward trend will not continue in the future, although it is quite likely that it will be temporarily reversed by relatively short cycles of dollar revaluation. If central banks manage to smooth out the dollar's soft reduction of status, the monetary and financial hegemony of the United States will be allowed to recede without traumas.

Twentieth-century history, however, abounds with traumatic episodes that point toward sudden declines. Great Britain is the foremost example. It stopped being the center of the financial world after World War I. After World War II, sterling was kept afloat for a while by semicompulsory sterling balance holding. There were, however, two very sharp devaluations and finally all that was left of British monetary hegemony disappeared. The British found the famous Wimbledon simile as a solace to their loss. Will the Americans take it as philosophically, as it starts to apply to them, too?

# 7

# TOWARD A LEADERLESS CURRENCY SYSTEM

Benjamin J. Cohen

The dollar presently reigns supreme as an international currency. Can its dominance be challenged? Many observers foresee the rise of significant rivals for global currency leadership—the euro; possibly a revived yen; perhaps, in the longer run, even the Chinese yuan. My aim in this essay is to assess the prospects of the greenback's main competitors and implications for the broader monetary system.

Do any of the dollar's potential rivals represent a truly serious challenge? Like other contributors to this book (Calleo, de Cecco, Kirshner), I accept that the global position of the dollar is weakening. Essential to the greenback's dominance until now has been a widespread and remarkably durable faith in the currency's value and usefulness. Sooner or later, confidence in the dollar is bound to be undermined by the chronic payments deficits of the United States, which add persistently to the country's looming foreign debt. But that by itself will not ensure the success of some alternative. The decline of one currency does not automatically guarantee the ascendancy of another. In fact, potential challengers have considerable deficiencies of their own, which are likely to limit their appeal, too. There is no obvious new leader lurking in the wings, an understudy just waiting to take center stage.

Author's note: I am indebted to William Grimes, Eric Helleiner, and Jonathan Kirshner for helpful comments. The research assistance of Heather Arnold is also gratefully acknowledged.

So what, then, should we expect? We should anticipate something like the interregnum of the period between the two world wars, when Britain's pound sterling was in decline and the dollar on the rise, but neither was dominant. Coming years, I submit, will see the emergence of a similarly fragmented monetary system, with several currencies in contention and none clearly in the lead—an increasingly *leaderless* mix of currency relationships. We know that the absence of firm monetary leadership during the interwar period was a contributing factor to the financial crisis and Great Depression of the 1930s. The economic and political impacts of a leaderless monetary system in the twenty-first century could also be considerable.

I begin with a brief review of prospects for the dollar, setting the stage for the analysis to follow. Contrary to the more sanguine views of observers such as Harold James (chapter 2) or Ronald McKinnon (chapter 3), I do not consider the persistent buildup of America's foreign debt as sustainable for long. Unless reversed by significant policy reform in Washington, the U.S. economy's dependence on foreign capital must be expected in time to erode the advantages historically enjoyed by the greenback, creating an opportunity for possible challengers.

Three currencies are most frequently mentioned as potential contenders for the dollar's crown—the euro, yen, and yuan. Prospects for each are considered. Overall, my assessment is skeptical. None of the three candidates appears capable of mounting a serious challenge to the dollar; certainly none is likely to surpass the greenback in the foreseeable future. Rather, the more plausible outcome is one in which the dollar's supremacy is eroded but no other single money emerges to replace it. In Jonathan Kirshner's terms (chapter 9), the dollar will become one of several "peer competitors" in a fragmented currency system, with no dominant leader.

I then turn, in conclusion, to the implications of a fragmented currency system for international monetary stability. A heightened struggle for leadership seems probable, threatening an increase of tension in currency affairs. Much will depend, however, on how aggressive policymakers choose to be in promoting their respective monies. The most likely battlegrounds are the Middle East, where the dollar and euro will contend for supremacy, and Asia, where the greenback can expect determined efforts on behalf of both the yen and the yuan. In both locales, the most likely outcome is intensified rivalry but not outright conflict.

## Assumptions

I focus on the *market* role of the dollar and its potential challengers—that is, the extent to which alternative currencies are used by market actors as a medium of exchange, unit of account, or store of value in international transactions. Hence the competition for monetary leadership is treated here as primarily a function of economic constraints and incentives. Politics in this context enters only through what Eric Helleiner (chapter 4) calls the "indirect" channel of political influence: the role that public policy may play in shaping economic constraints and incentives, thus helping to determine the relative attractiveness of alternative currencies for private market use. Only in the final section do I bring in what Helleiner calls the "direct" channel of political influence—the part that politics may play in seeking to sway the behavior of *state* actors in the currency system.

Underlying my analysis are four working assumptions, all well documented in practice. First, echoing Helleiner, is the assumption that for market actors international currency choice is shaped, above all, by a trio of essential attributes. First, at least during the initial stages of a money's cross-border adoption, is widespread confidence in its future value backed by political stability in the economy of origin. No one is apt to be attracted to a currency that does not offer a reasonable promise of stable purchasing power. Second are the qualities of "exchange convenience" and "capital certainty"— a high degree of liquidity and predictability of asset prices—each of which is essential to minimizing transactions costs. The key to both qualities is a set of broad and efficient financial markets, exhibiting depth and resiliency. Third, a money must promise a wide transactional network, since nothing enhances a currency's acceptability more than the prospect of acceptability by others. Historically, this factor has usually meant an economy that is large in absolute size and well integrated into world markets. The greater the volume of transactions conducted in or with an economy, the greater will be the economies of scale to be derived from the use of its currency.

Second is the assumption that currencies in the global economy tend to be distributed hierarchically in what I have elsewhere called the Currency Pyramid.[1] At issue is the geography of money—the spatial organization of currency relations. Driving the geography of money is the force of competition—the constraints and incentives that shape market demand for currencies for either foreign or domestic use. Under the force of competition, the monetary universe becomes stratified, assuming the appearance of a vast

---

[1] Cohen 1998, 2004.

pyramid: narrow at the top, where the strongest currencies dominate, and increasingly broad below, reflecting various degrees of competitive inferiority. In the nineteenth century, sterling stood at the peak of the Currency Pyramid. Today, of course, the top currency is the dollar.

Third is the assumption that monetary preferences are "sticky," characterized above all by path dependence and a noticeable tendency toward inertia. Currencies derive their popularity, in part, from scale economies in use—what specialists call network externalities. Network externalities may be understood as a form of interdependence in which the choices of any one actor depend strategically on the practices adopted by others in the same network of interactions. The same scale economies that encourage use of a currency in the first place are also responsible for "hysteresis" or "ratchet effects"—a marked resistance to change reflecting the high cost of switching from one money to another. Stickiness of preferences gives leading currencies a natural advantage of incumbency. This does not mean that change in the hierarchy is impossible. But it implies that when change does occur, it most likely will come relatively slowly. It took decades for the dollar to supplant sterling atop the Currency Pyramid.

Fourth—and following directly from the third—is the assumption that at any given moment, more than one currency may be widely used for international purposes. There is a common view, as one recent commentary put it, that "at any one point in time, there tends to be a single dominant currency in the financial world, not two or more. . . . In the currency markets the spoils go to the victor, alone; they are not shared."[2] But that scenario is patently inaccurate. It was certainly not the case during the interwar period, as the dollar gradually eclipsed the pound. Typically, it has not even been the case when one currency was clearly dominant, as during the decades before World War I. Though sterling was then the world's leading money, both the French franc and German mark also enjoyed widespread popularity, particularly on the European continent. Likewise, even as the dollar has dominated in more recent times, a considerable share of market activity has been accounted for by the deutsche mark (now the euro) and Japanese yen. Competition tends to be as keen at the peak of the Currency Pyramid as it is below. As Barry Eichengreen writes, the "argument that competition for reserve-currency status is a winner-take-all game holds little water either analytically or historically."[3]

[2] Persaud 2004, 1.
[3] Eichengreen 2006, 145.

## The Dollar

No one questions that the dollar today still enjoys top rank in the Currency Pyramid. In most categories of international market use, the greenback continues to dominate. In currency trading, the dollar remains the most favored vehicle, appearing on one side or the other of some 86 percent of all foreign-exchange transactions.[4] The dollar is also the most favored vehicle for the invoicing of world trade, used for just over half of all exports, and still accounts for some two-fifths of the international bond market, roughly one half of the international banking market, and two-thirds of central-bank reserves. No other currency today comes close to matching the greenback's global reach.

The threat to the greenback's dominant status is obvious. In the short term it comes from the great financial crisis that started in America's subprime mortgage market in 2007, which has thrown the security of the entire U.S. financial structure into question. Over the longer term, the threat comes from America's chronic balance-of-payments deficits, which are unprecedented by historical standards. As measured by the current account of the balance of payments, the gap in recent years has widened markedly; in 2006 it surpassed $850 billion, equivalent to some 6.5 percent of gross domestic product (GDP). Every year, the United States spends considerably more than its income, relying on foreign capital to make up the difference. In effect, Americans have outsourced their saving to the rest of the world. Although now shrinking a bit, the shortfall continues to add to America's foreign debt, absorbing as much as two-thirds of the world's surplus savings. On a gross basis, external liabilities now exceed $20 trillion. Net of America's own assets abroad, the debt reached $2.5 trillion at the end of 2007, equal to nearly a fifth of GDP.

Can the process be sustained? Many, optimistically, have tried to make a case for sustainability. One popular argument points to the attractiveness of the U.S. economy as a market for goods of all kinds. America's deficits, it is said, are the direct result of export-led development strategies promoted by governments in East Asia and elsewhere, which are unlikely to be abandoned any time soon. A second argument stresses the attractiveness of the U.S. economy as a haven for investments. The growth of debt is said to be the direct result of a growing "global savings glut" seeking high returns in a secure environment—a long-term trend that the *Economist* has labeled the "great thrift shift."[5] Either way, America's deficits are seen as a sign not of disequilibrium

---

[4] Bank for International Settlements 2007a.
[5] Economist 2005.

but rather as a form of equilibrium that we might expect to be sustained for a long time to come. James (chapter 2) goes even further, suggesting that in these patterns can be found the conditions for a new preeminence of the dollar in global affairs.

Such optimism, however, hardly seems justified. James discounts the importance of market confidence as a factor underlying America's ability to persistently live beyond its means—what Charles de Gaulle had in mind years ago when he referred to America's "exorbitant privilege." For how long can the United States go on building up a mountain of debt before doubts finally begin to take over? Some amelioration is possible, of course. The rate of growth of net liabilities already appears to have slowed somewhat since 2006, as a result of exchange-rate shifts that have stimulated exports and discouraged imports; and further adjustments are no doubt possible given the celebrated flexibility of the U.S. economy. But not even the most sanguine observers expect to see America's deficits disappear completely under the influence of market forces alone. In the absence of significant policy reforms to raise the domestic savings rate, spending will continue to exceed income, sooner or later eroding the world's trust in the dollar. The exorbitant privilege obviously cannot endure forever.

The case for sustainability, in short, is not nearly as persuasive as optimists such as James would have us believe. In fact, the probability that the dollar can long avoid a significant loss of confidence is sadly low. A fall from grace is unlikely to happen suddenly, as Kirshner (chapter 9) suggests; Kirshner seriously underestimates the stickiness of monetary preferences. Much more probable is a gradual, cumulative erosion of the greenback's appeal, opening the door to a possible challenge by others. Is any other currency capable of seizing the opportunity?

## The Euro

The most obvious candidate is of course the euro, the joint currency created in 1999 by Europe's Economic and Monetary Union (EMU). Many have predicted a bright future for the euro as an international currency. Europe is the equal of the United States in output and trade. Why should it not be America's equal in monetary matters, too? Typical is the cheerful enthusiasm of de Cecco (chapter 6), who suggests that we are at a turning point in world monetary history. Europe's new currency, he avers, is a "rising star" that is destined to play a role in the twenty-first century comparable to that of gold in the nineteenth century.

In reality, however, such enthusiasm seems misplaced. De Cecco asserts that Europe's new currency will be attractive—especially as a store of value—because, like gold, it is not an expression of national sovereignty. But that is simply wrong. Europe's governments have not *renounced* monetary sovereignty, as de Cecco puts it. Rather, monetary sovereignty has been *pooled*—an important distinction. The euro is the expression of the *joint* sovereignty of a group of governments and therefore can be considered only as good as the political agreement underlying it—an example of what one scholar calls a "sovereignty bargain."[6] Because the euro zone lacks the clean lines of authority traditionally associated with the management of money by individual states, it will always be at a structural disadvantage in global markets. James (chapter 2) is right when he contends that there are more uncertainties about the future of the euro than of the dollar.

Briefly updating a previous analysis,[7] I argue that only in the immediate neighborhood of the European Union (EU), where trade and financial ties are especially close, does the euro enjoy any special advantages. That is EMU's natural hinterland—"the euro's turf," as Charles Wyplosz calls it.[8] Elsewhere, the joint currency's star lacks luster.

## Critical Shortcomings

Admittedly, the euro is blessed with many attributes necessary for competitive success, including a large economic base, political stability, and an enviably low rate of inflation, all backed by a joint monetary authority, the European Central Bank, that is fully committed to preserving confidence in the money's future value. Much room, therefore, does indeed exist for the euro's star to rise. But because of its base in a sovereignty bargain, the euro is also handicapped by several critical shortcomings, all structural in character, that limit the currency's attractiveness as a rival to the greenback. These include relatively high transactions costs; a serious antigrowth bias; and, most important, ambiguities at the heart of the monetary union's governance structure.

*Transactions Costs*    First is the cost of doing business in euros. Transactions costs directly affect a currency's attractiveness as a vehicle for exchange transactions or international trade. From the start, it was clear that the dollar would be favored by the natural advantage of incumbency unless euro trans-

---

[6] Litfin 1997.
[7] Cohen 2003.
[8] Wyplosz 1999, 89.

actions costs, which began high relative to the widely traded greenback, could be lowered to a more competitive level. That, in turn, would depend directly on what could be done to improve the structural efficiency of Europe's financial markets. In practical terms, much has been accomplished to knit together previously segmented national markets. Efficiency gains have been substantial. Yet for all that effort the dollar's cost advantage has persisted, discouraging wider use of the euro.

The core problem is evident. The euro is condemned to remain at a disadvantage vis-à-vis the dollar so long as the EMU is unable to offer a universal financial instrument that can match the U.S. Treasury bill for international investor liquidity and convenience. This is a deficiency that will be impossible to rectify so long as the euro zone, with its separate national governments, lacks a counterpart to the federal government in Washington. The best the Europeans could hope to do was encourage establishment of selected benchmark securities for the public debt market. Gradually three euro benchmarks have emerged: the German Bund at ten years, the French bond at five years, and the Italian bond at two years. But such a piecemeal approach falls far short of creating a single market as large and liquid as that for U.S. government securities. The greater depth and convenience of the U.S. Treasury bill market continues to give an advantage to the greenback.

*Antigrowth Bias*    Second is a serious antigrowth bias that appears to be built in to the institutional structure of the EMU. By impacting negatively on yields on euro-denominated assets, this bias directly affects the euro's appeal as a long-term investment medium.

When the EMU first came into existence, eliminating exchange risk within the European region, a massive shift was predicted in the allocation of global savings as compared with holdings of European assets in the past. But as the ECB has ruefully noted, international portfolio managers have in fact been quite slow to commit to Europe's new money, despite some cyclical uptick of euro-zone growth in 2007.[9] Liquid funds have been attracted when there was a prospect of short-term exchange-rate appreciation. But underlying investor preferences have barely budged, in good part because doubts persist about the longer term growth prospects in EMU countries, which have been trending downward for decades. Many factors, as we know, contribute to the slowing of Europe's trend rate of expansion—aging populations, which limit manpower increases and stress old-age pension systems; rigid labor markets, which hinder economic adaptability; and extensive government regulation,

---

[9]  ECB 2008.

which can constrain innovation and entrepreneurship. The EMU, regrettably, adds yet one more brake on growth.

The core problem here, as is well known, lies in the EMU's institutional provisions governing monetary and fiscal policy, two key determinants of macroeconomic performance. In neither policy domain is priority attached to promoting output. Rather, in each, the main emphasis is on other considerations that tend to tilt policy toward restraint, producing a distinct anti-growth bias for the euro zone as a whole. On the monetary policy side, the European Central Bank is mandated to focus exclusively on fighting inflation, even if over time this might be at the cost of stunting growth. Similarly, on the fiscal policy side, euro-zone governments have formally tied their hands with their controversial Stability and Growth Pact, which sets a strict cap on national budget deficits at 3 percent of GDP, inhibiting contra-cyclical stimulation. Though the pact is by no means airtight, empirical evidence suggests that overall it has in fact exercised a significant discipline, particularly on some of the EMU's smaller members.[10] Is it any wonder, then, that the anticipated shift of global savings has turned out to be illusory?

*Governance*    Finally, there is the governance structure of the EMU, which for the euro's prospects as an international currency may be the biggest handicap of all. The basic question is: Who is in charge? The answer, regrettably, has never been obvious. From the start, as is well known, uncertainty has reigned concerning the delegation of monetary authority among governments and EU institutions.

Who, for example, controls monetary policy? Practical operational control lies in the hands of the ECB's Executive Board, made up of the president, vice-president, and four other members. Overall managerial authority, however, is formally lodged in the Governing Council, which in addition to the six-member Executive Board includes the heads of the central banks of all the member states, each participating fully in discussions and sharing voting rights. The large size and mixed representation of the Governing Council are clearly inconsistent with efficient or transparent governance. No one really knows how critical decisions are arrived at.

Or consider the question of financial stability. Who, ultimately, is responsible for crisis prevention or the management of financial shocks? Under the Maastricht Treaty, the EMU's founding document, no specific tasks are assigned to the ECB to help forestall crises. Though linkages have grown among national financial markets, increasing the risk of contagion should troubles

---

[10] Annett 2006.

hit, the ruling principle remains decentralization, otherwise known as sub-
sidiarity—the notion that the lowest level of government that can efficiently
carry out a function should do so. Formal authority for prudential supervision and regulation continues to reside at the national level, as it did before
the EMU. Each central bank is charged with responsibility for the financial
institutions based within its own national borders. No one can be sure that
such a decentralized arrangement can be counted on to assure the smooth operation of the overall system. The possibility that central banks might work
at cross-purposes, provoking or aggravating a crisis, is certainly not outside
the realm of possibility.

Finally, there is the issue of external representation. Who is to speak for the
euro zone on broader macroeconomic issues such as policy coordination, crisis management, or reform of the international financial architecture? Here
the Maastricht Treaty has no answer at all, leaving a vacuum at the heart of
the EMU. At a minimum, the treaty's silence compounds confusion about
who is in charge. At worst, it condemns the euro zone to lasting second-class
status, since it limits the group's ability to project power on monetary matters.

## A Regional Destiny

For all these reasons, it should be no surprise to find that the euro's experience as an international currency to date has been underwhelming (even allowing for the characteristic stickiness of monetary preferences). In most
categories of international market use, adjusting for the elimination of intra-
EMU transactions, the euro has managed roughly to hold its own as compared with the past aggregate shares of the EMU's "legacy" currencies. This
means that Europe's joint money has smoothly taken its place as the successor to Germany's old deutsche mark, which among international currencies
had already attained a rank second only to the dollar. But that is about all. Evidence from the ECB indicates that after an initial spurt of enthusiasm for the
new currency, use in most market segments has leveled off or even declined
in recent years.[11] Moreover, since its birth the euro's only enduring gains have
been in the EMU's natural hinterland, including the EU's newest members
before they joined as well as other actual or potential candidate countries. In
the ECB's words, analysis "confirms the largely regional character of the
euro."[12] Beyond the European region, the euro remains very much in the dollar's shadow.

[11]  ECB 2008.
[12]  Ibid., 7.

None of this, therefore, adds up to a serious challenge to the greenback. The dollar's appeal may be eroded by America's persistent payments deficits. But that by itself does not ensure success for the euro so long as the new currency's own deficiencies remain uncorrected. The euro clearly does have a future as an international currency. But its appeal is not unqualified and, worse, seems limited mainly to the EU's own backyard. The currency's destiny appears to be regional, not global.

## The Yen

Less need be said about Japan's yen—once thought to be the dollar's heir apparent, now looking more like a sad, faded also-ran. During the 1970s and 1980s, when the fast-growing Japanese economy seemed destined for superpower status, international use of the yen accelerated significantly. But then at the end of the 1980s came the bursting of Japan's "bubble economy," which abruptly halted the currency's upward trajectory. Years of domestic stagnation dampened foreign interest in the yen, despite some highly visible attempts by the government in Tokyo to promote internationalization. Today the yen appears to face a gradual erosion of market standing not unlike sterling's long decline in an earlier era.

The appeal of the yen in its heyday was obvious. Postwar recovery had transformed Japan into the second largest economy in the world, an exporting powerhouse with extensive trade ties in just about every corner of the globe. The potential for network externalities was considerable. Moreover, the country suffered from neither political instability nor high inflation; and its financial markets had come to rank among the largest anywhere. Most of the ingredients for success were present.

Yet even at the peak of its popularity, enthusiasm for the currency was limited. Internationalization was strongest in the banking and securities markets, where a record of seemingly endless exchange-rate appreciation made yen-denominated claims especially attractive to investors. But the yen never came close to surpassing the dollar, or even the deutsche mark, in trade invoicing or as a vehicle for exchange transactions. The central problem could be found in the Japanese financial system, which long lagged behind the American and even many European markets in terms of openness or efficiency. Until the 1990s, Japan's capital markets remained the most tightly regulated and protected in the industrial world, preventing wider use of the yen. Strict controls were maintained on both inward and outward movements of funds; the development of a domestic securities industry was retarded by the historic reliance of Japanese enterprise on bank lending for capital investment; and financial institutions were rigidly segmented. Neither exchange convenience nor reasonable capital certainty could be assured.

Worse, since the end of the "bubble economy," foreign use of the yen has in relative terms actually decreased rather than increased. The currency's appeal has clearly waned, mirroring Japan's broader economic troubles. Challenges include not only anemic growth and a rapidly aging population but also a fragile banking system and a level of public debt, scaled to GDP, that is now the highest of any industrial nation. Japanese government bonds are scorned by rating agencies, discouraging investors and inhibiting the use of the yen in lending markets. In exchange markets, the percentage of transactions involving the yen has shrunk from a high of 27 percent of global turnover in 1989 to barely 20 percent in 2004. Overall, the yen's position near the peak of the Currency Pyramid has slipped dramatically vis-à-vis both the euro and the dollar.

Can the yen's appeal be revived? Belated efforts by the Japanese government to promote greater internationalization of the yen have largely proved futile. Today, even the most ardent of the currency's supporters appear to have lost their enthusiasm for the struggle. Like the euro, the yen might still realistically aspire to something of a regional destiny. But outside Asia, it poses no serious threat to the dollar.

Ironically, a determined government interest in internationalization did not even emerge until the yen's popularity had already begun to wane. Intermittent discussions started as early as the mid-1970s, but for many years widespread foreign use was resisted on the grounds that it might destabilize the yen's exchange rate or compromise domestic monetary management. Official policy, as C. H. Kwan puts it, could best be described as "neutral if not passive."[13] It was only after the economy nose-dived that the authorities started to focus more on the potential advantages of an international currency. A greater role for the yen could help jump-start stalled growth. It might also enhance Japan's political standing in the global pecking order. In the words of one informed source: "Success at internationalizing the yen would be tantamount to achieving greater political prominence. . . . [It is] a bid to expand Japan's global political influence."[14] Policy shifted from passive to active.

In substantive terms, most effort has been put into modernizing Japan's financial system, accelerating a modest program of liberalization that, under

[13] Kwan 2001, 110.
[14] Castellano 1999, 5.

pressure from the United States, was initiated as long ago as the 1970s. Capital controls have been loosened, new instruments and markets have been developed, and institutional segmentation has been relaxed. Most dramatic was a multiyear program announced in 1996, dubbed the Big Bang in imitation of the swift deregulation of financial markets that had taken place a decade earlier in Britain. Under the Big Bang all remaining capital controls were eliminated and a variety of other ambitious measures were set in motion to enhance the general attractiveness of the yen as a vehicle for exchange transactions or international investment. Further reforms were initiated in 1998–99.

In geographic terms, policy has taken on a distinctly regional cast. Any pretense that Japan's currency might challenge the dollar on a global scale has plainly been abandoned. But, officials hope, it might still be possible to cultivate Japan's neighbors in East Asia—what could be thought of as the yen's natural turf. The EU is bound to dominate financial relations in the European hinterland. So why not counter with an Asian strategy for the yen, to consolidate a region of its own? Particular impetus came from East Asia's financial crisis of 1997–98, which seemed to create an opportunity for broadening the yen's role in the area. Internationalization of the yen, comments one source, "became a national cause célèbre for Japanese elites after the financial crisis."[15] Most notable was Tokyo's proposal for a new Asian Monetary Fund (AMF), a regional financial facility that would have done much to institutionalize Japanese dominance in Asian currency relations. When the AMF initiative got shot down, owing mainly to opposition from Washington, the Japanese soon followed up with ideas for other regional schemes, culminating in creation of a network of swap arrangements dubbed the Chiang Mai Initiative after the town in Thailand where negotiations took place.

In practice, however, results have been discouraging. Asian governments prefer to hedge their bets as they watch China emerge as a rival to Japan for regional economic and political dominance. As Saori Katada observes, "Asian countries still try to avoid any attempts by Japan that might result in locking those countries into power relations."[16] These days, even Japan's own policy elites now seem resigned to a diminished future for the yen. Japanese aspirations today seem limited to little more than holding onto a piece of regional leadership.

[15] Green 2001, 260.
[16] Katada 2002, 105.

## The Yuan

As the yen declines, could China's yuan rise? The notion that the yuan could one day become the key currency of Asia—or beyond—is widely shared. But is it justified? The renminbi (the "people's money" or RMB) certainly has much going for it and has already begun to step out onto the world stage. International use, however, remains rudimentary at best and is retarded by obstacles far more severe even than anything blocking the euro or yen. In time, the currency's handicaps might well be surmounted. But the time required is likely to be measured not in years but decades, if not generations. For the foreseeable future, the yuan poses no threat to the dollar.

The potential is there, of course. Years of double-digit growth have already made China's economy, in purchasing-power terms, the second largest in the world after the United States; as an exporter, China now ranks ahead of both the United States and Germany. With such a huge and well-connected economic base, the opportunity for network externalities is obvious. Few observers seem to doubt that international use of the yuan will eventually follow. As the *Financial Times* puts it, "The emergence of the RMB as an international currency will be . . . a natural result of China's booming economy."[17]

But that reckons without the other attributes essential to cross-border adoption—in particular, the qualities of exchange convenience and capital certainty that are so critical to the usability of a currency. China's financial sector is still at the very earliest stage of development, offering limited investment opportunities. The level of transparency and efficiency lags far behind all of the more established financial powers; markets are thin and liquid assets are few. Worse, the yuan itself remains tightly regulated, not easily accessible for international transactions. Convertibility for trade in goods and services was introduced only in 1996. Cumbersome capital controls are still nearly universal.

Not surprisingly, therefore, yuan internationalization to date has been negligible. A certain amount of Chinese paper currency has begun to show up in neighboring economies as a result of growing cross-border trade and tourism by Chinese citizens. But the totals remain small—no more than $2–3 billion at the end of 2004 according to one recent estimate, equivalent to roughly 1 percent of China's overall cash circulation.[18] By comparison, as much as two-thirds of Federal Reserve notes are in permanent circulation outside the

[17] *Financial Times*, June 2, 2003, 2.
[18] Zhang 2007.

United States. Beyond the borders of China the RMB is rarely used for trade invoicing or as an investment vehicle.

To its credit, China's government acknowledges its currency's limitations and seems determined to do something about them. Unlike the Japanese prior to the 1990s, the Chinese have long welcomed prospective internationalization as a logical corollary to their country's reemergence as an economic superpower. As one prominent academic in the authoritative *People's Daily* declared, "China has become a world economic power and the RMB has to be internationalized."[19] But for reasons as much political as economic, nothing like Japan's Big Bang has ever been mooted. In their typically cautious manner, the authorities prefer to move only gradually to widen use of the yuan.

In 2005, for example, multilateral agencies such as the Asian Development Bank and International Finance Corporation (a subsidiary of the World Bank) were authorized for the first time to issue yuan-denominated bonds inside China. The so-called Panda bonds, it was hoped, would encourage greater use of the RMB as a borrowing vehicle. Two years later, domestic borrowers were given permission to issue RMB bonds in Hong Kong, with the aim of broadening the range of potential buyers as well. Steps like these are essential if the yuan is ever to attract significant international interest. At the present pace, however, it clearly will be many years before any kind of serious challenge to the dollar can be mounted.

## Fragmentation

In short, prospects for the dollar may be discouraging (barring significant policy reforms in the United States), but the outlook for any of the greenback's main competitors appears little better. Neither the euro in Europe nor the yen or yuan in Asia seem ready to seize the dollar's mantle. Rather, a much more fragmented system appears in the offing, with much competition and no money clearly dominant. For years to come, the world will have to learn to live with a leadership vacuum at the peak of the Currency Pyramid.

## Cooperation?

The dangers of fragmentation are clear. Without some form of leadership to assure a minimal degree of compatibility among national policies, the global

---

[19] Li Daokui, "Internationalization of the RMB to Be Accelerated" People's Daily Online, 2006, http://english.people.com.cn/other/archive.html.

monetary system will be at constant risk of instability or worse. Among public agencies there is no "invisible hand" to assure mutually beneficial outcomes. Decentralized decision making among sovereign governments without some manner of coordination is potentially a recipe for disaster.

To be sure, a leaderless currency system would not necessarily be a bad thing. Some have argued it could even turn out be an improvement. Few knowledgeable observers doubt that the greatest threat to monetary stability today is to be found in America's mammoth payments deficits. As the supplier of the world's most popular currency, the United States is in the position of a monopolist that has grown complacent abusing its "exorbitant privilege." But once the dollar's supremacy is eroded by emergent challengers, America would finally be forced to curb its appetite for foreign savings, lowering the risk of crisis. As C. H. Kwan puts it, "The emergence of international currencies that compete with the dollar may help impose discipline on the economic policy of the United States by rendering the international environment less forgiving of its mistakes."[20]

Much depends, however, on the kind of relationship that develops among the competitors. The last time that the world was obliged to live with a leaderless system, during the interwar period, the outcome was—to say the least—dismal. A lack of cooperation between the British, with their weakened pound, and a self-consciously isolationist United States was a critical cause of the financial calamities that followed the stock-market crash of 1929. As Charles Kindleberger wrote in his classic *The World in Depression,* "The international economic system was rendered unstable by British inability and United States unwillingness to assume responsibility for stabilizing it."[21] Can we expect better this time around?

Optimists might emphasize how much conditions have changed since the interwar period. In contrast to the years after World War I, an array of multilateral organizations and forums have developed to institutionalize cooperative practices, from the International Monetary Fund to the Group of Seven. Past experience has provided some pointed lessons about the costs of unbridled competition. Governments have a much better sense of where their enlightened self-interest lies. A system lacking a single dominant leader, therefore, might not lack for effective leadership if the principal players can learn to work together for the common good.

Monetary cooperation, however, is notoriously difficult to sustain, as I have suggested previously.[22] The issue is monetary autonomy, which govern-

[20]  Kwan 2001, 7.
[21]  Kindleberger 1973, 292.
[22]  Cohen 1993.

ments greatly prize for its importance to domestic economic management. In times of crisis, when the benefits of coordination take precedence, governments may for a time be willing to enter into significant policy compromises. But once a sense of threat subsides, the desire to maintain control over domestic monetary conditions tends to reassert itself, encouraging defection. Despite the lessons of the past, cooperation among sovereign states tends to be episodic at best, with commitments ebbing and flowing like the tides.

Moreover, this time there are not just two major players involved, as there were after World War I, but as many as four. Worse, one of the four, the EMU, has still not resolved the issue of external representation; while two others, Japan and China, are in open contention for monetary influence in their regional neighborhood. In these circumstances, the probability that effective joint leadership could be successfully cultivated seems decidedly low.

### Leadership Struggle

Much more likely is a heightened struggle for leadership. Rational policymakers understand the benefits of widespread international use of a currency. The United States may be expected to resist any compromise of the greenback's historical dominance. The contenders in Europe and Asia may be expected to make every effort to defend or enhance the status of their own monies. Life at the peak of the Currency Pyramid will undoubtedly be tense.

But will it be dangerous? That depends on how aggressive policymakers choose to be in promoting their respective monies. As I have noted elsewhere, a critical distinction must be drawn between two different kinds of leadership aspirations: *informal* and *formal*. Much rides on the difference.[23]

Informal leadership refers to dominance among *market* actors—the scope of a currency's use for private market purposes. At this level, a competitive struggle may be said already to exist, operating through what Helleiner (chapter 4) calls the "indirect" channel of political influence. In the EMU as well as in the two Asian contenders, public policy is already actively engaged in trying to improve the appeal of the dollar's rivals, particularly via financial market reform; in defensive reaction, the United States will do what it can to sustain the popularity of the greenback. The consequences of an informal leadership struggle, however, are apt to be largely benign, since governments take this sort of contestation very much in stride. Rivalry to promote or sustain each currency's competitiveness can be regarded as a natural feature of a decentralized monetary system based largely on market principles. The global

---

[23] Cohen 2004.

community might even benefit if the result is lower transactions costs and
more efficient capital markets.

But what if the players elect to go a step further, to seek to alter the behavior of *state* actors—what I term formal leadership? This option corresponds
more closely to what Helleiner describes as the "direct" channel of influence.
The aim here is alter currency choices at the official level: to induce governments to switch to a different reserve currency or perhaps even to adopt the
foreign currency domestically in place of their own national money ("dollarization"). The result, ultimately, would be the formation of organized currency blocs, not unlike the old sterling area that coalesced around Britain's
pound in the interwar period. The world would face the "new geopolitical reality" of a "variety of regional systems" that David Calleo (chapter 8) predicts.

As in interstate relations generally, tactics in a formal leadership struggle
in monetary affairs may involve either coercion or persuasion, depending on
circumstances. Currencies might be directly imposed on client states in a
manner similar to what Susan Strange meant by a "Master Currency."[24] In the
language of Jonathan Kirshner, countries could be threatened with *enforcement* or *expulsion* if they do not align themselves monetarily—a threat of
sanctions, say, or a withdrawal of past commercial or financial privileges. Al-
ternatively, attractive inducements of an economic or political nature might
be offered to reshape policy preferences in manner analogous to Strange's notion of a "Negotiated Currency"—what Kirshner describes as *entrapment*.[25]

Whatever the tactics used, the consequences for the global monetary system could indeed be dangerous. In a formal leadership struggle, by definition,
competition becomes more overtly politicized and hence less easy to contain.
Economically, increasingly antagonistic relations could develop between mutually exclusive groupings, reversing decades of multilateral liberalization in
trade and financial markets. Politically, currency rivalry could become transformed into serious geopolitical conflict.

Many observers discount the probability of a formal leadership struggle,
pointing to the evident perils involved. Any efforts to alter currency choices
at the state level would imply a cutback of dollar accumulations, which in turn
could lead to a sharp depreciation of the greenback, causing massive losses on
existing reserve holdings. Would governments truly risk such self-inflicted
wounds? To avert a doomsday scenario, it makes more sense for state actors
to support the greenback—or, at least, not undermine it—whether they like
it or not. Optimists see this as nothing more than enlightened self-interest.

---

[24] Strange 1971b.
[25] Kirshner 1995.

Others, however, see it as more like the notorious balance of terror that existed between the nuclear powers during the cold war—a "balance of financial terror," as former treasury secretary Larry Summers has described it.[26] A fear of mutually assured destruction is surely a powerful deterrent to overtly destabilizing behavior. But fear cannot rule out the possibility of miscalculation or even mischief by critical players. As Kirshner (chapter 9) points out, today's challengers for currency supremacy, unlike in earlier years, are not all political allies of the United States bonded together by the glue of the cold war; indeed, one of them, China, is deemed America's greatest potential adversary. In fact, the balance of financial terror is inherently unstable and could conceivably break down at any time.

## Battlegrounds?

Will the balance break down? Prediction is hazardous, of course (particularly, as the joke goes, when the future is involved), and a doomsday scenario can hardly be excluded. But I am less persuaded than some observers, such as Kirshner, that the wolf is actually at the door, ready to wreak systemic havoc. Certainly the foundations for a confrontation over formal leadership are in place, suggesting that a threat somewhere, at sometime is possible. There seems little reason to worry in the Western Hemisphere, where a dollar bloc has effectively existed for some time; there, the greenback remains largely unchallenged. Nor do many question the euro's increasing dominance in the EMU's European hinterland as well as in much of Africa. But elsewhere room does indeed exist for serious clashes, though my expectation is that in the end most risks will be held in check by broader geopolitical considerations. The greatest dangers are to be found in the Middle East and East Asia.

*Middle East*    In the Middle East, where the greenback has long reigned supreme, Europe could be understandably tempted to seek a greater role for the euro.[27] With its concentration of wealthy oil exporters, the region would seem a prize well worth fighting for. At the moment, the U.S. dollar is not only the standard for invoicing and payments in world energy markets; it also accounts for the vast majority of central bank reserves and government-held investments in Middle Eastern countries. Overall, however, the region's commercial ties are far more oriented toward Europe—a disjunction that many Europeans find anomalous, even irrational. Repeatedly, the question is asked:

[26] Summers 2004.
[27] Cohen 2006.

Would it not make more sense for the area to do business with its largest trading partner, Europe, in Europe's own currency rather than the greenback? And if so, would it not then make sense to switch to the euro as a reserve currency as well? Europe is well placed to make the Middle East a currency battleground.

Certainly, the possibility of a switch to the euro is tempting from a European perspective. Displacement of the dollar might go far to restore a measure of Europe's historically privileged position in the region. Arguably, the prospect might be tempting from the perspective of Middle Eastern governments, too, for sound economic reasons as well as to curb the presently overweening strategic influence of the United States. It is well known that from time to time oil exporting states have actively explored alternatives to the dollar, only to be discouraged by the lack of a suitable substitute. Now, with the arrival of the euro, they see the possibility of a truly competitive rival for their affections. Talk of a switch to the euro (or to a currency basket heavily weighted toward the euro) has been particularly intense lately as a result of the greenback's most recent bout of weakness. Should Europe seek to capitalize on the dollar's travails, directly promoting use of the euro by regional governments, it might find itself pushing against an open door.

Any effort along these lines, however, would surely provoke determined opposition from the United States, which has long linked the region's use of the dollar to broader security concerns. For Washington, there is no higher politics than the Great Game being played out today in the energy-rich Middle East. America needs both the region's oil and continued support for the greenback; regional governments, in turn, need protection against enemies both within and without, which Washington has promised under a series of unwritten understandings dating back to the first oil shock in the 1970s. With so much at stake, the level of U.S. tolerance for a formal currency challenge from Europe would be correspondingly low, making geopolitical conflict a virtual certainty.

Indeed, for some observers, the conflict has already begun. Theories abound that America's 2003 attack on Iraq, following as it did shortly after Saddam Hussein's decision to demand payment in euros for Iraqi oil exports, was motivated above all by a desire to sustain the dollar's role in the region. Though the idea is wholly unsubstantiated by plausible evidence, as Kirshner (chapter 9) notes, one need not be a sensationalist to recognize the seeds of truth that it contains. A battle of currencies in the Middle East could get nasty.

Would Europe risk it? In the end, however strongly tempted, the Europeans are more likely to keep their aspirations in check, averting direct confrontation with Washington. Even after the Bush administration's decision to promote "regime change" in Iraq, there is no consensus among Europeans to risk the broader political and security relationship that they have long enjoyed with the United States. Beyond their currency's natural home in Europe's immediate neighborhood, therefore, they will most probably act with restraint. Maneuvering for advantage in the Middle Eastern region will undoubtedly persist. But the euro's challenge to the dollar is unlikely to be allowed to get out control.

*East Asia*   In East Asia, where both Japan and China continue to aspire to regional leadership, it is easy to imagine a three-way contest developing between the greenback, still dominant for now, and its two regional counterparts, the yen and yuan. Here also the U.S. dollar still accounts for the vast majority of central bank reserves and government-held investments. Hence here also there is much room for a vigorous campaign by either Tokyo or Beijing to promote a greater role for its currency at the greenback's expense. Japan, despite recent disappointments, has by no means given up on its Asian strategy for the yen, while China, taking the long view, clearly has committed itself to a policy of gradual internationalization of the RMB. These countries are well placed to make their neighborhood a currency battleground, too.

Determined opposition from the United States must be expected here as well, given America's long-standing security interests in the region. Much is at stake here, too. Washington has long enjoyed an impressive ability to project power in East Asia, based on an extensive network of military bases and alliances as well as deep commercial and financial ties. For decades America has in effect played the role of sheriff in the area, preserving a degree of stability among unfriendly, even hostile neighbors. More recently, Washington has also aimed to contain the rise of China as a potential global rival. To a significant degree, all this has been made possible by the unquestioned acceptability of the dollar, which allows the United States to spend whatever it feels it needs to promote its policy ambitions. Washington is hardly likely to take any challenge from the yen or yuan lying down.

In the case of the yen the risk is actually quite modest. That is because of America's decades-old defense alliance with Japan, which neither Washington nor Tokyo would wish to jeopardize. Like the Europeans, the Japanese are most likely to keep their aspirations in check rather than confront the United States directly. Ever since World War II, Japan's foreign policy has involved a delicate balancing act, seeking to play a leadership role in East Asia while also keeping the United States engaged in the region as a counterweight to China. Tokyo has no interest in seriously alienating its most powerful ally for the sake of a putative yen bloc.

In the case of the yuan, by contrast, the risk is greater. That is because of China's evident superpower aspirations, which color every dimension of Beijing's relationship with Washington. China has already gained a great deal of clout throughout East Asia as a result of its rapid economic growth and shows every sign of intending to reclaim what it regards as its rightful place as the dominant power in the region—a strategy that we know includes a wider role for the RMB. Given its limitations, the yuan is clearly unready to replace the dollar as yet. On the other hand, with Beijing's enormous dollar accumulations that could be diversified at any time, the Chinese do have the means to undermine the greenback should they so desire. The question is: Would they so desire, knowing that they could themselves suffer massive losses in the process? The answer ultimately will depend on broader trends in Sino-American relations, which cannot be predicted in advance.

## Prospects

Prospects for the future, therefore, are clouded at best. A weakening dollar is unlikely to be replaced by any other single currency. The outlook, rather, is for a more fragmented currency system, with three or four monies in direct competition in different parts of the world. Sustained cooperation among the major players is unlikely, except in the event of a serious crisis. Much more probable is a prolonged leadership struggle, particularly in such contested regions as the Middle East and East Asia, though for the most part there seems little risk of an escalation into outright geopolitical conflict. Once again, as during the long interregnum following the start of sterling's decline, it could be decades before the final outcome becomes clear.

# 8

# TWENTY-FIRST CENTURY GEOPOLITICS AND THE EROSION OF THE DOLLAR ORDER

David P. Calleo

Since World War II, America's geopolitical imagination has grown "unipolar." Americans take for granted that their country is the predominant world power and natural leader of the global system. Several generations have never known any other view. This imperious perspective also assumes a special international role for the dollar—one that reflects America's economic as well as geopolitical primacy, and is an important instrument for preserving both. By the same reasoning, signs of the dollar's weakness are seen to imply a corresponding decline in America's geopolitical rank. Because of this linkage, the dollar's periodic "crises" have regularly piqued the interest of foreign policy analysts. This was especially true throughout the 1970s and 1980s, when the dollar's exchange rate was highly unstable (see table 8.1). By the late 1980s economic problems, including a volatile dollar, had generated a "declinist" school of historians and political economists who were attracting widespread attention in the popular media.[1] Reagan's America, they argued, was suffer-

Author's note: This essay was written with the help of several research assistants at the Johns Hopkins Nitze School of Advanced International Studies, most notably David Beffert, Kai Behrens, Daniil Davydoff, Necmeddin Bilal Erdogan, Mark Huberty, and Kelly O'Malley. This chapter, written for this book, raises themes that are also engaged in my recent book, *Follies of Power: America's Unipolar Fantasy* (Cambridge: Cambridge University Press, 2009).

[1] See Peter Schmeisser, "Taking Stock: Is America in Decline?" *New York Times Magazine*, April 17, 1988, 96.

TABLE 8.1.
Dollar's average annual exchange rate with major currencies, 1971–2007

| Year | DM-Dollar | Dollar-Pound | Franc-Dollar | Yen-Dollar | Dollar-Euro |
|------|-----------|--------------|--------------|------------|-------------|
| 1971 | 3.4830 | 2.4442 | 5.5100 | 347.79 | |
| 1972 | 3.1886 | 2.5034 | 5.0444 | 303.12 | |
| 1973 | 2.6715 | 2.4525 | 4.4535 | 271.31 | |
| 1974 | 2.5868 | 2.3403 | 4.8107 | 291.84 | |
| 1975 | 2.4614 | 2.2217 | 4.2877 | 296.78 | |
| 1976 | 2.5185 | 1.8048 | 4.7825 | 296.45 | |
| 1977 | 2.3236 | 1.7449 | 4.9161 | 268.62 | |
| 1978 | 2.0097 | 1.9184 | 4.5091 | 210.39 | |
| 1979 | 1.8343 | 2.1224 | 4.2567 | 219.02 | |
| 1980 | 1.8175 | 2.3246 | 4.2251 | 226.63 | |
| 1981 | 2.2632 | 2.0243 | 5.4397 | 220.63 | |
| 1982 | 2.4281 | 1.7480 | 6.5794 | 249.06 | |
| 1983 | 2.5539 | 1.5159 | 7.6204 | 237.55 | |
| 1984 | 2.8455 | 1.3368 | 8.7356 | 237.46 | |
| 1985 | 2.9420 | 1.2974 | 8.9800 | 238.47 | |
| 1986 | 2.1705 | 1.4677 | 6.9257 | 168.35 | |
| 1987 | 1.7981 | 1.6398 | 6.0122 | 144.60 | |
| 1988 | 1.7570 | 1.7813 | 5.9595 | 128.17 | |
| 1989 | 1.8808 | 1.6382 | 6.3802 | 138.07 | |
| 1990 | 1.6166 | 1.7841 | 5.4399 | 145.00 | |
| 1991 | 1.6610 | 1.7674 | 5.6468 | 134.59 | |
| 1992 | 1.5618 | 1.7663 | 5.2935 | 126.78 | |
| 1993 | 1.6545 | 1.5016 | 5.6669 | 111.08 | |
| 1994 | 1.6216 | 1.5319 | 5.5459 | 102.18 | |
| 1995 | 1.4321 | 1.5785 | 4.9864 | 93.96 | |
| 1996 | 1.5049 | 1.5607 | 5.1158 | 108.78 | |
| 1997 | 1.7348 | 1.6376 | 5.8393 | 121.06 | |
| 1998 | 1.7597 | 1.6573 | 5.8995 | 130.99 | |
| 1999 | | 1.6172 | | 113.73 | 1.0653 |
| 2000 | | 1.5156 | | 107.80 | 0.9232 |
| 2001 | | 1.4396 | | 121.57 | 0.8952 |
| 2002 | | 1.5025 | | 125.22 | 0.8454 |
| 2003 | | 1.6347 | | 115.94 | 1.1321 |
| 2004 | | 1.8330 | | 108.15 | 1.2438 |
| 2005 | | 1.8204 | | 110.11 | 1.2449 |
| 2006 | | 1.8434 | | 116.31 | 1.2563 |
| 2007 | | 2.0020 | | 117.76 | 1.3711 |
| 2008[a] | | 1.9243 | | 105.30 | 1.5052 |

Source: Federal Reserve historical exchange rate data available at http://www.federalreserve.gov/releases/h10/hist/default1989.htm.
[a]As of the end of October.

ing from economic "overstretch," provoked by heavy military spending, in-adequately financed. Overstretch was embodied in the country's habitual "twin deficits"—one fiscal and the other external. The fiscal deficit indicated that America's federal government was spending more than its income, and therefore adding to the national debt. The external or current account deficit

TABLE 8.2.
National Defense Outlays, FY 1979–FY 2009 (by fiscal year, in billions of dollars)

| Year | Current dollars | FY 2009 dollars[a] | As percent of GDP | Real change (%) |
|---|---|---|---|---|
| 1979 | 116.3 | 296.3 | 4.7 | 3.0 |
| 1980 | 134.0 | 313.7 | 4.9 | 5.9 |
| 1981 | 157.5 | 335.9 | 5.2 | 7.1 |
| 1982 | 185.3 | 369.8 | 5.8 | 10.1 |
| 1983 | 209.9 | 401.2 | 6.1 | 8.5 |
| 1984 | 227.4 | 419.2 | 5.9 | 4.5 |
| 1985 | 252.7 | 451.3 | 6.1 | 7.6 |
| 1986 | 273.4 | 477.0 | 6.2 | 5.7 |
| 1987 | 282.0 | 479.5 | 6.1 | 0.5 |
| 1988 | 190.4 | 478.7 | 5.8 | (0.2) |
| 1989 | 303.6 | 481.7 | 5.6 | 0.6 |
| 1990 | 299.3 | 458.0 | 5.2 | (4.9) |
| 1991 | 273.4 | 403.2 | 5.4 | (12.0) |
| 1992 | 298.4 | 429.2 | 4.8 | 6.5 |
| 1993 | 291.1 | 409.5 | 4.4 | (4.6) |
| 1994 | 281.6 | 387.8 | 4.1 | (5.3) |
| 1995 | 272.1 | 366.9 | 3.7 | (5.4) |
| 1996 | 265.8 | 351.7 | 3.5 | (4.2) |
| 1997 | 270.5 | 351.8 | 3.3 | 0.0 |
| 1998 | 268.2 | 344.6 | 3.1 | (2.0) |
| 1999 | 274.8 | 348.5 | 3.0 | 1.1 |
| 2000 | 294.4 | 366.0 | 3.0 | 5.0 |
| 2001 | 304.8 | 370.1 | 3.0 | 1.1 |
| 2002 | 348.5 | 415.3 | 3.4 | 12.2 |
| 2003 | 404.8 | 472.8 | 3.7 | 13.9 |
| 2004 | 455.8 | 519.0 | 3.9 | 9.8 |
| 2005 | 495.3 | 546.4 | 4.0 | 5.3 |
| 2006 | 521.8 | 557.2 | 4.0 | 2.0 |
| 2007 | 552.6 | 574.6 | 4.0 | 3.1 |
| 2008[b] | 607.3 | 619.5 | 4.2 | 7.8 |
| 2009[b] | 675.1 | 675.1 | 4.5 | 9.0 |

Sources: "Historical Tables, Budget of the United States Government, Fiscal Year 2009," table 8.4, and Steven Kosiak, "Historical and Projected Funding for Defense: Presentation of the FY 2009 Request in Tables and Charts," Center for Strategic and Budgetary Assessments, March 31, 2008. Available at http://www.csbaonline.org/4Publications/PubLibrary/U.20080331.FY_09_Request_in_T/U.20080331.FY_09_Request_in_T.pdf.
[a] Derived using GDP deflator.
[b] Estimates.

meant that the United States, as an economy, was consuming and investing more than it produced, and importing the difference. Through most of the 1980s, military spending was close to its postwar high, while both fiscal and current-account deficits had become very large by historical standards (see table 8.2 and figure 8.1). Logically, the "twins" were thought to be closely linked.[2] The fiscal deficit, registering the government's deficit spending, ex-

---

[2] Of course, fiscal and current account deficits are each subject to distinctive factors and therefore do not necessarily move in tandem. See figure 8.1.

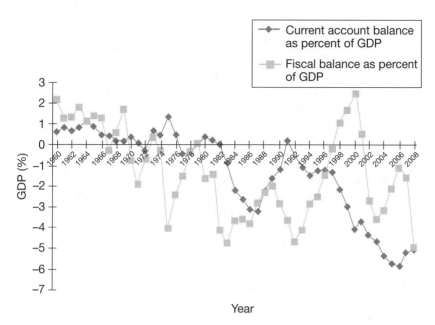

**Figure 8.1.** U.S. fiscal and current account balances (percentage of GDP), 1960–2008
(second quarter data for the year 2008)
U.S. Treasury, Bureau of Economic Analysis

acerbated the external deficit, which registered the overspending of the national economy as a whole.

Each of the deficits could be financed either by borrowing or by printing money. Each course had different consequences for the dollar and the overall economy. Government borrowing, when not accompanied by a commensurate increase in the money supply, tended to push up interest rates and strengthen the dollar and to "crowd out" private investors from capital markets and thus slow economic growth. Financing deficits by merely printing more money, or otherwise increasing the supply of credit, pointed toward inflation and a weak dollar.

Unlike the fiscal deficit, the external deficit, an excess of imports in goods and services over exports, had ultimately to be financed by foreigners—principally by allowing Americans to pay for their imported purchases with dollars. As America's external deficit continued to mount, so did the rest of the world's supply of dollars. Declinists feared that foreigners would grow nervous about holding more and more dollars.[3] Investors would begin to diver-

---

[3] For an influential explanation of how the gold exchange standard, with the dollar as principal reserve currency, "exported" inflation, see Rueff 1972, 283–87. See also Triffin 1960; Triffin 1966.

sify, and the dollar's exchange rate would fall—a decline that would tend to accelerate. Shoring up the dollar, while continuing to run a large external deficit, would require higher real interest rates, which might attract capital from abroad but also would raise the price of servicing debt in general and thus curtail investment and growth. Historians invoked the unhappy financial experiences of earlier empires. In the most popular of the declinist writings, *The Rise and Fall of the Great Powers* (1989), Yale's Paul Kennedy saw Reagan's profligate America following in the footsteps of Habsburg Spain and Bourbon France.[4]

I myself wrote two "declinist" books. *Beyond American Hegemony* (1987) discussed how the international monetary system had periodically been manipulated to finance America's heavy world role during the cold war. *The Bankrupting of America* (1992) analyzed our big twin deficits—how they were linked to geopolitical overcommitment and how they disturbed capital markets and led to economic damage and decline.[5]

### From Johnson to the End of the Cold War

Lyndon Johnson's Vietnam War and Great Society were together an illustration of the simultaneous pursuit of guns and butter, typical of cold war America. During this time the fiscal deficit began to swell, inflation to accelerate, and the external balance to deteriorate (see figure 8.1 and table 8.3). Johnson nevertheless struggled to sustain the fixed exchange rate established at Bretton Woods. By 1971, Johnson's successor, Richard Nixon, was abandoning Bretton Woods and letting the dollar's exchange rate float, as it has ever since.[6] During the Nixon and Carter presidencies the floating exchange rate was generally accompanied by an easy monetary policy. In President Reagan's era, by contrast, floating was generally accompanied by tight money. In effect, these cold war administrations exhibited three distinct formulas for

[4] Kennedy 1987. For others sometimes lumped into the declinist school of the time, see Rosecrance 1979; Gilpin 1981; Mead 1987. See also Keohane 1984.

[5] Calleo 1987, chaps. 6–7; Calleo 1992, chaps. 6–7. I examined these issues affecting the dollar in a series of books stretching back to the 1960s: Calleo 1968, chap. 5; 1970, chap. 6; 1976; 1982 chaps. 3–5; Calleo and Rowland 1973, chap. 5.

[6] The war in Vietnam and President Johnson's Great Society program led to a rapid acceleration of inflation in the United States; a deterioration of the trade and current-account balances made the gold exchange mechanism of the Bretton Woods system increasingly unsustainable. On August 15, 1971, in response to a market crisis of the dollar, President Nixon closed the "gold window" and imposed price and import controls. The subsequent 1971 Smithsonian agreement failed to salvage the Bretton Woods system and eventually all major currencies started floating against the dollar. Finally, in March 1976, the Bretton Woods system was officially ended. See Calleo 1982, chap. 4.

TABLE 8.3.
Changes in U.S. fiscal deficits, inflation rates, and gross national product, 1960–1975

| Year | Budget[a] (+/−) | CPI[b] | GNP[c] |
|------|------|------|------|
| 1960 | 0.1 | 1.6 | 2.2 |
| 1961 | −0.6 | 1.0 | 2.6 |
| 1962 | −1.3 | 1.1 | 5.8 |
| 1963 | −0.8 | 1.2 | 4.0 |
| 1964 | −0.9 | 1.3 | 5.3 |
| 1965 | −0.2 | 1.7 | 6.0 |
| 1966 | −0.5 | 2.9 | 6.0 |
| 1967 | −1.1 | 2.9 | 2.7 |
| 1968 | −3.0 | 2.9 | 4.6 |
| 1969 | 0.3 | 4.2 | 2.8 |
| 1970 | −0.3 | 5.4 | −0.2 |
| 1971 | −2.2 | 4.3 | 3.4 |
| 1972 | −2.0 | 3.3 | 5.7 |
| 1973 | −1.2 | 6.2 | 5.8 |
| 1974 | −0.4 | 11.0 | −0.6 |
| 1975 | −3.5 | 9.1 | −1.1 |

Source: Economic Report of the President 1981, p. 233.
[a]Budget surplus or deficit as a percentage of GDP; source: Budget of the United States Government, 1992, table 1.3, part 7: 17.
[b]Consumer Price Index, Economic Report of the President 1981, p. 267.
[c]1972 dollars; percent change from prior year.

managing the dollar: a fixed exchange rate with expansive macroeconomic policies (Johnson), a floating exchange rate with expansive macroeconomic policies (Nixon), and a floating exchange rate with expansive fiscal but restrictive monetary policy (Reagan).[7] Each formula was able to finance deficits and manage the dollar, but each also had its own particular weaknesses that eventually forced it to be abandoned. In the Nixonian era, when monetary policy was generally loose, the United States was exporting dollars freely into world markets. The dollar was weak and inflation became a serious problem. Monetary policy tightened and a recession followed. The Carter years manifested a similar pattern, with growing inflation and sharply tightened monetary policy at the end. Tight money continued under Reagan, but early on was complemented by an unusually loose fiscal policy—with large "supply-side" tax cuts and a major defense buildup. With a big fiscal deficit and tight money, interest rates were exceptionally high. The United States began importing back from abroad the dollars it had exported earlier. An "overvalued" dollar

[7] Calleo 1987, chap. 6. This formulation ignores the Ford administration (August 9, 1974–January 20, 1977), which did try to return to more conventional and restrained macroeconomic policies. For an appreciation of Ford's efforts see Greenspan (2007, 65).

was the natural result. The high dollar exacerbated the current account deficit, damaged domestic industry, and risked a general financial crisis.

The critical lesson of this progression was the free hand it invariably provided the United States. From Johnson to Reagan, when the effects of any one formula grew intolerable, another was ready. Thus, the United States was able to live beyond its means for several postwar decades—in particular, to run an external deficit financed by the rest of the world. It is difficult to explain how this was possible without invoking geopolitics. The other rich capitalist countries of the world depended heavily on American military power to protect them from the Soviets. The American deficits were a kind of supplemental imperial tax needed to help support America's hegemonic burdens abroad and democratic lifestyle at home. So long as the cold war's bipolar strategic confrontation persisted, America's rich allies could not permit the dollar to crash, and thereby curtail America's geopolitical role. One way or another, they provided the money needed to finance America's external deficits. It also helped greatly, of course, that the dollar was by far the most important international currency. Most countries held the bulk of their reserves in dollars, and they were not eager to see their assets depreciate. In the short run, at least, there was no real alternative to the dollar.

By the late 1980s, however, declinists were predicting that this whole cold war process was becoming unsustainable.[8] Were they wrong? We shall never know, since it was the cold war itself that proved unsustainable. Mercifully, overstretch was much worse on the Soviet than on the American side. But had there been no Soviet breakdown and no Gorbachev, and if the cold war confrontation had continued, would the dollar's deterioration expected by the declinists have been realized?

At the time, many monetarist economists, including Paul Volcker—the strong-minded chairman of the Federal Reserve through most of the Reagan era—believed that the United States could cure itself of its twin deficits and unstable dollar and still continue with the traditional cold war foreign policy. A prolonged restriction of monetary policy would, it was hoped, "wring out" inflationary expectations from our financial markets.[9] Real interest rates

[8]  Kennedy (1987, 515) saw the United States facing a dilemma of "imperial overstretch" familiar to past great powers. Hence "decision makers in Washington must face the awkward and enduring fact that the sum total of the United States' global interests and obligations is nowadays far larger than the country's power to defend them all simultaneously." There were numerous distinguished critics of the declinists. See, for example, Huntington 1989; Waltz 1979; Russett 1985; Nye 1990; Strange 1987; and Nau 1990.

[9]  See Volcker 1979, 888–89. Volcker's era of high interest rates saw two formal recessions. The first came in 1980, following an increase in the federal funds rate from 7.9% to 13.4%, and saw the economy shrink 0.2%. The second arrived in 1981, when the federal funds rate was raised to 16.4%; it was more severe, with the economy shrinking 1.9%, the deepest recession since World War II. See US Gov-

would fall. Businesses could raise capital more cheaply, and solid, noninflationary growth would follow. Real growth would ease fiscal conditions and make it easier to balance future budgets. Steady monetary policy, matched by real growth and fiscal discipline, would mean a stable dollar.

Some declinists, or at least this one, while applauding Volcker's policy, did not believe the United States could embrace orthodox views of fiscal and monetary equilibrium without a serious adjustment of geopolitical roles, in particular with Europe, which I thought should be pressed to take the lead in defending its own territory against the Soviets. European troops at home would cost much less than American troops abroad.[10] I had been developing this argument in the 1970's. Reagan's huge defense buildup, and the consequent mushrooming of the fiscal deficit, appeared only to reinforce it. The end of the cold war, however, radically altered the geopolitical framework. On the one hand, it greatly diminished the military dependency of the Europeans and Japanese, which had formerly compelled them to support the dollar. On the other hand, it offered the United States the chance to cut military spending and rebalance fiscal policy, which would make it easier to stabilize monetary policy and the dollar. In many respects, the United States under the Clinton administration seized that chance. Deep cuts in defense spending led toward a fiscal surplus. And despite a still rising external deficit, the dollar stabilized.

## The Clinton Formula

Eliminating the fiscal deficit was an outstanding achievement of the Clinton years.[11] The process actually began in the Bush administration, as the end of the cold war brought the United States a large "peace dividend," while the extra costs of the Gulf War were covered by allied contributions. Clinton, at the outset of his administration, showed little sign of the older Bush's enthusiasm for globalist geopolitics. Interventions were carefully circumscribed by the

---

ernment 2007, table B73. The combined Reagan-Volcker formula had been prescribed as early as 1971, when the economist Robert Mundell, later a Nobel laureate, criticized Nixon's combined tight fiscal policy and loose monetary policy as the wrong mix for the U.S. economy. He urged combined fiscal stimulus and monetary rigor, which would together curb inflation, attract foreign capital, and promote growth that would reduce deficits. See Mundell 1971.

[10] See Calleo 1987, chaps. 6, 7, and Calleo 1992, 152, 175–80. For the theory of "free riders," see Kindleberger 1973, 301–8. See also Newhouse et al. 1971 and Treverton 1978.

[11] The U.S. budget switched from deficit to surplus in fiscal year 1998. Clinton left office in 2000 with a budget surplus of $166 billion projected for that year and $184 billion for 2001. US Government 2000, 397.

"Powell Doctrine."[12] America's geopolitical ambitions thus remained relatively modest. The rapid decline in defense spending continued and was not reversed for several years. Meanwhile, a Congress controlled by conservatives proved unsympathetic to Clinton's plans for more comprehensive and generous health care or to any expansion of welfare benefits in general. Faute de mieux, the peace dividend was invested in restoring the fiscal balance. A declining fiscal deficit lessened government borrowing and liberated capital for private borrowers.[13] By the later years of the decade, the boom in information technology was providing a powerful incentive for heavy private investment in the real economy. Rapid growth in the nation's GDP followed, along with major increases in productivity. And although America's consumer debt and foreign borrowing both reached record levels, GDP growth was such that the ratio of these debts to the size of the economy shrank steadily.[14]

Logically, heavy investment, together with record employment and consumption, easily could have translated into wage and price inflation. But there was little sign of either. There were two complementary explanations for the low inflation.[15] Both remain relevant to understanding the economy's later

[12] See Powell 1993. Daalder and O'Hanlon (2000, 212–13) summarize the Powell Doctrine as follows, "The United States should use military force only after exhausting all other alternatives and then only decisively, to achieve clearly defined political objectives." They note that it differs from the "Weinberger Doctrine" that "force should only be used in defense of vital U.S. interests."

[13] According to Robert E. Rubin, U.S. secretary of the treasury under President Clinton, the 1993 deficit-reduction program led to the longest period of continuous economic growth ever recorded (Rubin and Weisberg 2003; and US Government 1998, esp. 356–64).

[14] The total public debt of the United States shrank as a percentage of GDP throughout the Clinton administration, from 49.39% in 1993 to 33.20% in 2001, the year after Clinton's departure. Under Bush, that number has crept up again to 37.7% as of 2008 and is expected to surpass 40% by the end of 2009. See The Economist Intelligence Unit, the United States of America, Country Data 1980–present, EIU Limited, London, 2006, at www.eiu.com.

[15] The low inflation during the 1990s growth cycle was puzzling from the start. Early on, unemployment fell below the Non-Accelerating Inflation Rate of Unemployment (NAIRU) but price inflation did not follow. Economists wondered whether structural changes in the economy had pushed the inflation rate lower than in past expansions. The long period of low inflation following the 1970s was thought to have moderated inflationary expectations and therefore wage demands. But by the second half of the 1990s, with wages rising at twice the rate of inflation, inflation still did not accelerate.

Federal Reserve chairman Alan Greenspan argued in the mid-1990s that the rate of technology adoption meant that U.S. productivity growth made real wage increases possible without inflation, and at the same time also led to lower unemployment.

Critics blame Greenspan's confidence about productivity gains for his easy monetary policy that, they maintain, allowed stock market bubbles to develop. Greenspan himself seems to have recognized this danger, most famously in his 1996 "Irrational Exuberance" speech. The exuberance came to an end just as Greenspan had feared it might, with the fall of the stock market in the dot-com collapse. Meanwhile, the high consumer indebtedness of the 1990s remained.

For Greenspan's thinking at the height of the 1990s boom, see "Statement by Alan Greenspan, Chairman, Board of Governors of the Federal Reserve System, before the Joint Economic Committee of the United States Congress," June 17, 1999, at http://www.house.gov/jec/hearings/grnspn4.htm. For later reflections, see Greenspan 2007, chap. 8. For critics, see Roach 2005 and "Original Sin," Mor-

prospects. One, favored by Volcker's successor, Alan Greenspan, argued that even if wages did rise, costs were falling more. Thanks to high investment, and the dot-com magic, productivity growth was matching rising wages with proportionately greater output. In other words, new technology meant notably higher productivity, which made possible real wage increases and higher employment without provoking inflation. Having this view encouraged Greenspan to keep monetary conditions easy in order to elicit the investment that was boosting productivity.

The other explanation linked low inflation to the growing trade deficit. The United States was buying more and more manufactures from low-wage countries—from Mexico, thanks to NAFTA, and increasingly also from China.[16] Low-cost foreign manufactures were so prominent in the American market that domestic producers were in no position to raise prices, nor could their workers exact big wage increases. With such stiff competition, much of the American workforce was being shifted out of manufacturing jobs into service jobs. These tended to pay less and provide little security.[17]

---

gan Stanley Global Economic Forum, at http://www.morganstanley.com/GEFdata/digests/20050425 -mon.html.

[16] The reports of the Council of Economic Advisers argued that falling import prices did lower inflationary expectations, but only by 0.3 percentage points. See US Government 1999, 92. Later explanations gave more weight to the deflationary effects of cheap imports, Chinese in particular. As the World Bank has argued, excessive rates of private saving in China resulted in overinvestment and overcapacity in Chinese export industries. Between 1996 and 2002, the pressure on these industries to channel their excess output into global markets lowered Chinese export prices by an average of 15%. The result has been falling prices for many consumer goods within the U.S. economy. Hence, as the volume of Chinese exports to the United States jumped from $15.2 billion to $100 billion between 1990 and 2000, the United States, in effect, imported deflation into its economy. See World Bank 2002; also Yang 2002.

Critics of this view note that much of the Chinese import growth came at the expense of equally cheap imports from other developing economies. Therefore, given the already high volume of consumer goods imported from Asia, the deflationary impact should already have been present in the U.S. economy. For skepticism about China's disinflationary effect, see Kamin, Marazzi, and Schindler 2004 and IMF 2003.

Other studies suggest China's deflationary effect may be greater than previously thought, thanks to the changing nature of U.S. retailing, and in particular the role of giant firms like Wal-Mart that import heavily from China. A recent study from the National Bureau of Economic Research estimates that the effect of Wal-Mart's "everyday low prices" on local grocery markets was underestimated by 14–18.3%. Correcting for this in the Consumer Price Index would have lowered the official estimate of inflation by 15% (Haussman and Leibtag 2004).

[17] "As a share of current dollar GDP, manufacturing output has been in near continuous decline in the post–World War II era, falling from nearly 30% in 1950 to less than 16% in 2000. Employment in manufacturing as a share of total employment has also declined over this period, from about 30% in 1950 to around 14% in 2000. The corollary to these trends is an equally steady rise in the output and employment share of the service sector. That sector's share of GDP has increased from about 35% of GDP to about 55% over this time period, while its share of employment increased from 55% to 80%" (Elwell 2006).

This shift of employment to the service sector is said to have a created a new class system, where workers are less secure. Production workers, less mobile than capital, are trapped in a global competition for the cheapest and most docile labor. And workers who provide routine services are bound to

The Clinton administration embraced these employment trends as a means of converting the economy to high-productivity manufacturing and services. Rather than protecting less competitive industries, its preferred response to job losses was more training for the workforce and more education in general. America's competitive advantage was thought to lie in advanced manufacturing and services, supported by the nation's abundant educational and research resources.[18] Welfare reform was also part of the administration's basic strategy. Its aim was to accelerate the transformation of the work force by making prolonged unemployment uncomfortable.[19] As redundant industrial workers were prodded into service jobs, income inequality widened well beyond continental European standards (see table 8.4). Nevertheless, the United States avoided Europe's very high unemployment, which made it easier to balance fiscal policy. Moreover, even workers stuck in low-income jobs could benefit from the lower cost of many manufactured items. Meanwhile the country as a whole benefited from record GDP growth and productivity improvement. In short, Clinton's economic policy could present itself as a pantheon of classic liberal virtues: a peaceful foreign policy, combined with fiscal restraint, welfare reform, an efficient labor market, liberal trade, and heavy investment aimed at higher productivity. This felicitous combination appeared to enable and justify ever higher levels of private consumption, satisfied by heavy importing that encouraged the rapid growth of developing countries, above all in Asia.[20]

Thus, while Clinton's liberal formula eliminated the fiscal deficit, it also tended to swell the already large current-account deficit inherited from the Reagan era.[21] Clinton's apologists, however, saw the external deficit during his

the competitive fate of their localities. But globalization also creates a new elite of "symbolic analysts," those endowed with the knowledge to master the global economic web, and to combine and recombine globalized resources to create and serve globalized markets. See Reich 1991, 177–80. For a contrary view, see Peter S. Goodman, "In N.C., a Second Industrial Revolution, Biotech Surge Shows Manufacturing Still Key to U.S. Economy," *Washington Post*, September 3, 2007, A-01.

[18] US Government 1997, esp. chap. 5. See also Reich 1991.

[19] US Government 1998, 32, 80, 98.

[20] For more on the Clinton administration's economic strategy, see Rubin and Weisberg 2003 and US Government 1998, esp. chap. 2.

[21] According to the Congressional Budget Office: "The major changes in the U.S. trade deficit since 1970 can be traced to three primary sources, a long decline in saving as a share of gross domestic product GDP that began in the mid-1950s and accelerated in the 1980s, fluctuations in the business cycle, and relatively attractive investment opportunities in the United States in the 1990s. In the early 1980s, the percentage of GDP accounted for by gross saving fell rapidly and was reflected in a widening gap between the supply of saving and the demand for domestic investment. Inflows of capital from abroad partially filled the gap and permitted domestic investment to exceed saving. Those inflows also financed a trade deficit, allowing domestic consumption and investment to exceed domestic production. The trade deficit shrank as the economy slowed in the early 1990s but has increased since the current expansion began in 1992. Some evidence suggests that demand for private investment in the 1990s has grown beyond what would be expected to occur simply as a result of a normal upswing in

TABLE 8.4.
Gini coefficients of high-income OECD countries, 2007

| Country | Gini coefficent |
| --- | --- |
| United States | 40.8 |
| Portugal | 38.5 |
| New Zealand | 36.2 |
| United Kingdom | 36.0 |
| Italy | 36.0 |
| Australia | 35.2 |
| Spain | 34.7 |
| Ireland | 34.3 |
| Greece | 34.3 |
| Switzerland | 33.7 |
| Belgium | 33.0 |
| France | 32.7 |
| Canada | 32.6 |
| Netherlands | 30.9 |
| Austria | 29.1 |
| Germany | 28.3 |
| Finland | 26.9 |
| Norway | 25.8 |
| Sweden | 25.0 |
| Japan | 24.9 |
| Denmark | 24.7 |

*Source:* UNDP Human Development Report 2007/2008, available at
http://hdr.undp.org/en/reports/global/hdr2007-2008/.
*Note:* The Gini coefficient is the most commonly used measure of inequality. The coefficient varies between 0, which reflects complete equality, and 1, which indicates complete inequality (one person has all the
income or consumption, all others have none), www.worldbank.org.

administration as demonstrating America's economic strength rather than its
vulnerability. Roughly 85 percent of the current account deficit was matched
by a record wave of private direct investment from abroad, generated above
all by America's booming high-technology industries. Private foreign portfolio investment was more than enough to match the remainder of the external
deficit. Inflows of this kind contributed to the productive capital of America's
real economy, and not simply to its debt.[22] In short, the Clinton administra-

---

the business cycle. Regardless of whether that is true, substantial growth of private investment over
the past decade has combined with the longer-standing low saving rate to produce today's large current-account deficits." See "Causes and Consequences of the Trade Deficit, An Overview," Congressional Budget Office, 2000, at http://www.cbo.gov/showdoc.cfm?index=1897&sequence=0. The
current account deficit actually improved in the final Reagan years, as the dollar depreciated after the
conclusion of the Plaza Accord. Between 1985 and 1987 the real trade-weighted value of the dollar as
measured by the Federal Reserve's ten country index fell by 36%, with a corresponding 40% fall in the
trade deficit. For a discussion of the role of the dollar in U.S. trade balances, see Feldstein 1993.

[22] For the magnitude and significance of transatlantic foreign direct investment (FDI) from the
1980s onward, see Hamilton and Quinlan 2007. The authors note the huge reciprocal stock of transatlantic investments, together with the products and earnings of those investments.

TABLE 8.5.
Productivity, investment, and consumption growth, 1970–2006

| Year | Productivity growth (%) | Change in gross domestic investment (%) | Change in real personal consumption (%) |
|---|---|---|---|
| 1970 | | −1.9 | 2.3 |
| 1971 | | 12.2 | 3.8 |
| 1972 | | 13.8 | 6.1 |
| 1973 | | 16.4 | 4.9 |
| 1974 | | 4.9 | −0.8 |
| 1975 | | −4.1 | 2.3 |
| 1976 | | 22.2 | 5.5 |
| 1977 | | 19.6 | 4.2 |
| 1978 | | 20.1 | 4.4 |
| 1979 | | 12.9 | 2.4 |
| 1980 | | −0.3 | −0.3 |
| 1981 | | 17.2 | 1.4 |
| 1982 | | −7.3 | 1.4 |
| 1983 | | 9.2 | 5.7 |
| 1984 | | 27.3 | 5.3 |
| 1985 | | 2.3 | 5.2 |
| 1986 | | 2.8 | 4.1 |
| 1987 | | 5.4 | 3.3 |
| 1988 | 2.1 | 4.0 | 4.1 |
| 1989 | 1.0 | 6.4 | 2.8 |
| 1990 | 2.2 | 0.4 | 2.0 |
| 1991 | 2.6 | −5.0 | 0.2 |
| 1992 | 3.8 | 6.3 | 3.3 |
| 1993 | 2.6 | 7.8 | 3.3 |
| 1994 | 3.5 | 12.5 | 3.7 |
| 1995 | 4.5 | 4.4 | 2.7 |
| 1996 | 3.6 | 7.9 | 3.4 |
| 1997 | 5.5 | 10.6 | 3.8 |
| 1998 | 5.4 | 7.9 | 5.0 |
| 1999 | 4.5 | 8.0 | 5.1 |
| 2000 | 4.1 | 6.7 | 4.7 |
| 2001 | 1.6 | −5.0 | 2.5 |
| 2002 | 6.9 | −0.6 | 2.7 |
| 2003 | 6.2 | 4.9 | 2.8 |
| 2004 | 2.2 | 12.0 | 3.6 |
| 2005 | 4.9 | 9.4 | 3.0 |
| 2006 | 1.1 | 6.8 | 3.0 |

Source: Bureau of Labor Statistics, http://www.bls.gov/data/#productivity; and Bureau of Economic Analysis, http://www.bea.gov/national/nipaweb/SelectTable.asp.

tion seemed to be creating an American economy remarkably well adapted to the post–cold war world. Domestic investment and productivity growth were high; the dollar was reasonably stable, despite the growing current account deficit and the big external deficit fed by America's avid consumers (see tables 8.1 and 8.5, and figure 8.1). And unlike the earlier formulas of the cold war, the dollar's strength was more economic than political. Foreign savings flowed in, it was believed, because the United States held a decisive lead in those new industries and services that were expected to dominate the coming era. That lead depended not only on the country's advanced firms but also on its heavy investment in education and research. Thus, for the first time since the 1960s, the United States featured a macroeconomic formula combining balanced fiscal policy with what appeared to be restrained monetary policy. Accordingly, through most of the 1990s the dollar enjoyed a reasonably stable exchange rate, sustained less by the interventions of central banks than by its own appeal in the market, arguably a status not durably enjoyed since the 1950s. In other words, Clinton's political-economic formula sustained the dollar without demanding special privileges from the international system as a whole. Clinton's policies succeeded because they could be characterized mainly by their restraint. A minimalist foreign policy made it possible to keep defense spending not only at historically low levels but also directed toward acquiring new technologies rather than accumulating manpower for global interventions.[23] So long as the Clinton administration lived within this restrained liberal paradigm, the new euro seemed unlikely to pose a serious threat to the dollar's international status.

## The Limits of the Clinton Approach

There were, however, vulnerabilities in Clinton's policies that would eventually undermine his accomplishments, including the stable dollar. His fiscal success depended initially on a restrained defense budget. But the restraint lacked an enduring geopolitical foundation. A "unipolar" worldview grew increasingly pervasive among American political elites. After 9/11 this was to lead the succeeding Bush administration to large-scale global interventions and back to big fiscal deficits. But the shift in geopolitical mood was present in Clinton's presidency as well. Already in 1993, Clinton had himself become a fervent partisan of NATO enlargement.[24] As NATO's horizons kept expanding, relations with Russia resumed their old antagonistic character. Eu-

---

[23] The Clinton administration reduced American military forces from 2.2 million to 1.45 million active soldiers between 1993 and 2002. Aggregate U.S. outlays for military procurement during the 1990s were 76 percent of the total for the 1980s. As a proportion of GDP, defense expenditures amounted to an average of 3.5% of GDP between 1993 and 2002, considerably less than the average of 5.8% of GDP during the 1980s. However, funding for advanced military technology like the Joint Direct Attack Ammunition program, the GPS-guided Tomahawk cruise missile, and unmanned aerial vehicles like the Predator and Global Hawk originated during the Clinton years. See SIPRI Military Expenditure Database, October 2005, http://www.sipri.org/contents/milap/milex/mex_data_index.html

[24] See Calleo 2001, 310–13, notes 27–29, 39.

rope's political and military weakness also played a critical role. After Europe's dismal performance in Yugoslavia, the United States found itself intervening militarily in the Balkans. America's military success, following the failure of European states to coordinate effectively, fed a wave of American triumphalism that put the administration's lingering geopolitical diffidence on the defensive. In his second inaugural address, Clinton launched the phrase "indispensable nation."[25] By the end of his second term, defense spending was on the rise, and the United States was renewing its vocation for world peacekeeping.

Meanwhile, serious problems with Clinton's economic model also grew increasingly visible. Outsized consumption meant a very low rate of private savings, but compensated for by heavy investment from abroad. Heavy investment and heavy consumption combined to fuel America's soaring GDP (see table 8.5). Investment assets mushroomed in the celebrated dot-com stock-market boom of the later 1990s. A hyperactive financial industry not only leveraged capital for more investment but also made it easy to convert rapidly appreciating assets into disposable income for still more consumption. As time went on, asset growth was self-evidently transforming itself into asset inflation.[26] A widely expected stock market crash came in 2001, at the start of the new Bush administration. The Fed quickly countered with a flood of fresh liquidity, followed by Bush's large tax cuts to redistribute Clinton's anticipated fiscal surplus.[27] Consumer spending quickly recovered and the

[25] President Clinton used the phrase in his second inaugural address in reference to America's geopolitical position over the preceding four years. Madeline Albright employed it later to justify using force in the Balkans: "If we have to use force, it is because we are America. We are the indispensable nation. We stand tall. We see further into the future." For Clinton's address, see http://www.yale.edu/lawweb/avalon/presiden/inaug/clinton2.htm. For Albright's comments, see transcripts from the February 19, 1998, broadcast of *The Today Show,* from the National Broadcasting Company. For a good example of the triumphalism generated by the Balkan interventions within the administration itself, see also Holbrooke 1998.

[26] For a neoclassical economist like Friedrich Hayek, booming corporate profits with a concomitant rise in stock prices risk becoming an embedded expectation, which cannot be satisfied except by increasing inflation. See Hayek 1978, 331–32. Alan Greenspan expressed apprehensions about "irrational exuberance" during a speech he gave at the American Enterprise Institute on December 5, 1996; his memoirs suggest he erred on the side of indulgence: Greenspan 2007, chap. 8.

Robert Shiller's 2000 book, named after Greenspan's memorable phrase, argues that stock markets were overvalued at the time. The second edition of the book, published in 2005, warned of a housing bubble soon to burst. For a general discussion on inflation in the Clinton boom, see notes 16 and 17.

[27] The prime rate plummeted after 2001 and remained low for several years. In its first year in office, the new Bush administration ran a fiscal surplus of 1.3% of GDP. In subsequent years, tax cuts and security spending helped drag the budget back into the red, with the deficit reaching a high point in 2004 of 3.6% of GDP. The fiscal deficit thereafter recovered considerably, thanks to high GDP growth and increasing federal revenue, reaching 1.9% of GDP as of 2006. Since then the trend has reversed itself and a deficit of at least 5% of GDP is expected for the year 2008. See Bureau of Economic Analysis, http://www.bea.gov/national/nipaweb/SelectTable.asp?Selected=N#S3, The White House, Mid-Session Review, Budget of the U.S. Government, Fiscal Year 2008, p. 1. For a Congressional Budget Office longer-term view, see note 40.

recession was mild and brief. Rapid GDP growth resumed. With the dot-com boom deflating, asset growth shifted to the housing market. A very large part of America's gross fixed investment was going into residential construction—35 percent in 2003, 37 percent in 2004, and 38 percent in 2005.[28] Mortgages were abundant as cheap credit substituted for savings. Generous home equity loans transformed rising property values into credit for more spending.[29]

GDP growth, however, was again more than matching the mounting debt. The expanding economy so lifted government revenues that the budget deficit, even though much enlarged in real terms, fell from 2.6 percent of GDP in 2005 to only 1.9 percent in 2006.[30] The U.S. economy had become a magic machine for turning stones into bread. Americans regularly absorbed substantially more than they produced. They borrowed the difference from abroad.[31] But the more Americans consumed, invested, and borrowed, the more their economy grew. Indeed, the economy grew faster even than its debts, which thus shrank in relation to its growing net wealth. The Clinton administration saw the growth as real—the product of advanced technology, of a better distribution of labor and capital—all leading to ever-greater advances in prosperity. For a conservative monetarist, however, such a pattern might seem too good to be true. It would strongly suggest not real growth but asset inflation fueled by a complacent central bank. American monetary policy, morbidly fearful of recession, had remained extremely loose following September 11, 2001. As one bubble popped, another was under way. First came the "irrational exuberance" of the dot-com boom, in due course succeeded by a frenzied housing market. From a Hayekian perspective, the process was likely to end in deep financial disorder.

Unfortunately, subsequent events have confirmed conservative apprehensions. By mid-2007, housing prices, then at record levels, grew stagnant and started to fall in many parts of the country. A wave of foreclosures followed in the greatly overextended "subprime" mortgage market. Dubious mort-

---

[28] U.S. Department of Commerce, Bureau of Economic Analysis, http://www.bea.gov/national/nipaweb/SelectTable.asp?Selected=N#S5.

[29] For the credit for consumer spending generated by home equity loans, see Greenspan and Kennedy 2007.

[30] US Government 2007, 324.

[31] The United States entered the 1990s with a household savings rate of 7% of disposable income. By 2000 the rate was 2.3%. On average, Americans in the 1990s saved 5.2% of disposable income. In comparison, the Japanese saved 13.9% in 1990 and 10.7% in 2000, the Germans 13.9% and 9.5%, respectively. See "Macroeconomic Trends, Economic Growth, Household Saving," in *OECD Factbook 2006, Economic, Environmental, and Social Statistics,* http://lysander.sourceoecd.org/vl=8881248/cl=13/nw=1/rpsv/factbook/. Consumption has continued to play a dominant and relatively steady role in driving GDP, even as the other components—government spending and investment—have fluctuated.

gages, based on inflated property values and "securitized" in rickety financial structures, had come to form a significant part of bank assets all around the world. As bloated real estate prices fell, the value of these opaque mortgage based assets plummeted and banks posted enormous losses. Fearing a general drying up of credit, they hoarded their cash from each other.[32] The ingredients were at hand for financial chaos. Beyond the mortgage market, further "subprime" shocks were in prospect from bubbles still to burst—perhaps hedge funds facing mass redemptions, or the huge consumer credit-card debt held in the banking system, or perhaps money market funds, suddenly insolvent because of heavy withdrawals from deteriorating assets.[33] Anxious American banks began seeking big capital infusions, often from foreign investors, including non-Western sources tied to authoritarian governments.

In the early fall of 2008, when I am writing this, the process has threatened to spin out of control. Some big financial institutions in the United States and Europe are tottering. Banks, American banks not least, have lost much of their credibility. The market for short-term capital has grown extremely tight. To prevent a general financial collapse, Western central banks have issued enormous credits to their banking systems. In recent weeks, the U.S. Treasury has proposed and Congress has authorized up to $700 billion for the government to purchase "toxic" assets from the faltering financial industry. This, it is hoped, will permit financial firms to stabilize their balance sheets and restore their credit. In due course the government can hope to recoup by selling the tainted assets after the market has recovered. European governments have pledged $2.56 trillion to shore up their crumbling financial sectors. It remains to be seen how effective these measures will prove. Meanwhile, the Bush administration has called for raising the ceiling on the national debt by another trillion to a total of $11.3 trillion—almost half of which has been acquired during the Bush administration.[34]

At this point, it is difficult to speak with much assurance about the future course of events. The basics are not promising. Probably the worst fear is that issuing funds on such a colossal scale may eventually call into question the creditworthiness of governments themselves. To be sure, America's formal

[32] For a good contemporary survey of the subprime loan crisis of 2007–08, see Gillian Tett, "Draining Away: Four Problems That Could Beset Debt Markets for Years," *Financial Times,* November 28, 2007, 9. For broader implications, see Martin Wolf, "Why the Credit Squeeze Is a Turning Point for the World," *Financial Times,* December 12, 2007, 11, and also Wolf 2008.

[33] Estimates of the total of obligations at risk run into several trillions. Also see Wolfgang Münchau, "This Is Not Merely a Subprime Crisis," *Financial Times,* January 14, 2008, 9.

[34] The original proposal would raise the national debt ceiling to $11.3 trillion: *New York Times,* September 21, 2008, 1. At the beginning of the first Bush administration in 2001 the national debt ceiling stood at $5.95 trillion; see "Another Possible Bump to the Debt Ceiling," *Washington Post,* May 9, 2006, A21.

federal indebtedness in relation to GDP appears moderate in comparison with many other advanced countries.[35] But adding the federal government's new and ever-widening guarantees for failing banks, money market funds, and insurance companies together with the formal guarantees for the debt of various agencies—like Fannie Mae and Freddie Mac—produces a more alarming but perhaps realistic picture of the federal government's debt burden, as do calculations of the rapidly rising obligations under Social Security and especially Medicare.[36] And whereas in the Clinton years at least the short-term fiscal situation was in good order, knowledgeable estimates of the end of year federal deficit for the last year of the Bush administration were as high as one trillion dollars, or over 7 percent of GDP, with official figures at the end of the second quarter standing at close to 5 percent.[37]

Nor was any quick relief in sight. Quite apart from the unprecedented costs of the financial crisis, large deficits were already in store from traditional military and civilian spending. Following 9/11, real military outlays had come to surpass those of the cold war.[38] And with a good part of America's political class—Democratic as well as Republican—reluctant to retreat from global geopolitical engagements, the Bush administration's high military spending will be difficult to reverse. Civilian entitlements, of course, form a much larger part of public spending. Here an aging population calls for growing expenditures requiring serious tax increases, all the more onerous if the present financial instability translates into a protracted period of slow growth.[39] Given such tight fiscal conditions, and the anticipated heavy debt service, governments will be tempted, perhaps compelled, to use inflation to ease the way. At the moment, of course, with housing prices still falling and the normal machinery of domestic credit expansion reversing itself, the more urgent fear is

[35] Among the G8 countries only Russia has a lower public debt to GDP ratio at 8.8% in 2006 than the United States at 37% in 2007, whereas the rest are 43% United Kingdom, 63.9% France, 64.2% Canada, 64.9% Germany, 104% Italy, and 170% Japan.

[36] According to the Congressional Budget Office, Social Security, Medicare, and Medicaid spending stood at 8.2% of GDP at the end of 2006 and is expected to grow to 18.1% of GDP by 2050. CBO, "The Long Term Budget Outlook, December, 2007," http://www.cbo.gov/doc.cfm?index=8877. The U.S. Federal Reserve also moved to provide $540 billion in guarantees to money market funds. See *Financial Times*, October 21, 2008.

[37] Alan Beattie, "Taxpayers Shoulder Trillion-Dollar Deficit," *Financial Times*, September 22, 2008. Also see U.S. Department of Commerce, Bureau of Economic Analysis, http://www.bea.gov/national/nipaweb/SelectTable.asp?Popular=Y.

[38] See "Historical Tables, Budget of the United States Government, Fiscal Year 2008," table 6.1, p. 118. Available at http://www.whitehouse.gov/omb/budget/fy2008/pdf/hist.pdf; also see figure 4.

[39] According to the Congressional Budget Office's long-term projections, "unless changes are made to current policies, growing demand for resources caused by rising health care costs and the nation's expanding elderly population will put increasing pressure on the budget." Congressional Budget Office, "The Budget and Economic Outlook, an Update," September 2008; http://www.cbo.gov/ftpdocs/97xx/doc9706/09-08-Update.pdf.

of severe recession. With unemployment rising, and so many assets collapsing, there is little sign of wage and price inflation. Nevertheless, with the United States creating credit and injecting liquidity into the economy on an unprecedented scale, while also running giant and growing fiscal deficits, it would not be surprising to see eventually heavy pressure on America's long-term interest rates, which might even reflect a growing loss of confidence in the government's own creditworthiness.

### What Effects on the Dollar?

How will these prospects affect the dollar? Over the years 2000 through 2007, there was a sharp depreciation of the exchange rate—roughly 50 percent against the euro.[40] Foreign investment figures shed light on the mechanics of the dollar's decline. By 2003, net foreign inflows had fallen to one-fifth of their value in 2000. Nevertheless, America's consumption remained high and its external deficit kept growing.[41] Logically enough, the dollar fell sharply, particularly against the euro. At this point, foreign central banks upped their interventions to support the dollar and, for a time, the exchange rate stabilized.[42] By 2005, American consumption was setting new records and the United States was in the middle of a new bubble—the real estate boom. The heavy inflow of foreign private money had resumed.

By far the most significant holders of long-term U.S. treasury and agency debt are Japan and China (see table 8.6).[43] Both Asian countries were widely thought to be supporting the dollar in order to subsidize their own exports. For Japan, this was an old habit going back to the "dirty floating" of the 1970s—a common Japanese and European response to Nixon's falling dollar. For a stagnant but very rich and well-developed country like Japan, supporting the dollar to boost exports is perhaps not an irrational policy. For a poor country like China, however, it seems less sustainable. Although China's rapid growth has depended heavily on its export markets, growing protectionism against Chinese products, together with mounting social unrest in China it-

[40]  From 2000 through 2007, the dollar fell 48.6% against the euro and 32% against the pound. See the OECD Statistics Databank, http://stats.oecd.org/wbos/default.aspx?querytype=view&query name=168. Also see figure 1.

[41]  Since 2000 U.S. personal consumption expenditures grew at an average of 3.1% per year. For the U.S. current account balance, see figure 2.

[42]  Euro-dollar exchange rates were relatively stable between 2004 and 2006. Average annual exchange rates were 1.2438, 1.2449, and 1.2563, respectively. U.S. dollars per "Euro Federal Reserve Statistical Release," http://www.federalreserve.gov/releases/G5A/current/.

[43]  Several European countries and some others exceeded both Japan and China in holdings of U.S. equities and corporate long-term debt, and exceeded China in holdings of short-term debt.

TABLE 8.6.
Value of foreign holdings of U.S. securities, by major investing country and type of security, as of June 30, 2007 (in billions of dollars)

| Country | Total | Equity | Treasury long-term debt | Agency long-term debt | | Corporate long-term debt | | Short-term debt |
|---|---|---|---|---|---|---|---|---|
| | | | | ABS[a] | Other | ABS[a] | Other | |
| Japan | 1,197 | 220 | 553 | 103 | 126 | 30 | 89 | 76 |
| China, mainland[b] | 922 | 29 | 467 | 206 | 170 | 11 | 17 | 23 |
| United Kingdom | 921 | 421 | 43 | 18 | 10 | 142 | 263 | 24 |
| Cayman Islands | 740 | 279 | 23 | 46 | 6 | 190 | 157 | 38 |
| Luxembourg | 703 | 235 | 45 | 23 | 16 | 81 | 259 | 44 |
| Canada | 475 | 347 | 18 | 1 | 3 | 23 | 62 | 22 |
| Belgium | 396 | 25 | 14 | 2 | 31 | 54 | 267 | 3 |
| Ireland | 342 | 81 | 14 | 20 | 6 | 56 | 80 | 85 |
| Netherlands | 321 | 185 | 16 | 20 | 3 | 44 | 40 | 13 |
| Switzerland | 262 | 145 | 33 | 4 | 6 | 28 | 37 | 9 |
| Middle East oil exporters[c] | 308 | 139 | 79 | 12 | 18 | 7 | 10 | 44 |
| Country unknown | 214 | * | * | * | * | 1 | 211 | 2 |
| Rest of world | 2,904 | 995 | 659 | 113 | 336 | 230 | 325 | 246 |
| Total | 9,772 | 3,130 | 1,965 | 570 | 735 | 902 | 1,835 | 635 |
| Of which: Holdings of foreign official institutions | 2,823 | 266 | 1,452 | 236 | 515 | 44 | 55 | 256 |

Source: "Foreign Portfolio Holdings of U.S. Securities as of 6/30/2007," United States Department of the Treasury, at http://www.treas.gov/tic/shl2007r.pdf.
*Greater than zero but less than $500 million.
[a] Asset-backed securities. Agency ABS are backed primarily by home mortgages; corporate ABS are backed by a wide variety of assets, such as car loans, credit card receivables, home and commercial mortgages, and student loans.
[b] Excludes Hong Kong and Macau, which are reported separately.
[c] Bahrain, Iran, Iraq, Kuwait, Oman, Qatar, Saudi Arabia, and the United Arab Emirates.

self, is pressuring the government in Beijing to focus inward—to develop the country's own infrastructure and immense home market. Under these circumstances, expecting China to go on indefinitely accumulating vast quantities of surplus dollars seems an uncertain prospect.[44]

By mid-2007, however, the Chinese government was already elaborating a further strategy for using its huge and rapidly increasing dollar reserves, reported by the fall of 2008 to have reached roughly $2 trillion.[45] Substantial portions of these reserves were to be gathered into a "sovereign wealth fund" and invested in America's private economy.[46] Investing in the U.S. private economy has, of course, long been the practice for Japan and also for western European and other countries with large accumulated dollar holdings.[47] By the end of 2007, the unfolding subprime mortgage crisis had left numerous Western financial institutions undercapitalized and strapped for cash. America's corporate doors were open and China, along with several other non-Western countries, began making large investments in America's private economy.[48]

To some analysts, these inflows from dollar-laden developing countries suggested a new paradigm was governing the global financial system. Rapidly developing non-Western countries were "oversaving." Instead of consuming or investing more in their own home economies, they were seeking investment opportunities in other countries. In particular, immense pools of volatile capital were available for the "undersaving" American economy. Non-Western savings provided the United States with the "endogenous liquidity"

[44] For an analysis of how internal macroeconomic challenges will effect China's external imbalances, see "China Quarterly Update, September 2007," Beijing World Bank Office, September 2007; http://siteresources.worldbank.org/CHINAEXTN/Resources/318949–1121421890573/cqu_09_07 .pdf.

[45] See Satyajit Das, "Insight, Shattered Illusions of Liquidity," *Financial Times*, October 21, 2008, online edition.

[46] For an analysis of China's new management of its dollar reserves and the potential implications, see "China's New Sovereign Wealth Fund, Implications for Global Asset Markets," Henderson Global Investors, Ed. 14–17, July 2007; http://www.hendersongroupplc.com/content/singapore/restricted/ documents/research/2007–07–17_chinasnewsovereignwealthfund.pdf.

For earlier indications that China was moving in this direction, see Peter S. Goodman, "China Set to Reduce Exposure to U.S. Dollar," *Washington Post*, January 10, 2006, D01. More recently, the governor of the People's Bank of China remarked that "many people say that foreign exchange reserves in China are large enough. We do not intend to go further and accumulate reserves." See Lucia Mutikani, "China Reserve Comments Unsettle Dollar vs. Yen," Reuters News Agency, March 20, 2007, at http://www.reuters.com/article/wtMostRead/idUKT6842120070320.

[47] See Hamilton and Quinlan 2007; see also Calleo 1992, 117–19. For a further analysis of how western European and Japanese savings helped finance U.S. debt during the cold war, see Cleveland 1990.

[48] Recently China Investment Corporation has invested $3 billion in Blackstone Group, $5 billion in Morgan Stanley, and $100 million in VISA. See Ben White, "US Banks Get $21 billion Foreign Bailout," *Financial Times*, January 16, 2008, 1; "China Seeks External Help for Wealth Fund," *Wall Street Journal*, December 14, 2007; "Great Wall Street of China," *Wall Street Journal*, December 20, 2007.

its economy requires.[49] America's deficits were thus self-sustaining: high consumption in the United States was sparking prosperity and oversaving in the non-Western world. American military spending, adding further to the country's beneficent overconsumption, was also maintaining geopolitical stability in the world at large, and reinforcing the image of the United States as a safe and profitable haven for foreign savings. So long as this self-reinforcing pattern persists, dollar hegemony could expect a new lease on life.[50] This seems a new version of America's familiar "stones into bread" paradigm—economic magic that brings growth without saving. Under present circumstances, it is perhaps overly sanguine, particularly in its expectations of Chinese behavior.

To begin with, a policy of investing surplus dollars in the United States will meet resistance from those in China who wish capital savings directed toward domestic improvements in China itself. And given the Chinese government's intrusive role in its own society, and the American government's traditional aversion to sharing advanced technology with potential military rivals, heavy Chinese investment in corporate America, particularly using a sovereign wealth fund, should also expect mounting resistance from Americans.[51] If China is thereby blocked from a satisfactory way to invest its surplus dollars in the United States, and equally massive but more acceptable dollar investors do not miraculously appear, it seems logical that the dollar will continue to depreciate. With its exchange value already halved in less than a decade, how

[49] See Mohamed El-Erian, "A Route Back to Potency for Central Banks," *Financial Times,* January 17, 2008, 9. He argues that the new paradigm limits the effects of interest rate changes and requires different tactics from central banks.

As Paul Krugman notes, in a speech by Ben Bernanke in early 2005, before becoming Federal Reserve chairman, he lists oversaving in third world countries as the cause of U.S. heavy borrowing in international capital markets. Krugman's remedy for the resulting rash of unsound investment is "adult supervision over markets running wild." But blaming the present turmoil on lack of regulation perhaps overemphasizes China's enthusiasm for saving and underestimates the effects of America's enthusiasm for heavy consumption and world management. One view sees too much supply of capital, thanks to China's oversaving. Another might blame America's excessive appetites financed by adding dollars to the reserves of those countries that satisfy America's demand. See Paul Krugman, "Don't Cry for Me, America," *New York Times,* January 18, 2008, A23. See also Bernanke 2005.

[50] Harold James (chapter 2) offers a variation of the new paradigm, and sees it as favorable to the dollar's international role. James notes how the end of the cold war coincided with a surge in world savings that has created the conditions for a new preeminence of the dollar. Despite recent dollar depreciation, James believes that the dollar will remain a reliable store of value, because sales of U.S. Treasury bills will increasingly be replaced by purchases of other dollar assets like securities, real estate, and hedge and buyout funds. Capital inflows will thus continue to be strong, not because of higher expected returns than in the rest of the world, but because of greater security offered by the unique depth of U.S. markets, the political and security position of the country, and low business cycle volatility. Therefore, James concludes, military spending and tax cuts are actually strengthening the dollar and there is little sign that the U.S. economy and the dollar itself is, or should be, perceived as more vulnerable to crisis than the European economy or than the rapidly growing Asian economies.

[51] See Steven R. Weisman, "A Fear of Foreign Investments," *New York Times,* August 21, 2007, C1; and Tony Tassell and Joan Chung, "The $2,500bn Question," *Financial Times,* May 25, 2007, 7.

long can a falling dollar be expected to retain its international role as a store of value?

The 2008 financial crisis, raging as I write, appears to belie this prognosis. Frightened investors apparently have returned to their old cold war habits and are seeking safety in U.S. government obligations. Investors apparently fear that the euro, the obvious alternative, lacks the political framework and backing sufficient to sustain it through the severe crisis that many expect. As a result, in the weeks since the banking crisis began in earnest, the dollar has appreciated rapidly—over 15 percent between September and November 2008. This appears to reaffirm the old cold war pattern. During much of that time the dollar's exchange rate also depended heavily on foreign support. But despite occasional periods of decline, foreigners remained willing to hold their rapidly increasing surplus of dollars as reserves useful for international transactions or as investments in the American economy. Why should the dollar's position be any less sustainable now than in the past?

The most obvious answer, as we have seen, is that the U.S. currency has lost two critical structural supports that formerly helped to sustain it: the Soviet threat and the absence of any plausible alternative reserve currency. The loss of these supports reflects new geopolitical realities—the disappearance of the Soviet Union and the rise of others, not least a more powerful and coordinated Europe, with its euro. From this perspective, the monetary crisis is, at heart, also a geopolitical crisis. Without the Soviets, the United States has lost its world role. As our experience in Afghanistan and Iraq suggests, America's lingering hegemonic power over friends and foes alike already seems considerably less than our political elites have imagined. As a result of our post-Soviet geopolitical decline, the overextended dollar, once a powerful economic complement to our global power, now threatens to be a major liability for ourselves and for the world in general.

Market forces do not seem to offer a comfortable way out. According to the customary laws of economics, a sharp depreciation of the dollar, especially when accompanied by a recession, should change American behavior. It should reduce consumption, give incentive to exports, and squeeze funding for military interventions. Accordingly, the current account should move toward balance. Eventually the dollar's exchange rate should stabilize and perhaps reverse, particularly if buying cheap dollars comes to seem an attractive speculation.

What stands in the way? Political scientists like to speak of "path dependency"—denial, inertia, the willful persistence of old habits. Americans, it appears, have grown deeply habituated to our exorbitant postwar privileges. Our political elites are addicted to managing the world. They have no intention of retreating from what they believe to be their historic duty. Grand imperial projects thus continue despite big fiscal deficits and a weak dollar. America's consumers are no less self-righteous and determined. Given our world position, saving seems an anachronism. Free-spending habits fuel our own national economy's exemplary growth and are critical to the rapid rise of the developing countries that export to us, above all China. Thus, our high consumption justifies itself. More saving would lower our own standard of living and impoverish the world. In short, since the orthodox cure for our unstable dollar and massive twin deficits appears to involve a diminishing of our military power in the world and our prosperity at home, not surprisingly we resist the cure. Instead of consuming less and exporting more, we prefer exporting more dollars.[52] We have long seen the world as unipolar; we will resist becoming a mere normal country.

Of course, taking a lesser role in a different world will depend not only on our own preferences but also on the world's broader economic and geopolitical trends. If a more plural geopolitical order is emerging, that implies a commensurate monetary framework. Indeed, the current global financial crisis may conceivably assign monetary policies a key role in shaping whatever new world order emerges. Just as Bretton Woods helped to crystallize the postwar hegemony of the United States over much of the global system, so the monetary order that emerges out of today's crisis may reflect and help organize a different hegemony or a more plural world.

## Toward a New World Monetary Framework?

The decline of American global hegemony does not automatically mean the hegemony of someone else. For those habituated to a unipolar view, it is perhaps less challenging intellectually to imagine some new superpower taking over from the old—something like the Pax Americana succeeding the Pax Britannica. But who now could succeed the United States as monetary hegemon? Of course, the issue is at least as much geopolitical as it is economic. If it were only economic, today's European Union does now have what might seem an ideal global currency. Like the dollar, the euro serves a very big market and, unlike the Federal Reserve, the European Central Bank is forbidden to underwrite the fiscal policies of the EU's member states. This makes the euro seem almost deliberately designed to play the role of global currency, particularly for an integrated but nonhegemonic system. Indeed, as Marcello

---

[52] See table 8.1 and figure 8.1.

de Cecco points out (chapter 6), the euro is today's functional equivalent of gold. But although, in theory, the European Union may have the necessary resources, universal cultural appeal, and attractive political formula needed to play a global hegemonic role, Europe's states do not have, or want, a centralized federal structure to gather and focus their power to manage the world. For now, European states still seem to lack the collective will to play such a role. Similarly, although China and probably India are on the way to becoming major global powers, neither has, as of yet, the resources, universalist pretensions, or ambitions of the West.

With the United States weakened and a new global hegemon unlikely, perhaps it is time to think seriously about a global constitutional order that is pluralist rather than hegemonic, one that better accommodates the increasingly diverse world in which we actually live. The United States will almost certainly remain a leading power in that world for the foreseeable future. Before a collapsing dollar presents the United States with stark and humiliating alternatives, a competent government ought to be able to negotiate a new world monetary framework with a decent resting place for the dollar. Few countries have any real interest in provoking the dollar's further collapse. But bringing order to an increasingly plural system will require multilateral and rules-based institutions that engage states in seeking common interests and in keeping disputes from growing unmanageable. Since World War II, the world has made great progress in building such institutions. In the early postwar era, globalist institution-building was principally the product of America's cold war hegemony, practicing its own multilateral ideology. The results were, among others, the United Nations, the World Bank, the International Monetary Fund, and the North Atlantic Treaty Organization.

In more recent decades European states have taken the lead, building with the European Union—an intensely integrated but more genuinely pluralist structure for their own region. That structure now comes complete with a common currency and technocratically managed central bank, but without the dominance of a leading state, whose "exorbitant privileges" bend the monetary system to a broader hegemonic agenda. Could such a technocratic structure be adapted to a global monetary system? Technocratic control over the world's money is an old idea found, for example, in John Maynard Keynes's plans for the IMF. In practice, however, the IMF has reflected the de facto hegemony not only of the dollar but of the United States in general. Could Europe's pluralist model now be adopted for an integrated global monetary system, in a world without the overwhelming American hegemony of the postwar era? Such a system, even if not managed unilaterally by Washington, might preserve the dollar as the principal global currency. But this probably would require, as Ronald McKinnon suggests, stabilizing the dollar by tying it, like the euro, to a Stability and Growth Pact.

For the United States, adopting Europe's monetary discipline—favoring lower inflation over higher growth—would have some of the same consequences as a continuing depreciation of the dollar. If the sharply devalued dollar turned the economy away from consumption and toward exporting, the standard of living would decline for much of the population. Economic costs would weigh more heavily on military and diplomatic decisions. As a consequence, American foreign policy might begin to look more "European," that is to say, more limited by the lack of resources and the consequent need for support from a broader consensus.[53] Conversely, Europe's foreign policy, if seriously allied with America, might itself grow more forceful. A renewed American—European global partnership, linking the dollar and the euro in dedication to monetary and fiscal balance, could provide a weighty balance wheel and regulator for an integrated global political economy. Like France and Germany in Europe, the EU and the United States might be able to exercise a leadership together that neither can expect to achieve alone.

After decades of adventurous and highly successful unilateralism, however, it is not easy to see America's political system remaining faithful to such a pact, unless compelled by the threat of a collapsing dollar. Writing in the early fall of 2008, crisis is raging around the world, and the consequences cannot be foreseen with confidence. The United States may well be compelled to evolve toward a more balanced macroeconomic policy. Probably, however, European states are more likely to preserve their monetarist discipline than the United States is to adopt it. Can Europe's own unity survive the crisis?

Europe's great experiment with monetary union is still in its early stages. A monetary bloc undoubtedly offers many advantages to European states, including some protection against the gyrations of unilateralist American policies. So far, moreover, the European Central Bank has responded deftly to the banking crisis. But Europe's states are still groping for the coordinating mechanisms and regulatory framework to end the chaotic conditions of recent weeks. They may, of course, fail. Events may move too quickly. Beyond the potential weakness of its monetary order, Europe has serious problems with high unemployment, flagging competitiveness, fiscal overstretch, aging populations, and immigration pressures. Insofar as European states cannot find consensus on broader political-economic policies, their monetary union will be troubled. And as other currencies remain highly unstable, Europeans may feel it necessary to imitate the Americans and manipulate their currency to

---

[53] See Kirshner (chapter 9).

improve their own commercial prospects. Meanwhile, environmental concerns and material shortages seem likely to prevent growth on the scale needed to accommodate the combined goals of the rich West and the hungry East. As Asian competition increasingly squeezes Western wages and profits, protectionism seems likely. How protectionism might affect future trade patterns is unclear. Given that the United States and Europe are competing to dominate high-tech industries and high-value-added services, monetary and trade relations across the Atlantic may take on a more mercantilist cast.

These uncertain prospects suggest a rethinking of fashionable globalist visions of the future. It may be wrong to imagine a world economy surpassing or even sustaining today's level of intense but relatively uncontrolled interdependence. Financial relations already show alarming signs of chaotic disorder—an overwhelming of the world's present capacity for integrated direction or even regulation. Given the difficulties of absorbing China and India into a closely integrated global system, or of reconciling the United States, Europe, or Japan to declining standards of living, it may be wiser to imagine a more articulated global order, one separated into a variety of regional systems. A region like Europe, whose states share strong collective institutions, has so far been able to negotiate the necessary rules and structures to sustain close economic integration, including even a common currency, and over a large and diverse area. Probably Europe's model will continue to inspire imitation elsewhere. But like the European Union itself, regional experiments sooner or later discover boundaries to the economic, political, and cultural consensus that sustains their union.

Perhaps the most likely outcome is a plural world articulated into a number of more or less coherently integrated blocs. Abrupt discontinuities of interest between such blocs will keep this global political economy a loose agglomeration of subsystems, with little immediate prospect of durable hegemony over them all. Nevertheless, economic conflicts among subsystems will have to be negotiated politically—and before they grow unmanageable and generate violent solutions. These negotiations should reflect a broader geopolitical vision—a global system consciously based on bargaining and mutual appeasement rather than hegemony. The monetary system is perhaps a good place to start embodying such a vision. There is no shortage of institutions for blocs to meet regularly to anticipate and negotiate their bargains. Harder to find will be the mutual modesty, self-restraint, and generosity needed to coexist together peacefully without a hegemon. The overriding challenge will be to make a plural world also collegial.

# 9

# AFTER THE (RELATIVE) FALL

## Dollar Diminution and the Consequences for American Power

Jonathan Kirshner

Why does it matter, for world politics in general but for American power in particular, if there is a diminution in the dollar's international role? Each of the chapters in this volume has addressed the question of the future of the dollar, and in particular whether there will be continuity or change in the dollar's role. I participate in this discussion, but I then turn to and focus on the more prospective question of geopolitical consequences. In broad brush, I expect a sudden contraction in the scope of the dollar's international role, probably in the wake of an international financial crisis. I expect a crisis to be resolved not by continuity but rather by change—due to the brittle prospects for international monetary cooperation, rooted in sharply divergent political preferences among those states whose cooperation would be necessary to smoothly reconstitute some variation on the status quo. Dollar diminution would significantly affect international power politics, in particular by presenting new and underappreciated restraints upon American political and military predominance.[1]

Author's note: I thank Eric Helleiner, Jerry Cohen, Herman Schwartz, Chris Way, Hubert Zimmerman, and all of the participants in the Cornell Dollar Workshops.

[1] The "system" here refers to the basic customs, understandings, routines, and practices by which international monetary affairs are conducted.

## Dollar Pessimism in Context

My baseline expectation is that a serious international financial crisis, set off by some unforeseen shock and snowballing as it implicates the dollar, will be met by a failure of international political cooperation that will both exacerbate the crisis and fail to contain and reconstitute the international monetary system in an orderly fashion. When the dust from this upheaval settles, the dollar will no longer be the undisputed and dominant international currency, but instead would become one of several key currencies that could be called "peer competitors." In such a future—the "leaderless currency system" predicted by Benjamin Cohen in chapter 7—the dollar would most probably remain the world's most widely used international currency. But its status would undergo a crucial and fundamental shift, in the framework developed by Susan Strange and elaborated by Eric Helleiner, from a "top" currency to a "negotiated" currency.[2]

These expectations are *contra* those of Ronald McKinnon and especially of Harold James in this book, and largely in agreement with the contributions of Cohen and David Calleo—and in particular with the factors that those authors stress: the ambitions of other states, the problem of very high levels of American consumption, and the crucial role that politics does and will play in shaping the pattern of international monetary relations. I part company with Calleo and Cohen in my expectation of a sudden rather than a gradual contraction of the dollar's international role—but it is important to emphasize that the consequences for U.S. power and world politics will be similar, if perhaps less immediately salient, if the change does take place at the slower pace they anticipate. That is, my expectation is that a dollar crisis will lead to a sudden, rather than a gradual, contraction in the dollar's international role, but, absent such a crisis, I expect a gradual diminution of the dollar's international role with similar if less dramatically apparent consequences.

James's excellent and well-reasoned chapter makes four strong arguments in favor of continuity: (1) the continuing attractiveness of the enormous and sophisticated U.S. economy, both in terms of its size and stability, a claim supported by evidence that foreign investors understand that they "buy security in return for lower yields" when they invest in the United States; (2) the "cry and sigh" syndrome, whereby the death of the dollar has been repeatedly (and erroneously) forewarned, here supported by data that the international use of the dollar has fallen in the past, only to rebound; (3) the fact that China,

---

[2]  Strange 1971b. Other dollar "pessimists," with emphases on the consequences for power politics and the likelihood of sudden change, include Thompson 2007 and Wade 2003, esp. 79, 86.

with its enormous dollar holdings, has every incentive to support rather than undermine the greenback; (4) the conclusion that "the United States remains the world's largest concentration of political and military might as well as of economic potential."

McKinnon buttresses the case for sustainability by adding arguments about inertia and natural monopoly, and with his sophisticated variation on the instrumental interpretation, which he finds rooted not in Asian mercantilism but in the important role of the dollar as a monetary anchor for these states.[3] For McKinnon, to safeguard their economic well-being, surplus countries are "trapped into acquiring dollar assets from the savings deficient United States." And since exchange rate adjustments will not resolve trade deficits anyway (an important argument that I think is right on the economics but underestimates the role of expectations and is crucially wrong on the politics, issues I return to below), the entire arrangement is sustainable.

The two principal bases of my disagreement with James and McKinnon are that their analyses are not wrong, but static, and that they give insufficient weight to crucial geopolitical factors. On the first point, these deductive arguments about sustainability make sense in the abstract at almost any particular point in time. But surely there is some threshold, if unknown a priori, at which point the dollar's position becomes unsustainable. An essential variable, then, in shaping expectations about the dollar are the dynamics—what is the trend? Even though major recession in the United States has done what nothing else could do—tamped down domestic demand and reduced the size of America's current account deficits—these deficits are still large and ongoing and financed by the continued accumulation of dollar assets abroad. And a fundamental question is, how robust is the current system? That is, if disturbed, would current arrangements tend to self- correct or to unravel? McKinnon may be right that "as long as the American price level remains stable, there is no well-defined ex-ante restraint on the amount that the U.S. can borrow internationally." But again, this does not mean that there is no limit, even if that limit is poorly defined. Rather, the dollar seems primed for a Wile E. Coyote moment—it can keep going until holders suddenly look down and realize that there is no ground underneath. As McKinnon notes, if, for some reason, the monetary anchor strategy was abandoned, it "would leave the dollar in free fall."

In general, arguments for sustainability that appeal to some version of a Bretton Woods II–type argument need to address the unnerving fact that, however plausible this envisioning of the international monetary system,

---

[3] On natural monopoly, see Kindleberger 1967.

Bretton Woods I collapsed. Jeffrey Frankel and others suggest that there is good reason to believe we are much closer to 1971 than to 1944—and in 1971 the United States had a current account *surplus* and capital mobility was considerably less than it is today. How close might we be to the edge? Without a push, it's hard to say. "Fixed exchange rates with heavy intervention," Lawrence Summers observes, "have enormous capacity to create an illusory sense of stability that could be shattered very quickly."[4]

What then, does this mean for the future of the international role of the dollar? The willingness of actors to hold and rely on dollars (or any international money) depend on three calculations: some confidence that the dollar will retain its value and stability indefinitely into the future; an assessment of the attractiveness of the dollar compared to plausible alternatives; an additional calculation on the part of public authorities assessing the political implications of the use of international currencies.

For the first time, in each of these three foundations, cracks are visible and widening. This is obvious with regard to expectations about the future of the dollar, and just as important, guesses about what other people are guessing about its future value. The American trade deficit reached an all-time high of $166 billion in 1998, increased by 60 percent in the following year, and then set a new record in each of the first six years of the twenty-first century, reaching $758 billion in 2006. As a percentage of GDP, the U.S. current account deficits have reached annual levels at or above 6.5 percent—more than 1 percent of global GDP—and they absorb almost two-thirds of the current account surpluses of all the world's surplus countries. As Summers notes, "All of these figures are without precedent."[5]

As suggested above, for the dollar, in the near term, one possible "silver lining" of the serious recession in the United States is that it has inhibited the magnitude of those external deficits. Nevertheless, at a minimum, the still massive and cumulating imbalances in American external accounts are much more consistent with expectations of a long-run trajectory of depreciation rather than of appreciation. Nor do other variables suggest confidence. U.S. net national savings, which averaged about 10 percent in the 1960s, 8 percent in the 1970s, and 4 percent in the 1980s, has in recent years continued to fall, scraping close to 1 percent of GDP, its lowest rate in American history. (In this context, shifting the blame to a "global savings glut," an interpretation championed by Federal Reserve chairman Ben Bernanke, sounds like an alcoholic

---

[4] Frankel 2006, 658; Summers 2004, 9–10.
[5] Obstfeld and Rogoff 2004, 1, 5, 7, 18; Mussa 2005, 175–76, 186, 194–95, 201–3; Cline 2005, 3, 66, 85, 99, 154, 168–71, 275–77; Edwards 2005, 2–3, 11–12, 26, 40–42; Summers 2004, 3 (quote), 4. Trade deficit figures are from the U.S. Census Bureau, Foreign Trade Division, June 8, 2007.

on a bender insisting it's just that everybody else isn't drinking enough.) Public sector trends offer no respite: although James rightly points out that other advanced industrial countries face similar problems, he notes that fiscal problems in the United States (from a 1.3% surplus in 2000 to a 4.9% deficit in 2004) "pose a long-term threat", a threat that will only loom larger as a result of the massive stimulus packages the United States will need to stabilize its reeling economy. In sum, as Cohen argues, "the probability that the dollar can long avoid a significant loss of confidence is sadly low."[6]

Despite the proliferation of red flags about the future trajectory of the dollar, the greenback is still *relatively* attractive as an international currency. The political stability of the United States, its enormous and dynamic economy, its rich and deep financial markets and institutions—not to mention simple inertia—give the dollar profound advantages over potential competitors. The star of the Japanese yen, one-time heir apparent to the dollar, has faded considerably; the Chinese yuan is a very long way from being ready for prime time, and political rivalry between the two states will complicate the emergence of either currency. The euro bears its own political, economic, and institutional burdens, and it is still finding its voice. Nevertheless, underlying trends again point away from the dollar. Whatever its current limitations, the euro does represent "the first real competitor" to the dollar, and in the longer run other states do aspire to greater international use of their currencies— and thus will be alert to opportunities that present themselves. The key point is that there are more alternatives now (and likely increasingly) than there were in the past—and the dollar does not need to be supplanted for there to a consequential contraction in its international role.[7]

Finally, and crucially, there has been a basic change in the political contours of the international monetary system, and this has seriously weakened the dollar's third pillar of support: political calculations on the part of other states and their preferences regarding international money (and the intensity of those preferences). Politics has always and will continue to shape the monetary order—dollar optimist James notes how the United States (and Britain in the sterling system) pressured military dependencies to support its currency. Yet as Calleo notes, with the Soviets gone and the euro in place, "since the end of the cold war both the strategic and financial imperatives that compelled others to sustain the dollar have faded." Once again, this suggests an underlying weakness that could suddenly be revealed under stress. And periodic stress is typical in international monetary affairs. But resolving disequi-

---

[6] Bernanke 2005; Congressional Research Service 1994; Summers 2004, 6.

[7] Cohen 2004; McNamara and Meunier 2002; Eichengreen 2005b, 7–8. On the euro as a peer competitor, see Bergsten 1997, 83 (quote); Henning and Carlo 2000, 22–28; Henning 2006, 130.

libria in international monetary affairs requires some determination about how the considerable burdens of adjustments will be distributed. As Robert Gilpin has argued, such "adjustment mechanisms do and will reflect the interests of powerful states and groups." In the most recent major episodes, the unilateral (1971) and coordinated (1985) adjustments involving the dollar took place between the United States, western Europe, and Japan. Following Helleiner's analysis (chapter 4), follower states in the dollar order at those times had a high level of political commitment to the greenback. All of the main players in both 1971 and 1985 were political and military allies of the United States. During the cold war, then, macroeconomic conflicts took place exclusively between friends, and beyond that the high politics of the bipolar world order served as an "emergency break" that placed a limit on just how far monetary squabbles between the Western allies could go.[8]

Current global macroeconomic imbalances are greater today than they were in 1971 or 1985, suggesting that states will at some point be confronted with an urgent need to coordinate a response, negotiate a burden-sharing agreement, or, failing that, duck for cover. If a currency crisis emerges, or if and when international negotiations take place over the nature of the international monetary order, the high political context will be profoundly different. Certainly China, as well as other states more easily defined as military and political adversaries of the United States than as allies, would have to play an important role; and even old friends in Europe, eyeing a greater international role for the euro and sensing less geopolitical harmony with unipolar America, will less instinctively rush to the dollar's defense, willingly shoulder fewer costs, and likely extract a higher price for any future support of the dollar.[9]

Although it is not certain that an international financial crisis that implicates the dollar will occur, the preconditions for such a crisis are certainly in place—there may not be a party, but the room has been rented, the band has been hired, and the caterer engaged; all that is left is for the invitations to go out. Paradoxically, one legacy of the dollar's historical attractiveness is that it has increased its vulnerability. Because the U.S. dollar has served as the world's "key currency," there are an enormous amount of dollars held abroad.[10] China, Japan, and other states in East Asia hold, literally, trillions in highly liquid dollar-denominated assets. Many others, including Saudi Arabia, also have significant dollar reserves.[11] Thus, if there was a spark, some-

---

[8] Gilpin 2001, 245; Kirshner 2003.

[9] Zimmerman 2004; Walter 1999; Katada 2002; Bowles 2002.

[10] For discussions of the economic and political origins and maintenance of the contemporary international dollar order, see McKinnon 2005a and Schwartz 2003, 333, 343, 345, 348.

[11] Genberg et al. 2005; Murray and Labonte 2005; Burdekin 2006, 6; Truman and Wong 2006.

where, that touched off a financial crisis that implicated the dollar, given the state of underlying expectations about its future value, and the number of greenbacks (and other dollar liabilities) out there, a tidal wave of dollars could flood the market. In the aftermath of this much larger crisis, the United States would find itself, suddenly, in a very different international financial position.

Is the global financial crisis of autumn 2008 that crisis? It is too soon to tell (events are still unfolding as I write this), but I suspect not. Mitigating against a run on the dollar in response to the crisis of 2008 are the truly global nature of the upheaval, recasting the crisis as a global rather than an American one (and limiting safe haven options); the related manifestation of salient international interdependencies; and the likelihood that public authorities abroad holding dollars could see little to gain in taking actions against the greenback narrowly that would most certainly exacerbate an already extremely serious global financial crisis.[12] However, although it does not appear likely at this time, such an unraveling could still occur as an aftershock of this crisis, or in the wake of a subsequent crisis that is more limited to the dollar. In any event, the U.S. financial crisis of fall 2008, and the resources committed to the bailout (the famous $700 billion, for openers) can't possibly add to confidence in the dollar. Rather, just the opposite; it will, when the dust settles, raise still further doubts about the robustness of the U.S. economy (and thus the dollar), and these new additions to the U.S. federal debt will further highlight already doubtful expectations about the long-term trajectory of the value of the dollar. In sum, those actors planning, over time, to diversify their portfolios away from the dollar probably view that strategy as even more wise now than they did before.

Thus, as a result of this crisis, or a subsequent crisis, or from the long-term consequences and expectations of the way the crisis was contained, it is even more likely that there will be in the coming years a relative contraction, rather than a maintenance (or relative expansion), of the dollar's international role. Indeed, the former prime minister of Thailand has already called on the big dollar holders in East Asia to create an "Asian bond to contain the fallout from a weak dollar," and to hold their reserves in the form of those bonds.[13]

In sum, if not this crisis (for reasons outlined above), a future crisis involving the dollar would be suddenly transformative of the dollar's interna-

---

[12] On the global nature of the crisis, see, for example, Chris Giles et al., "Markets Routed in Global Sell Off," *Financial Times,* October 6, 2008; David Jolly and Keith Bradsher, "European and Asian Stocks Fall Sharply," *New York Times,* October 7, 2008; Carter Dougherty, Nelson Schwartz, and Floyd Norris, "Financial Crises Spread in Europe," *New York Times,* October 7, 2008; Andrew Wood and John Aglionby, "Shares Tumble in Black Day for Asia Markets," *Financial Times,* October 8, 2008.

[13] Thaksin Shinawatra, "An Asian Bond Could Save Us from the Dollar," *Financial Times,* October 6, 2008.

tional role because of the distinct political context in which international political efforts to contain the crisis and then reconstitute the international monetary system would take place. In particular, the role of the dollar from the perspective of actors in Asia, Europe, and the Middle East would be reevaluated. Moreover (and again, here in accord with Calleo and Cohen), *even in the absence of such a sudden crisis* the hardening of political fault lines regarding the dollar in each of these three regions suggest a long-run trajectory of a relative contraction of the dollar's international role.

## The Brittle Politics of Contemporary Monetary Cooperation

In general, international monetary relations are predisposed toward discord even when states recognize the benefits of coordinating their policies. Different national circumstances and contrasting beliefs about the economic attractiveness of various arrangements and regimes complicate negotiations. When understandings are reached, they are often fragile, because ultimately they entail distributing the burdens of macroeconomic adjustment, and thus implicate basic decisions about domestic monetary policy, growth, stability, and distribution. And due to the public nature of macroeconomic externalities (interest rate changes, for example, have a general effect on the international economy), macroeconomic "bads" tend to be overprovided and are relatively difficult to contain.[14]

This provides the context for international monetary relations in the best of circumstances, and the politics of the coming years, as the dollar's fate is being determined, suggest anything but the best of circumstances. Indeed, the contemporary system is conditioned for conflict. The problem is more subtle, and more ingrained, than often characterized. The danger comes not from fire (things like boat-rocking confrontations about dumping dollars, or wars to protect the hegemony of the greenback), but from ice: continual unresolved monetary disagreements that dissatisfy all sides and increasingly calcify international monetary relations, making it less and less likely that currency problems and crises, when they arise (as they will), will be resolved cooperatively.

Concerns have been raised that China might threaten to dump its enormous dollar holdings as an act of political coercion against the United States. This possibility is severely circumscribed, however, because it is not in China's interest to do so. China has not been accumulating dollars as an act of phil-

---

[14] Cooper 1975; Keynes 1971 [1930], 272; Oye 1992.

anthropy, but rather as a calculation of national interest. Despite its remarkable record of economic growth, China's economy has visible fragilities, especially with regard to the weakness of its financial sector and importance of
exports to the United States. Significant dollar depreciation would be a blow
to China's economy; a collapse in the dollar that caused a recession in the
United States or undercut its ability to finance imports would be a disaster.
Thus, China could conceivably dump its dollars, but this would be the economic equivalent of the nuclear option. It is possible to imagine scenarios, especially regarding confrontations over Taiwan, where China might engage in
dollar brinksmanship or even pull the currency trigger—based on the gam-
ble that the United States would be hurt even more than China would be.
Short of that, however, China's vested interest in the dollar undercuts the potential political advantages of such a gambit.[15] And other than the "nuclear
option," more modest efforts at currency manipulation of the dollar by China
(presumably in the service of less ambitious goals) would be an extremely
risky strategy, given the rapid and unpredictable ways in which financial crises
can develop and get out of control.[16]

Nevertheless, more routine and quite consequential exchange rate conflict
between the United States and China is likely to emerge. From 1994 to 2005
the renminbi traded at the fixed rate of 8.28 yuan/dollar, and Chinese authorities have intervened heavily in the market, purchasing dollars to sustain
the yuan peg. In July 2005 China shifted the management of the RMB from
a hard dollar peg to an unspecified basket of currencies, which initially revalued the yuan by about 2 percent against the dollar, to 8.11, and was then followed by a slow but steady appreciation, with the yuan trading at 7.3 at the
end of 2007. China's exchange rate policies, massive dollar purchases (which
do seem to violate IMF provisions against protracted, one-sided interventions in the market), and enormous and burgeoning trade surplus with the
United States have led to considerable agitation in the United States for much
more ambitious action on the exchange rate front.[17]

Unfortunately, while the yuan is certainly overvalued (in that absent any
intervention, it would appreciate), as McKinnon has argued here and elsewhere, changes in the exchange rate will have little effect on the balance of
trade between the United States and China. There are a number of technical

---

[15] A similar conclusion is reached in Liss 2008, 29, 32–33.

[16] Note, however, that for the dollar the China problem is overstated, but not nonexistent. If the
dollar does continue on a trajectory of depreciation, which seems more likely than not, Chinese authorities will eventually decide that it is in their interest to diversity their reserve portfolio; this will
further weaken the dollar, and this in turn will reinforce the decision to cautiously ease off dollar holdings.

[17] Goldstein and Lardy 2007.

reasons for this, but in broad brush China's trade surpluses with the United States are to some extent natural—given the characteristics of each economy and the relative stages of development of the two countries. Even if U.S. trade was in balance overall, it would likely have a deficit with China. And beyond that, China's surpluses are largely a function of the differential savings and consumption rates between the two countries. As long as these disparities continue, U.S. external accounts will remain unbalanced. A dramatic change in the yuan/dollar rate would be more likely to have a larger effect on the composition of U.S.-China trade than it would on its overall balance. As the U.S. Congressional Budget Office concluded, "China's exchange rate policy has only a modest influence on the overall trade deficit."[18]

Nevertheless, the United States is likely to press for yuan appreciation. Monetary relations between the United States and Japan during the cold war illustrate the types of problems that will aggravate future Sino-American exchange rate politics: the failure of exchange rate movements to resolve trade imbalances and the absence of a shared security vision to serve as an inhibitor of monetary conflict. During the first two decades of the cold war, the United States was eager to stimulate the development of the Japanese economy. Pressure built, however, by the end of the 1960s, as the undervalued yen and overvalued dollar produced large sustained trade surpluses with the United States. In the 1970s, with détente and the easing of the cold war, the United States pressed repeatedly for yen appreciation in an effort to stem the flood of inexpensive Japanese imports, while Japan desperately resisted, often intervening in foreign exchange markets to limit yen appreciation. In fits and starts, from 1971 to 1978 the yen appreciated from 360 to the dollar to 180 to the dollar, although trade remained imbalanced. This pattern was later repeated with the resurgence and then end of the cold war during the 1980s, with trade frictions contributing to demands for yen appreciation, which again failed to resolve the trade balance (but contributed to Japan's economic malaise during the 1990s.)[19]

The United States will routinely call for revaluation of the RMB, demands that will grow more strident during challenging phases of the business cycle. But China will resist, more forcefully and successfully than did Japan. Moreover, since I agree with McKinnon regarding the (limited) influence of the exchange rate on the trade balance, even when the RMB is revalued, the basic

[18] Statement of Douglas Holtz Eakin, director, Congressional Budget Office, "Economic Relationships between the United States and China," before the Committee on Ways and Means, U.S. House of Representatives, April 14, 2005, quote; see also Hale and Hale 2008, 57, 62; Goldberg and Dillon 2007.
[19] McKinnon and Ohno 1997. For a more elaborate discussion of the influence of the cold war on U.S-Japan monetary relations, see Kirshner 2007b.

problem will remain the same, and soon enough the United States will come knocking for another revaluation. But rather than suggesting sustainability, as policymakers learn not to fret about the exchange rate, the dollar/yuan controversy will not go away, and the limited influence of the exchange rate will instead serve as a constant irritant in Sino-American relations.

China will be more inclined, and more capable, of resisting appreciation than Japan was during the cold war. Authorities in Beijing will view exchange rate policy through the lenses of its somewhat more balanced global trade accounts, the desire to retain the stability of the RMB as a welcome policy anchor for its unbridled domestic economy, and an acute sensitivity to the weakness of its internal financial sector. As de Cecco neatly suggests, although contemporary China is often compared to late nineteenth-century Germany, in many ways it is similar to the American economy during the first blush of its ascendancy, with a booming industrial sector and backward financial sector—as illustrated by the terrible banking crises of 1893 and 1907 that upended the American economy. In any event, in the words of one observer, China "clearly intends to maintain tight control over the pace at which the RMB appreciates."[20]

In sum, the United States will continue to press for yuan revaluation; moreover, American demands will not be a one time thing, since there will inevitably be disappointment about the results of any changes that are made. At the same time, China will resist U.S. pressure; if faced with credible threats of significant American protectionism, it will probably make grudging adjustments. But monetary conflict will be chronic, and become acute at the worst possible (economic) times, and, unlike the U.S.-Japan relationship, there is no "emergency break" of high politics to contain macroeconomic squabbles. Moreover, current arrangements seem fragile—as Calleo argues, "expecting China to go on indefinitely accumulating vast quantities of surplus dollars seems an uncertain prospect," and sustained dollar depreciation will at some point influence these choices as well.

Further complicating matters, especially over the years, will be China's own monetary ambitions, and this will further color the way in which Beijing views both the dollar and international monetary conflict. Although the yuan is far from ready to take on an important international role, as Cohen notes, China's long-run strategy certainly "includes a wider role for the RMB."[21] For

[20] McKinnon 2005a, 10–11, 129, 147, 248; McKinnon 2006; Goldstein and Lardy 2007, 12, 18, 20, 22, sift through many of these issues with less alarm; see Leverett 2008 for quote.

[21] See also Leverett 2008, who notes that "Chinese officials speak privately about their longer-term ambitions to form an Asian economic 'zone' organized around China, in which the RMB would emerge as a leading transactional and reserve currency"; Chin and Helleiner (2008) also anticipate that China will, over time, emerge as a financial power.

a host of reasons, then, Sino-American currency conflicts will thus be harder to resolve, and any understandings reached will be brittle.

Although relations between the United States and its traditional allies and friends in Europe are certainly much warmer, better, and more robust than they are with China (even assuming an optimistic trajectory for Sino-American relations), nevertheless, in international monetary affairs the reservoir of goodwill they share is shallower than at any time since World War II. The dollar has already depreciated considerably against the euro, in fits and starts from 1.1 to 1.3 from the end of 2002 to the end of 2004, and then, after recovering to 1.2 in 2005, falling like a stone over the following two years, reaching 1.5. And as a number of scholars have noted, with many countries linked to the dollar, those currencies that float freely against the dollar will bear a disproportionate burden of the downward pressure on the value of the dollar.[22]

Three factors, then, have left little space for monetary cooperation between the United States and Europe and calcified likely perspectives if and when there is a pressing (or even latent) need to address the problems of the dollar. First, given the extent of the euro's appreciation against the dollar that has already taken place, it is hard to imagine there is much more give in that direction. Second, with the end of the cold war, and especially with the Iraq War and general divergence of the geopolitical visions of the United States and Europe during this century, monetary coordination, so dependent on international political foundations, would likely become more difficult under any circumstances. Finally, whatever the relative weaknesses of the euro as an international currency, the appetite for greater structural monetary power and ambitions for the euro to play a greater international role are certainly there. Thus, a crisis of the dollar may look to many less like an opportunity to rally around the greenback and more like the moment for the euro to grab a larger share of the limelight.[23]

Cohen has identified East Asia and the Middle East as "two battlegrounds" over the use of international money—in the latter arena, he writes, "Europe could understandably be tempted to seek a greater role for the euro." This raises yet another source of potential vulnerability for the dollar. However (as Cohen also notes), there is some confusion with regard to this aspect of the high politics of the dollar, typically related to the idea that the United States might use force in an effort to impose the use of the dollar on others; it is occasionally suggested (without foundation) that the United States went to war

[22] Roach 2003, 8; Wyplosz 2003, 8; Barysch 2004, 31; Summers 2004, 9.
[23] On increasing political space between Europe and the United States, see Kupchan 2002; Pape 2005; 7–45; on euro ambitions, see notes 8 and 10 above; on latent competition for structural monetary power, see Helleiner 2006a.

in Iraq to protect the international role of the greenback.[24] But there is simply no plausible logic that can connect the dots between this preference and the decision to go to war.[25] In fact, the opposite is true. Although, conceivably, the United States could through conquest and colonization impose the use of the dollar on foreign subjects under its rule, such measures would undermine, not advance, the global role of the dollar. The decision to use the dollar internationally is determined first and foremost by anonymous investors scattered throughout the globe—to the apolitical investor, the costs of war and occupation make the dollar marginally less attractive, not more attractive. The decision to price oil in dollars is determined by oil producers making a political-economic calculation about their best interests—here again, except for those directly conquered, U.S. wars would more plausibly nudge such states away from the dollar, not toward it.[26]

Dismissing half-baked conspiracy theories does not mean that there are not real stakes over the future of the dollar here. And these stakes have been recognized: it is indeed the case that the United States prefers that the price of oil is denominated in dollars—during the Carter administration, the United States went to considerable and secret diplomatic lengths to assure that this would be sustained.[27] James notes that the denomination of commodity prices in dollars (a function of the size of the U.S. market) provides "an obvious rationale for many countries to continue to hold reserves in dollars." Thus, a change in that denomination would erode the dollar's international role. Even though the commercial ties of Middle Eastern countries are oriented more toward Europe than the United States, Cohen does not expect the Europeans to pick a fight with the United States over this issue. But he does conclude that a "battle of currencies in the Middle East could get nasty."[28] It is not necessary to anticipate a strategic thrust by Europe to con-

[24] This argument is advanced in Clark 2005. For a good place to start to sift thoughtfully through some of these issues, see Momani 2008. Momani argues that the use of dollars in the oil trade is an important source of support for the dollar as an international currency, and she also concludes that the U.S. security guarantees to the region, in particular the Carter doctrine and the first Gulf War, play a role in shaping the incentives gulf oil exporters face in using the dollar. But the second Gulf War was different (298), and, if anything, contributed to a reassessment of the oil-dollar link. Momani concludes that gulf states are inhibited by either capacity or preference in taking steps that would undermine the dollar (295, 297, 309); see also Essayyad and Algahtani 2005.

[25] On diplomacy of the dollar after the Iraq War, see Taylor 2007, esp. 212; on prewar currency manipulation, see Kirshner 2006.

[26] If preserving the international role of the dollar was such a high national priority that it was worth going to war over, the United States had a much more powerful and less expensive option available—reducing the federal budget deficit. But the Iraq War—with uncertain consequences on third-country dollar choices at best—made those federal deficits even larger.

[27] Spiro 1999, 121–24; Momani 2008, 293, 296.

[28] See also Leverett 2008, and Essayyad and Algahtani 2005, 73–74, on the erosion of enthusiasm for the dollar in the Middle East.

clude that the conditions are again in place for a positive feedback loop that would reinforce any dollar difficulties that might surface in the coming years, and accelerate a decline in the international use of the dollar.

Changes in economics and politics as they relate to the international pricing of oil represent the third important calcification of contemporary international monetary relations. The economic indicators suggest that the dollar is vulnerable to crisis and ripe for the contraction of its international use, if not suddenly, then gradually. The political preconditions for dollar diminution are also in place—discord over international monetary affairs and more wary political relations among all the key players, which have set in place preconditions, in Europe, Asia, and the Middle East, that do not in and of themselves threaten the dollar, but leave the now vulnerable dollar without the mechanisms of support that would have sustained it through difficult times in the past. The stage seems set for a contraction of the international role of the greenback. How does that matter?

## Dollar Primacy and Its Contents

Assessing the consequences of dollar diminution rests on two questions— one "static" and the other "dynamic." The first question asks abstractly, "What are the costs and benefits to a country when its currency of issue is used extensively abroad"? The answer depends on the levers of power (and possibly their cost) that accrue to a "key currency," and that the United States therefore stands to lose, or at least will be less able to employ. The second question asks more specifically, "What (if any) costs will the United States bear as a result of the transition away from dollar primacy?" The answer to this question describes the price that comes from losing one's perch upon the throne, which, as elaborated below, is a separate matter and one that is more contingent on the specific attributes and political and economic context of the transition.

Each of these issues leads the analysis back to the 1960s. In the '60s, concerns about the sustainability of the Bretton Woods system, along with political tensions among its participants, stimulated a wave of academic literature on the costs and benefits of serving as the "world's currency." At the same time, (actually, from the '50s through the '70s), Britain was confronted with the challenges of managing sterling as it faded from its international role, which also attracted considerable academic attention. Although there are fundamental differences between then and now with regard to each of these issues, the general contours of the analysis remain similar.

The debate in the 1960s was inspired by French critiques of the political implications of the dollar-centric international monetary system, a gold exchange standard where the greenback was designed to be used as the underlying reserve asset, in lieu of gold. Charles de Gaulle, to a large extent shopping for an issue that would provide a lever against American political influence, campaigned against the gold exchange standard and the "extraordinary advantage" it provided to the United States: "What it owes abroad, it pays for, at least partially, with dollars which it alone can issue." His chief economic advisor, Jacques Rueff, spoke of a deficit "without tears"—as the issuer of reserve currency, the United States could run a balance of payments deficit more or less indefinitely without facing the pressure that would be imposed automatically on other countries. With discord between the United States and its European allies over the Vietnam War, and the inflationary financing of the war, these disputes became more acute.[29]

Most observers readily agreed that the United States enjoyed advantages from its role at the center of the international monetary system, but there was considerable debate at the time about the magnitude of the gains, and about the extent to which these gains were mitigated by, or were even smaller than, the costs associated with managing the world's money. Scholars at the time considered the principal benefits that accrue to a reserve country currency to be seigniorage (the difference between the cost of creating new money—including interest payments—and its face value), balance of payments flexibility, and competitive advantages for the domestic financial services sector. The principal costs derived from the loss of discretion over aspects of macroeconomic policy. Some scholars argued that, to assure confidence in the fixed gold-dollar link, the United States was inhibited in the practice of expansionist monetary policies and was required to maintain higher interest rates than it would otherwise have needed to. As the hub of the fixed exchange rate system, the United States also could not resort to a balance of payments remedy readily available to other states—devaluation. These points were debated at some length, with competing conclusions often deriving from difficulties in reaching practical measurements of seigniorage and of the costs of constraints on U.S. policy.[30]

The demise of the Bretton Woods system in 1971 took the wind from the sails of the debate over the costs and benefits of the dollar-centric interna-

[29] General Charles de Gaulle, eleventh press conference, February 4, 1965, in de Gaulle 1967, 80; Rueff 1972, 78; Memorandum from Secretary of the Treasury Fowler to President Johnson, "Balance of Payments—1966," May 10, 1966, in U.S Department of State 1998, 257–62; Zimmerman 2002, 177–78.

[30] The most comprehensive assessment of the costs and benefits can be found in Cohen 1971a, chap. 2. See also Salant 1964; Aliber 1964; Grubel 1964; Karlik 1968.

tional monetary order. With no fixed rates to protect, there was no explicit need to hold dollars at all—and with no obligation to hold dollars, it was hard to level the charge of exploitation. Nor did the United States seem to be in any position to exploit the dollar: severed from the last vestiges of the cord that linked it to gold, the greenback tumbled in value. As noted, dollar depreciation is distinct from the dollar's international role, but it did influence perceptions about American power. From the official postwar rate of $35 to an ounce of gold that anchored the international monetary system, the dollar fell to $65/oz. in 1972 and $100/oz. in 1973 and approached $200/oz. in 1974. In the context of broader discussions about American decline, experts talked not of U.S. monetary power, but rather were more likely to proclaim that "the dollar is finished as international money"; and the international monetary disorder of the 1970s was attributed to declining American power.[31]

However, and especially in retrospect, it is much easier to argue that a huge chunk of "American decline" in the early 1970s was due not to the consequence of sectoral trends and the inevitable tides of history, but to bad domestic policies (a lack of macroeconomic discipline) and worse luck (the oil shocks).[32] Looking beyond the monetary disorder of the decade and revisiting the costs and benefits of issuing key currency reveals that the shift to floating exchange rates actually enhanced the prospects for the United States to gain from its position at the center of the international monetary order. By cutting itself loose from the obligations of the system, the Americans shed the costs of serving as the world's currency without significantly reducing the benefits. With regard to costs, no longer did U.S. macroeconomic policy need to be sensitive to the need to assure (however abstractly) the official gold-dollar link. No longer was it recused from employing or allowing devaluation (now depreciation) to take pressure off the dollar (and reduce the real burden of dollar-denominated debts). And no longer was it vulnerable, as it was throughout the 1960s, to efforts by states (such as France) to exploit weaknesses in the gold exchange standard as the Achilles' heel of American international power.[33]

In sum, as Susan Strange observed, "To decide one August morning that dollars can no longer be converted into gold was a progression from exorbitant privilege to super-exorbitant privilege; the U.S. government was exercis-

---

[31] Kindleberger 1976, 35 (quote); Krasner 1978, 82, "the fragility of the international monetary system is inherently related to the declining international power of the US." See also Kennedy 1987, 434.

[32] Nau 1990, 154–57; Keohane 1982, 11.

[33] On greater U.S. discretion and an increase in the excess return of its gross assets over gross liabilities after Bretton Woods, see Gourinchas and Rey 2005, 4, 10, 16, 25. On France's "strategic disruption" of the international monetary system in the 1960s, see Kirshner 1995, 192–203.

ing the unconstrained right to print money that others could not (save at un-acceptable cost) refuse to accept in payment."[34]

Thus, while shedding the costs of the dollar standard, given that, in prac-tice, there was still a considerable demand for international currency, the United States still enjoyed the benefits associated with the primacy of the dol-lar. Technically, the United States probably gained less seigniorage than be-fore, but the evidence strongly suggests that such seigniorage was always modest and not a significant source of power.[35] Two other sources of power, however, remained robust: the greater flexibility afforded the issuer of inter-national money, as well as something that was not emphasized in the 1960s debate—structural power. These two benefits remain the key perks of issu-ing international currency, and it is the loss of balance of payments flexibil-ity and the erosion of structural power that the United States stands to lose if significant dollar diminution takes place in the future.[36]

## Autonomy and Structural Power

During the 1960s it was understood that the "principal advantage" of the Bret-ton Woods system for the United States was that its balance of payments defi-cits "can be financed in part through increases in the dollar reserves held by foreign monetary authorities." To the extent that its deficits are financed in part by increased holdings of dollar reserves abroad, the United States could run larger balance of payments deficits than other states; moreover, and perhaps with even greater consequences, "it [could] take greater risks in adopting economic policies that might have adverse effects on the balance-of-payments."[37] This remains true for as long as the dollar retains its attrac-tiveness abroad; today, the principal overt benefits that the United States enjoys from the international role of the dollar are the ability to sustain defi-cits on its international accounts that others cannot, and the related and cru-cial ability not simply to run deficits at a certain magnitude but to take risks and adopt economic policies that would, anywhere else, elicit a withering "disciplinary" response from international financial markets.

The key currency role of the dollar also provides the United States not with only overt power via its enhanced autonomy and discretion, it increases the

---

[34] Strange 1987, 569; see also Calleo 1982, 63, 65, 78; Aubrey 1969, 16.

[35] McKinnon 1969, 5, 17, 21–22; Grubel 1969; Cohen 1971b; Kirschen 1974.

[36] The United States would also enjoy reduced international monetary power—that is, the ability to advance its interests by taking advantage of its position in the international monetary system. For a thoughtful overview of the nature of monetary power, see Andrews 2006; see also Cohen 2006b, esp. 31, 36, 45; and Kirshner 1995.

[37] Salant 1964, 165 (quotes); 166 (quote); Aliber 1964, 445, 454; Rueff and Hirsch 1965, 2–3.

political influence and capacity of the United States, via what has been called "structural power." There are two distinct (if related) strands of thought on structural power that are relevant here, one associated with Susan Strange and the other with Albert Hirschman.

Strange's conception of structural power owes something to Woody Allen; as with aspiring playwrights, for hegemons, 90 percent of structural power is just showing up. Simply by its enormous size, a dominant state creates the context in which political interactions take place—often without even the intention of doing so. Thus, for example, any discussion of the international monetary system takes place in the context of dollar primacy. Of course, structural power can also be quite purposeful, although it is expressed not by "relational" power or coercion over specific outcomes, but via agenda setting—"the power to decide how things shall be done, the power to shape frameworks within which states relate to each other."[38]

The strand of structural power associated with Hirschman emphasizes how the pattern of economic relations between states can transform the calculation of political interest. States (and private actors within states) that use the dollar (and especially those that hold their reserves in dollars) develop a vested interest in the value and stability of the dollar. Once in widespread use, the fate of the dollar becomes more than simply America's problem—it becomes the problem of all dollar holders (to varying degrees from case to case). Even those that simply peg to the dollar as part of a broader international economic strategy also have an interest in the future of the greenback even without signing on as "stakeholders" the way large holders of dollars have, advertently or not, as they accumulate dollar-denominated assets.[39]

In the contemporary system, then, dollar primacy increases both the "hard power" and the "soft power" of the United States. Regarding the former, America's coercive capacity is enhanced by its greater autonomy to run deficits and to adopt policies that would otherwise elicit a countervailing market reaction. As for the latter, the structural benefits afforded to the United States can be classified under Joseph Nye's definition of "soft power"—getting others to want what you want them to want. For Strange the weight of the dollar benefits the United States by necessitating that relevant political arenas will operate in such a way that they cannot but account for American interests. For Hirschman, the United States gains because participation in a dollar-based international monetary order both shapes the perceived self-interests

---

[38] Strange 1988, 25 (quote); Strange 1990; Strange 1994; see also Helleiner 2006a, 73–76.

[39] Hirschman 1980; Kirshner 1995, chap. 5; Abdelal and Kirshner 2000. States that accumulated dollars in the 1960s found themselves with a considerable stake in the viability of the dollar; see, for example, Salant 1964, 170; Cooper 1973, 11.

of states and of many private actors within states, and also, more concretely, creates stakeholders in the fate of the dollar.

### After the Fall—the Costs of Currency Contraction

The costs of the loss of monetary primacy are not limited to the end of the expanded powers afforded to the issuer of key currency. There are also additional costs associated with managing a currency in relative decline. Like living in the family mansion after all the money is gone, the costs of the vestiges of a once great lifestyle can be onerous, no matter how earnest an effort is made to rein in expenses. For landowners, even an empty estate bears property taxes and requires some basic upkeep; for issuers of a once-dominant international money, new burdens arise from the "overhang" and from a loss of prestige. These new burdens affect state power as much as the loss of old advantages and privileges do.

The overhang problem arises directly as a function of a currency's onetime greatness. At the height of its attraction, numerous actors are eager to hold international money—governments for reserves, and private actors in many countries use the world's currency as a store of value (and often as a medium of exchange) as a hedge against instability in and mismanagement of the home currency. But once the key currency is perceived to be in decline, it becomes suspect, and these actors will, over time, look to get out—to exchange it for some other asset. The need to "mop up" all this excess currency, even in the absence of a fixed exchange rate or other fiduciary commitment, creates chronic monetary pressure on the once great currency; and macroeconomic policy will take place under the shadow of the overhang.[40]

The loss of prestige is also a crucial consequence of managing a currency in decline. Prestige is a slippery concept that is very difficult to measure, but it is nevertheless important in international relations and an inescapable factor in matters pertaining to money. Defined by Robert Gilpin as "the reputation for power," prestige finds a home in monetary analysis under the rubric of credibility, which is generally acknowledged to play a crucial role in monetary affairs (even if ultimately it is as hard to measure as prestige).[41] The

---

[40] The informal term "overhang" was originally associated with the postwar British problem of "the notorious 'overhang' of official sterling balances over British reserves of gold and foreign exchange." In theory, with freely floating exchange rates, the "overhang" can be ignored and excess currency "mopped up" by greater depreciation. In practice, states are sensitive to the management of the overhang in any event, and in the past the management of the "dollar overhang" attracted considerable attention even in the absence of a fixed exchange rate or any formal commitments on the part of the United States. See Strange 1971a, 219 (quote); Kenen 1973, 194; Bergsten 1975b, 80; Cohen 1979, 42.

[41] Gilpin 1981, 31 (quote); see also Kindleberger 1970, 56, 204–5, 217–18.

unparalleled reputation and bedrock credibility of the key currency during its glory days is a key source of the power it provides. The implicit willingness of markets to tolerate imbalances in accounts and impertinent macroeconomic politics that would not be tolerated in other states rests on these foundations.

The loss of prestige and reduced credibility (which the challenge of the overhang contributes to and exacerbates) imposes new costs on the issuer of a currency in relative decline. Whereas in the past the key currency country was exempted from the rules of the game—that is, placed on a much longer leash by international financial markets than other states—the opposite becomes true. With eroding prestige and shared expectations of monetary distress, market vigilance is heightened and discipline imposed more swiftly by the collective expectations of more skeptical market actors. A presumption of confidence is replaced with a more jaundiced reading of the same indicators, and the long leash is replaced by an exceptionally tight choker.

Although the political and international monetary context is distinct, the experience of sterling illustrates these phenomena. In the nineteenth and early twentieth centuries, the pound served as the international currency of choice, with London as the world's financial hub. During World War II, Britain was able to quite explicitly cash in on its key currency status, employing the sterling area to its advantage, financing billions in military expenditures in ways that would not have been possible without the mechanisms that were already in place as a result of the pound's long-standing global role. The war forced Britain to scrape the bottom of the financial barrel, and its ability to essentially borrow at will in the sterling area and route the pounds back through London was an important element of the war effort. But after the war, the sterling balances became a vexing problem, complicating the management of Britain's relative economic decline and exacerbating its chronic financial crises in the 1960s.[42] With sterling invariably on the ropes in international financial markets the demand for a clean bill of macroeconomic health placed British budgets—and British military spending and overseas commitments—under constant pressure as a result. Susan Strange has argued that the challenges associated with the loss of "top currency" status were at the heart of Britain's postwar economic distress.[43]

---

[42] Kirshner 1995, 140–48; Shannon 1950; "The Sterling Balances," *Economist*, May 13, 1950, 1075; Hirsch 1969, 336–43.

[43] Strange 1971b; Fielding 1999, 633–37, 645, 651; Burk and Cairncross 1992, 20, 78, 105.

## What About the Dollar?

The sterling analogy is illustrative, but crucial differences between postwar sterling and the contemporary dollar limit the extent to which direct parallels between the two states can be drawn. First of all, Britain had exhausted itself financially over the course of two world wars; and after the war, it was no longer one of the world's elite powers. Although the United States has certainly lived beyond its means, which has made it easier for it to pursue an ambitious and often costly grand strategy (the circumscribing of which would take some edge off pressures on the federal budget and thus the dollar), it retains global military preponderance, and the geopolitical roots of currency distress between the two states is markedly dissimilar. Moreover, in the 1960s and 1970s, the British economy was sputtering and its share of global product was slipping further behind leading economies. The contemporary American economy, even in the context of the global economic crisis, remains relatively robust and enormous: nearly three times the size of the next largest economy (Japan), and about twice the size of the combined economies of Germany, France, and Britain. In its historical and economic context, Britain faced a more intimidating overhang than does the United States. Finally, a key difference between the two is that the international role of the pound was somewhat anachronistic—the dollar was a much more plausible international currency of choice. Today the dollar may face rivals on the horizon, and, as discussed, the emergence of the euro as a potential peer competitor matters. But sterling was going out of business as a reserve currency; the dollar is only faced with the need to scale back operations.[44]

Still, the United States would, nevertheless, face real consequences from the contraction of the international role of the dollar. They are reduced international political influence, the loss of the benefits it has become accustomed to enjoying (in particular, the ease with which it is able to finance its deficits), and the risk of reduced macroeconomic policy autonomy during international political crises. These latter two effects, which would directly affect U.S. power, would be more acute and salient if the change in the dollar's role comes about suddenly in the wake of an international financial crisis, and less dramatic, though still significant, if the dollar's relative primacy were to erode gradually. Either of these changes would take place in a domestic (American) political context that would likely magnify the extent to which dollar diminution contracts U.S. power.

[44] OECD 2005b, 13–14.

It is hard to quantify the reduction of political influence that would result from diminished global use of the greenback, but that does not make it any less real. The loss of dollar primacy, even to a (most likely) "first among equals" status, would erode the Hirschmanesque benefits that the United States garners as a result of the dollar's global role. In a world where fewer hold dollars, fewer would also have a stake in the dollar, and subtly, they would have less of a stake in the U.S. economy and U.S. policy preferences more generally. At the same time, the issuers of currencies that fill in the gaps where the dollar once reigned would see their own influence enhanced—as holders of, say, euros, see their interests more enmeshed in the interests of the European Union. As the dollar is used less in some parts of the world (including most likely Europe, Asia, and parts of Africa and the Middle East), the United States would lose twice, first, from the reduction in its own influence, and second, from the enhanced political influence of other powers.

More concretely, with the reduction in the dollar's prestige and thus its credibility, the United States would lose some of the privileges of primacy that it takes for granted and routinely, if implicitly, invokes. Here the shift in status from "top" to "negotiated" currency is paramount.[45] In a scenario in which the dollar's role receded, and especially as complicated by an increasingly visible overhang problem (as more actors get out of dollars), American policies would no longer be given the benefit of the doubt. Its macroeconomic management would be subject to intense scrutiny in international financial markets and its deviations from financial rectitude would start to come at a price. This would affect the ability of the United States to borrow and to spend. Federal government spending would take place under the watchful eye of international bankers and investors, whose preferences will always be for cuts. Borrowing from abroad would also come at a higher price. In the past, periods of notable dollar weakness led to U.S. borrowing via mechanisms that involved foreign currency payments and which were designed to insure creditors against the possibility of a decline in the value of the dollar. Each of these experimental mechanisms, the Roosa bonds of the 1960s and the Carter bonds of the 1970s, were only used on a modest scale; but they suggest the antecedents for future demands by creditors that would limit the ability of the United States to borrow in dollars.[46] It would also become more difficult to

[45] Strange's concept of a negotiated currency was principally a statist one—with an emphasis on political agreements between states. Here, the primary "negotiation" will likely be a tug-of-war between U.S. government officials and anonymous and disembodied market forces.

[46] Or more pointedly, to the ability to benefit from the fact that it is borrowing in dollars as opposed to foreign currencies. Makin 1971, 350–51; Schwartz 1997, 143; "Shrinking Role of U.S. Money," *Time*, October 15, 1979; Truman 2005b, 353, 354.

reduce the value of U.S. debts via devaluation and inflation, devices that have served the United States well in the past, but which in the future would both work less well and further undermine the dollar's credibility.

Increased (and more skeptical) market scrutiny of American macroeconomic policy choices would also affect the United States during moments of international crisis, and during periods of wartime. Markets tend to react negatively to the prospects for a country's currency as it enters crisis and war, anticipating increased government spending, borrowing, inflation, and hedging against general uncertainty.[47] Under dollar hegemony, the United States tended to benefit from the "flight to quality" during moments of international distress; but in the context of dollar diminution, with markets much more nervous about the dollar, the United States would find itself uncharacteristically under financial stress during crucial moments of international political confrontation. Here some analogy to Britain is illustrative. During World War II the international role of the pound was an important source of support, but after the war, with sterling in decline, the vulnerability of the pound left Britain exposed and forced it to abandon its military adventure over Suez in 1956.[48]

These new pressures on the dollar would take place in a distinct domestic political context. How would the U.S. political system react to life under the watchful and newly jaundiced eye of international financial markets, with reduced macroeconomic policy autonomy, greater demands that its economic choices meet the "approval" of international financiers and investors, and forced to finance its military adventures not by borrowing more dollars, but with hard cash on the barrelhead?

There is good reason to suspect that in response, the United States will scale back its international power projection, to an even greater extent than necessarily implied by the change to its underlying economic power. For the United States seems to be at the political limits of its fiscal will, consistent with theories that anticipate great powers will become addled by consumerism and the corroding consequences of affluence.[49] This is particularly notable with regard to America's recent wars. The 9/11 attacks revealed a real threat to the nation's security, yet the subsequent war in Afghanistan was undertaken with caution regarding risks taken and resources (both military and economic) expended; investments in homeland security have been relatively modest given

[47] Kirshner 2007a.

[48] Kirshner 1995, 63–82; Kunz 1991, 139–40, 143, 152–53; Johnman 1989, 176; Dooley 1989, 516–17; Klug and Smith 1999, 189–93, 200; Boughton 2001a, 435, 437–38, 440–41.

[49] Gilpin 1981, 153, 163–68; Kindleberger 1996, 32, 214–15; Cipolla 1970, 4–5, 13–14.

the needs at hand, and appropriations for securing "loose nukes" have been inadequate.[50] The yawning divergence between the government's rhetoric associated with the stakes of the Iraq War and the unwillingness of the Bush administration to call for any national sacrifices on its behalf strongly suggest that America's leaders were deeply skeptical of the nation's ability to mobilize its vast wealth in support of its foreign policy abroad. Indeed, the Iraq War is the only large war in U.S. history that has been accompanied by tax cuts. Major tax increases were associated with the War of 1812, the Civil War, World War I, World War II, the Korean War, and even, if with great reluctance on the part of President Johnson, the Vietnam War.[51]

From one perspective, military spending in the United States has not been at historically high levels. As a percentage of the Gross Domestic Product, U.S defense spending (4.0% in 2006 and in 2007) was in fact near post–World War II lows, and well below the levels associated with other wartime periods (13% in 1953, 9.5% in 1968). However, that amount of spending is nevertheless extremely high when considered in absolute dollars ($520 billion in 2006; 547.9 billion in 2007), and given that, at these levels, the United States comes close to spending as much on defense as the rest of the countries of the world combined.[52] It is these figures that are more likely to be decisive in the future when the United States is under pressure to make real choices about taxes and spending. When borrowing becomes more difficult, and adjustment more difficult to postpone, choices will have to be made between raising taxes, cutting nondefense spending, and cutting defense spending.

In sum, although dollar doomsayers have cried wolf repeatedly in the past, the currents of the massive, unprecedented, and unrelenting U.S. current account imbalances, the emergence of the euro (and the more distant ambitions of others), and, most important of all, the shift, across the board, to a distinct and less hospitable geopolitical setting, have caused the dollar to drift toward dangerous and uncharted waters. The financial crisis of 2008 has further weakened the dollar's footing, a deterioration that will be more salient when the global economy recovers. As a result, a reduced international role for the dollar is likely, either suddenly, in the wake of a financial crisis that more narrowly and directly implicates the greenback, for which all the preconditions are in place, or more gradually if by chance that crisis does not emerge. Either way, the diminution of the dollar would have significant political conse-

---

[50] On this last point, see Allison 2004.

[51] Dewey 1922; Stein 1996.

[52] "Historical Budget Data," Congressional Budget Office, September 2008, tables 7 and 8, http//www.cbo.gov/budget/historical.pdf; Chamberlin 2004, 28–29; Clayton 1972, 379, 393. U.S. military spending accounted for 47% of world military spending in 2004. Stockholm International Peace Research Institute 2005, chap. 8.

quences. A general downward recasting of U.S. political influence would be accompanied by much more novel and acute inhibitors on the willingness and ability of the United States to use force abroad—macroeconomic distress during international crises, and consistent pressure on federal budgets. The reduction in U.S. power and influence would be less salient if dollar diminution occurs gradually rather than suddenly, and if (after the economy recovers from major recession) the American public becomes willing to tolerate tax increases and cuts to other government spending.[53] But even these circumstances would mitigate, not eliminate, the consequences of the erosion of dollar primacy for the United States.

---

[53] Obviously, any efforts to "put the fiscal house back in order" have to be put on the back burner for the duration of the major recession that emerged in 2008; as noted, the measures necessary to stabilize and revive the economy will leave the dollar even more vulnerable in a few years. But there is no choice—aggressive measures must be taken to put this fire out, even though the water will cause damage that will have to be reckoned with in the future.

# 10

# SUMMING UP AND LOOKING AHEAD

## The Future of the Future of the Dollar

Eric Helleiner and Jonathan Kirshner

We conclude with a return to the motivating puzzle with which we began: Why do scholars, including those who have written with such authority and wisdom on monetary affairs and the international role of the dollar in the past, disagree so widely about the prospects for the future of the dollar as an international currency? What the preceding chapters have shown is that analysts have drawn on different underlying theoretical approaches—market-based, instrumental, and geopolitical—and, within the context of some of those models, they have made distinct judgment calls about which elements of evidence are to be privileged in explaining the dollar's fate. Those most pessimistic about the dollar generally reach first for geopolitical variables, such as the end of the cold war, the consequences of U.S. unipolarity and unilateralism, and the rise of new centers of economic and political power, in particular (but not limited to) the European Union and China. These scholars take as a point of departure the understanding that international monetary and financial affairs take place in the context of an underlying political order, and they are able to appeal to some market-based variables—especially U.S. debts and deficits—as providing further support for the expectation that the dollar-based international monetary order will erode in the coming years.[1]

[1] Gilpin 1987, 119; see also Strange 1976, esp. 354–56.

Potential weaknesses in the U.S. dollar, however, while not dismissed, are interpreted differently by those less pessimistic about the future prospects for the dollar as an international currency. Theorists whose first instinct is to employ instrumental interpretations of the dollar's international role focus more on whether the dollar, for better or worse, in appreciation or depreciation,[2] continues to be able to play its role for foreign governments either as a facilitator of export-led economic strategies or as a convenient and eminently logical nominal monetary anchor. The focus of attention here shifts away somewhat from the behavior of the United States as the issuer of the key currency toward the policy choices of those that have decided (implicitly or explicitly) to depend on it. The expectations of such scholars, therefore, more often than not are *contingent*. The fate of the dollar depends on whether it is still able to (or is perceived to be able to) deliver the goods; that is, to perform these instrumental functions in the international economic order.[3]

Those most optimistic about the dollar tend to throw even more of the spotlight abroad. While again acknowledging market-based challenges to the greenback, optimists are more likely to emphasize the *relative* market-based strengths of the dollar compared to possible alternatives—for example, the immaturity of the RMB and of China's financial system, the relatively modest size of the Japanese economy, and most pointedly, the impediments to European financial integration and the limited facility and dexterity with which the euro can serve as an international currency. Market-based dollar optimists also tend to emphasize the power of inertia in sustaining the dollar order, and can appeal, for additional reinforcement of their position, to some geopolitical variables that still underpin the dollar order (American military primacy, political rivalries in Asia, and the unwieldy nature of "European" foreign policy).[4]

In this concluding chapter, we continue the exercise, not of definitively declaring one perspective or set of assumptions the "best," but of clarifying our understanding of how and why different experts disagree on this issue. Our goals are to establish ever more clearly the bases of those disagreements, and to offer a guide to the future—not necessarily to the future of the dollar, but a guide to understanding and assessing the future of predictions about the dollar—by establishing a priori expectations of and potentially salient observations pertaining to competing models and the positions of scholars.

[2] This reference to the *value* of the dollar provides a good opportunity to remember that the focus in this book on "the future of the dollar" is in reference solely to its use as an international currency, and not to changes in its value (although contributors have discussed the way that the latter may influence the former).

[3] Cooper 2007; Dooley and Garber 2005.

[4] Posen 2008.

First, we reprise the principal arguments of the contending analytical approaches and how the perspectives of the contributors to this book are situated in that context. Second, we establish criteria of evaluation for each author: What are those future events or changes that would either reinforce or undermine their baseline expectations? We also briefly assess the (initial, preliminary) implications of the 2008 global financial crisis.[5] Finally, we finish with a few brief comments about the future of the future of the dollar—that is, what open questions remain that scholars interested in the future of the dollar should be pursuing.

### Reprise: Expectations about the Future of the Dollar

In the introductory chapter, we introduced and established the logic behind the market-based, instrumental, and geopolitical approaches to the question of the future of the dollar, and considered how each of these perspectives might be introduced to support expectations of sustainability *or* decline of the dollar's international role. We also situated the arguments of each of the contributors within that framework, which resulted in a broad spectrum of expectations. We revisit those models here, and reproduce the figure from the introduction that positioned each author compared to one another and illustrated how each author appealed to those models.

*Market-based* approaches that suggest a continuation of the dollar's international role call attention to the depth of U.S. financial markets, the absolute size of the U.S. economy, foreigners' confidence in the dollar, the tendency for international currency use to be self-reinforcing, and, importantly, to the absence of some of these attributes in those currencies that would aspire to encroach on the dollar's international role. On the other hand, market-based expectations can also be marshaled to make the opposite argument: concerns about the record-setting and unprecedented size of U.S. current account deficits, as well as the heavy burdens implied by the growing U.S. federal debt, combined with the emergence of new global centers of economic gravity, all raise red flags for those who would source the foundation of a currency's international use in economic "fundamentals."

*Instrumental* approaches see the sustainability of the dollar order coming

---

[5] The 2008 international financial crisis continues to unfold as we write this conclusion in October 2008. The dust has not yet settled—indeed, new dust may yet be thrown—obviously, it will be some time before confident conclusions can be drawn about the implications of the crisis for the future of the dollar. But the opportunity (and perhaps the reader's expectation) is too great not to take an initial cut at the issue, which might, in retrospect, offer the first test of our competing explanations.

from the services it provides—via "Bretton Woods II," by which states are content to accumulate dollar reserves in exchange for unfettered access to the voracious American market, or from pegging to the dollar as a monetary anchor, in order to provide a bedrock of macroeconomic stability and predictability in an otherwise rambunctious domestic economic environment. But the seeds of decline are also in place from this perspective, and just await proper cultivation in order to flower. The Bretton Woods II "system" would be immediately undermined by a surge in U.S. protectionism, and it is also vulnerable to possible underlying trends, such as a relative "decoupling" of Asian economies from the U.S. economy (should U.S. demand decline and consumption shares elsewhere increase, unrelated to protectionism), or from increased disenchantment with financial losses on dollar holdings should the dollar steeply depreciate.[6] Similarly, the dollar's role as a monetary anchor would be diminished if the dollar were to depreciate rapidly and/or U.S. inflationary pressures were to grow strongly.

*Geopolitical* approaches, as noted above, tend to take as a point of departure the unraveling of the cold war order, which provided the political foundation for the international monetary order of the second half of the twentieth century. From this perspective, a fundamental recasting of international monetary relations (and thus of the relative roles of international currencies) is a transformation waiting to happen, just waiting for a proximate cause of realignment to disrupt the inertia of the status quo—and nudged forward, perhaps, by instincts of adversaries (and even friends) to engage in "soft balancing" against the United States and its twenty-first century foreign policies (to date).[7] But geopolitical analysis can also point to a logic of sustainability: in particular, the enduring, indeed unprecedented, concentration of hard (military) power in, and the physical security of, the United States, which provides confidence in the endurance of the greenback unparalleled (and essentially unattainable) by any other issuer of international money. And although changes in balance-of-power variables and security concerns may have caused the dollar's cold war foundations to tremble, would-be competitors to the dollar face arguably even more daunting international political barriers to a greater global role. China and Japan, for example, seem particularly wary of each others' monetary ambitions.[8]

As noted above, the contributors to this book reach their divergent expectations regarding the future of the dollar because they reach for one (or more)

---

[6] International Monetary Fund 2007, 147–48.
[7] Kupchan 2002; Pape 2005.
[8] Grimes 2008 and "Asian Monetary Fund: Leadership Struggle Thwarts Regional Solidarity," *Korea Times*, October 6, 2008.

of the three perspectives, and, within the context of those perspectives, emphasize variables that lean more toward sustainability or decline. From that initial point of departure, the insights of the additional approaches, to the extent that they are appealed to, tend to fold in to the analysis in a complementary fashion.

Harold James anticipates continuity in the maintenance of the international dollar order. He appeals first to those factors that make the dollar attractive to market actors, in particular the size, the financial depth and sophistication, the certain stewardship of the U.S. monetary economy, and the country's stability and security, all factors that illustrate both the absolute and relative advantages underpinning the dollar. Ronald McKinnon also expects the dollar order to be sustained indefinitely, although, as an instrumentalist (he is a founder of the nominal anchor school), his expectations are more pointedly contingent on good public policy practices (American commitments to low inflation, a stable exchange rate, and free trade). He is cautiously optimistic that this will remain the case.

Eric Helleiner strikes an uncertain note about the dollar's future. Following the framework of Susan Strange, which he modifies and expands, Helleiner sees the dollar's trip from "top" to partially "negotiated" currency shifting the ground somewhat from market-based variables that suggest continuity toward political factors that open the door to the possibility of change. Herman Schwartz is also positioned in the middle ground. His novel analysis, which emphasizes the relative attractiveness of specific attributes of the U.S. economy and which as a result anticipates the maintenance of the dollar order, nevertheless emphasizes the extent to which the entire edifice depends on the prospect of the U.S. economy continuing to outpace other economies. Marcello de Cecco is also uncertain but slightly more pessimistic (indeed, uncertainty is an explanatory variable in his argument as much as it is an expectation). Stepping back from the specific attributes of the dollar proper, and drawing on historical analogy, he envisions a more turbulent and conflictual international monetary and financial order, in which the dollar's role can be sustained but which can also generate pressures for change.

Benjamin Cohen appeals to market factors, but stresses those that see weakness, rather than strength, in the foundations of the international dollar order. Coupled with geopolitical trends, he sees unsustainable U.S. external accounts raising doubts about the greenback and providing opportunities for some encroachment by (not ready to be peer) competitors to the dollar at the frontiers of the American system in the Middle East and Asia. This perspective is shared by David Calleo, whose analysis leans more heavily on geopolitical factors (the end of the cold war order) and on the (contingent)

TABLE 10.1.
Expectations about the future of the dollar

| What future for the dollar's international role? | Determinants of international currency standing | | |
|---|---|---|---|
| | Market-based | Instrumental | Geopolitical |
| Sustainable | **James**<br>Helleiner | **McKinnon**<br>James | |
| Uncertain | **Schwartz**<br>De Cecco<br>McKinnon | Helleiner<br>Schwartz | Helleiner<br>De Cecco |
| Decline | **Cohen**<br>Calleo<br>Kirshner | | Cohen<br>**Calleo**<br>**Kirshner** |

economic weakness of an America unwilling to bear the burdens implied by its appetites for military might and domestic consumption. Jonathan Kirshner shares the declinist assumptions underlying Cohen and Calleo's analysis, but with an even more pessimistic bent. He anticipates even greater external political opposition to (and lack of crucial support for) the dollar's role abroad, and sees a market environment conducive to a suddenly transformative crisis of the dollar.

## Looking Ahead: Establishing Expectations and Criteria of Evaluation

Although, as we have stressed, our goal is not to declare one of these arguments the most convincing, it is possible, and constructive, to consider what events in the future would arguably serve as confirming or disconfirming evidence for each argument, or at the very least would serve as a guide to the distinct expectations of each contributor.

As James sees a system in which all good things go together, and reinforce the rather robust international dollar order, that which sustains the dollar is that which has always sustained it—its relative attractiveness to market actors, an attractiveness based on the dynamism and growth of the American economy and financial markets, the role of U.S. consumption as an engine of global growth, and the U.S.'s unique role as stable and secure haven in which property rights are powerfully protected. An unexpected, sustained, relative decline of the U.S. economy or its broader power and security that appeared indicative of a new secular trend is probably the only possible real threat to the global preponderance of the greenback. For James, the United States could conceivably shoot itself in the foot and turn inward, but it is harder to imagine actors voluntarily turning away from America.

For McKinnon, potential threats to the dollar are largely home grown—not in the form of expanding defects, but from poor public policy choices. Particularly worrying policies would be those that would allow for macroeconomic mismanagement, a large depreciation of the dollar, or protectionism. In the absence of policy mistakes, continued confidence in U.S. economic stewardship should sustain the dollar. But if foreign governments began to abandon dollar pegs in this context, this could be considered evidence that challenges the argument.

Like James, Helleiner predicts that the relative market-based attractiveness of the dollar (based particularly on the unique liquidity of U.S. financial markets in this account) will enable it to remain the central global currency for some time. At the same time, he does see one potential danger in the near term to the dollar's international role: a severe dollar crisis provoked by the withdrawal of foreign political support for the currency (combined with the weak defense of the currency's global position from U.S. policymakers). The increasingly fragile instrumental and geopolitical bases of foreign support for the dollar have, according to Helleiner, made this more possible than in the past. Disconfirming evidence for Helleiner's overall argument would be a significant market shift away from the dollar in the absence of a severe exchange rate crisis for the currency.

Schwartz suggests that the future of the dollar's international role will depend above all on the relative growth rate differentials. If U.S. growth rates are faster than in Europe and Asia, the dollar will remain the central global currency for both market-based and instrumental (Bretton Woods II) reasons. But if U.S. growth rates are slower, then the dollar's international role is likely to diminish gradually. Schwartz's perspective would be disproved if the dollar's international role changed considerably in the absence of a shift in this key variable he has identified.

From de Cecco's perspective, the dollar's future depends on both market-based and geopolitical factors. With respect to the former, de Cecco worries about the reaction of increasingly powerful and volatile global financial markets to further depreciation of the dollar, particularly given the new presence of the stable euro. Uncertainty will only be compounded, he predicts, by the more unstable geopolitical environment that has been ushered in by the end of the cold war and the rise of new emerging powers. De Cecco's predictions would be disconfirmed if the dollar's global role did not erode much at all in a context of growing financial and geopolitical instability in the coming years.

Cohen, a market pessimist, expects a shift to a leaderless currency system because as the dollar order erodes, there is no plausible alternative. For Cohen, then, the gravest threat to the dollar would be an unexpected strengthening of potential alternatives, either due to dramatic reform of the management of the euro or international political developments in Asia that facilitate the emergence of broader and perhaps even institutionalized monetary cooperation there. The dollar could be bolstered by sharp improvement in U.S. accounts and/or economic distress abroad. What would be anomalous from this perspective would be any discontinuous, rather than gradual, shift in currency preferences by major actors.

Calleo's dollar could possibly be saved by the United States getting its financial house in order. Although Calleo is skeptical, this is within reach in theory—the Clinton 1990s, for example, took the United States from a federal budget deficit to a surplus and even to concerns about an overly large surplus. The 1990s also saw reductions in the U.S. defense burden. The dollar would, however, be undermined, from this perspective, by new spending and consumption, especially by the government on defense. It would be incongruous, from this perspective, if the United States embarked on a new military confrontation in the future without seriously undermining global confidence in the dollar, unless the EU began to break up and security or political-economic conditions in Europe deteriorated markedly.

For Kirshner, a serious threat to the dollar would be a further deterioration of U.S. external accounts, because absent a salient, shared security vision, states will quietly diversify away from the dollar if it seems to be skating toward ever thinning ice. Sharp political conflicts abroad, however, such as greater conflict between China and Japan, troublemaking by an increasingly assertive Russia, or some unraveling of European unity, would tend to bolster the dollar. From this perspective, it would be surprising if continued U.S. predominance, in the absence of the rise of sharper regional political rivalries, did not lead states to seek to find greater distance from the dollar order.

These expectations, counterfactuals, and anomalies are summarized in the table below. In each case, the columns refer to *future* expectations; that is, "sustaining factors" refer not to the basis upon which each author has argued that the dollar's international role will endure, but rather to those events that might occur that would be most likely to sustain the dollar. Similarly, "threats" refer not to prior analysis, but to prospective events that would be subversive of the dollar, from each author's perspective. Anomalies are those events that could not be easily explained.

TABLE 10.2.
Gauging the expectations

|  | Sustaining factors | Threats to the dollar's international role | Would-be anomalies |
|---|---|---|---|
| James | U.S. growth and attractiveness | Decoupling of global economy | Political balancing against the U.S. |
| McKinnon | Confidence in Federal Reserve | U.S. protectionism, inflation, or depreciation | Departure from dollar pegs in absence of U.S. policy mistakes |
| Helleiner | Liquidity of U.S. financial markets | Sudden withdrawal of foreign political support | Market shift away from dollar in absence of exchange rate crisis |
| Schwartz | Relatively higher U.S. growth rates | Relatively slower U.S. growth rates | Decline in dollar's role in absence of growth rate differentials |
| De Cecco | Inertia, U.S. global role | Dollar depreciation, financial instability, geopolitical uncertainty | Dollar endures as financial and geopolitical upheavals grow |
| Cohen | Distress in Europe, discord in Asia | Shift in 'battlegrounds" Mideast, Asia | Discontinuities in currency use |
| Calleo | U.S. policy reversals, 2010s like 1990s | More consumption, especially defense spending | Dollar stability in context of new military confrontation |
| Kirshner | International political conflict (non-U.S.) | Deterioration of U.S. fundamentals | Unmotivated bandwagoning with U.S. |

## A First Test? The Financial Crisis of 2008

In articulating and evaluating these various expectations, it is worthwhile (if admittedly somewhat premature) to consider how the international financial crisis of 2008 might support or undermine distinct perspectives on the future of the dollar. The crisis, after all, is the first big new disruption to the international financial system in the last decade or so, and thus the fallout for the various perspectives (to the extent that it can be determined at this time[9]) is worth considering briefly.

The financial crisis can be interpreted in three stages. In stage one, as it erupted in the fall of 2007 through the summer of 2008, the crisis looked to confirm the most pessimistic expectations about the future of the dollar. With the housing bubble at the epicenter of the crisis, Schwartz's analysis could be used to anticipate an unraveling of the dollar's advantages. And Kirshner expected that a financial crisis would be the spark that led to a sudden contraction of the dollar's international role. An immediate reaction to the crisis in

[9] See note 5.

the United States, then, was that it seemed to be in accord with pessimistic expectations about the prospects for the greenback.

Within a few months, however, as the U.S. financial crisis developed not into a broader dollar crisis but instead into a profoundly widespread international financial crisis, the opposite conclusion seemed more plausible—the global crisis revealed the weaknesses of alternatives and demonstrated, once again, the unique strengths and attributes of the U.S. economy and of the dollar. For market actors and central banks scrambling for liquidity, there was no obvious substitute for the U.S. T-bill. The euro suddenly seemed very much *not* ready for prime time, and as markets in Asia, Europe, and throughout the world suffered, panicked investors sought out the safest possible ports in which to ride out the storm—and those were found in the United States, and to some extent Japan.[10] As Eric Helleiner argued in chapter 4, one consequence of the crisis was to reveal crucial weaknesses in the euro's ability to challenge the dollar.

But a third phase looms—when the crisis passes (in the coming months or years), what will be the longer term consequences for the international role of the dollar? These events, of course, are yet to unfold, but here the pessimists are able to rearm. If the U.S. economy slows considerably, it might advance the decoupling of the global economy, creating fewer instrumental incentives to embrace the dollar. Of course, if the U.S. economy grows more slowly than other economies over the next ten years, its external balances would likely improve. From the market-based optimistic view of the dollar's future, this correction would be seen as one more illustration of the long-term health and stability and attractiveness of the U.S. economy, and of the system as a whole to tend toward equilibrium. But some instrumentalists, less concerned about the sustainability of U.S. deficits, would see a reduction in American demand as subversive of the dollar-based international financial order. Moreover, more pessimistic market-based analysts worry about how the long-term costs of the necessary bailout(s) and stimulus packages in the United States have added, and will add further, to the already high American national debt, which invites concerns about the long-term prospects for inflation rates and the relative value of the dollar.

And there also remain the long-term consequences of the policy implications (as opposed to the economic consequences) of postmortem analyses of decision makers in Asia, Europe, and the Middle East. The poor performance of the euro during the crisis might prompt European policymakers to

---

[10] David Jolly, "Financial Crisis Has One Beneficiary: The Dollar," *International Herald Tribune,* October 22, 2008; "The European Union's Week from Hell," *Economist,* October 9, 2008; Martin Fackler, "Edgy Capital Pours Back into Japan, and the Yen Soars," *New York Times,* October 28, 2008.

strengthen cooperation to solve some flaws in the Maastricht Treaty (especially crisis management mechanisms) that would pave the way for the emergence of a stronger and more capacious euro, better positioned to challenge the dollar. Elsewhere, those burned by the crisis (perhaps in Asia) or those nervous about putting too many eggs in any one basket (possibly the Middle East?) might conclude that some greater decoupling and diversification would actually be a good thing, and edge away from the dollar as a manifestation of disenchantment with the "American system."

In any event, it is possible, once again, to understand the crisis and future expectations about the dollar in the wake of the crisis through the lenses of the various approaches and analyses. They do not all point in the same direction, but we understand why they disagree and what type of evidence to look for in evaluating them.

## The Future of the Dollar (Studies)

If the future of the dollar remains uncertain, are there some broader lessons to be learned about the study of the future of the dollar? One lesson we have learned is the benefit of embracing a multidisciplinary approach. This book includes contributions from political scientists, historians, and economists, and we have seen how each brings a distinct perspective. Political scientists tend to look first at the politics, and expect the markets to follow suit. It might be suggested that political scientists underappreciate the driving power of market forces, and do so at great risk, especially when discussing contemporary financial markets, which are so large and fast moving. But the assumption of these analysts is not so much that they expect political forces to trump market forces, but rather that politics will shape the contours through which market forces exercise their power and influence and the context in which economic actors shape their expectations.

Historians, when they speak to the present, are often caricatured for bearing false analogies, or imposing rhythms on history that do not exist. Our experience has been that this is not the case, and that historians are especially well positioned to explain why some superficial analogies are misleading (for example, why the twenty-first century dollar is so different from postwar sterling). They can also suggest creative and thought-provoking analogies that bring attention to underappreciated issues and potential problems. For example, China is often compared with pre–World War I Germany, in that both could be seen as emerging great powers. But from a monetary perspective, China might be more comparable to the pre–World War I United States, a country whose burgeoning economic growth and underdeveloped banking system contributed to international financial instability in the 1890s and 1900s.[11]

The conclusion of economists might leave one, like Harry Truman, in search for a one-armed economist who would be unable to say "on the other hand." But the picture is not at all that dismal. Economists may come to divergent conclusions about the future of the dollar, but this is because they are privileging different variables and behavioral relationships. It is for this reason that experts can look at exactly the same data and reach different conclusions.[12] What we have hoped to clarify in this book is the basis upon which they can disagree, so that we might establish and evaluate, a priori, the criteria by which we can assess their prognostications.

In addition to the benefits of multi-disciplinarity, we have also learned that there are many more things to learn. We do not yet have access to careful studies of policymaking toward reserve management in key dollar-holding countries such as China or the Gulf states. Detailed scholarship on this topic would be of enormous assistance in helping us assess more effectively the relative usefulness of the market-based, instrumental, and geopolitical interpretations. There is also a need for much greater understanding of the ways in which international financial crises might generate continuities or discontinuities in the international currency arrangements. Although we understand that international financial systems seem prone to crises with some regularity, we know much less about their geopolitical consequences. There are, of course, many other issues requiring more scholarly attention if we are to better understand the dollar's future as an international currency. We only hope that this book, by highlighting key analytical issues underlying the contemporary debates on the topic, will encourage other scholars to take up the challenge of exploring the topic in more depth.

[11] Sprague 1910.
[12] Kirshner 2000.

# REFERENCES

Abdelal, Rawi, and Jonathan Kirshner. 2000. "Strategy, Economic Relations, and the Definition of National Interests." *Security Studies* 9, nos. 1–2: 119–56.

Aliber, Robert Z. 1964. "The Costs and Benefits of the U.S. Role as a Reserve Currency Country." *Quarterly Journal of Economics* 78, no. 3: 442–56.

Allison, Graham. 2004. *Nuclear Terrorism: The Ultimate Preventable Catastrophe.* New York: Times Books.

Andrews, David. 2006. "Monetary Power and Monetary Statecraft." In *International Monetary Power,* edited by David Andrews. Ithaca: Cornell University Press.

Annett, Anthony. 2006. "Enforcement and the Stability and Growth Pact: How Fiscal Policy Did and Did Not Change under Europe's Fiscal Framework." Working Paper WP/06/116. Washington, D.C.: International Monetary Fund.

Aoki, Kosuke, James Proudman, and Gertjan Vlieghe. 2004. "House Prices, Consumption, and Monetary Policy: A Financial Accelerator Approach." *Journal of Financial Intermediation* 13, no. 4: 414–35.

Aubrey, Henry G. 1969. *Behind the Veil of International Money.* Essays in International Finance 71. Princeton: International Finance Section, Princeton University.

Balogh, Thomas. 1949. *The Dollar Crisis: Causes and Cure.* Oxford: Basil Blackwell.

Bank for International Settlements. 2003. *72nd Annual Report.* Basel: BIS.

——. 2007a. *Triennial Central Bank Survey, Foreign Exchange and Derivative Market Activity 2007.* Basel: BIS.

———. 2007b. *Triennial Central Bank Survey of Foreign Exchange and Derivatives Market Activity in April 2007: Preliminary Global Results.* Basel: Bank for International Settlements.

Barysch, Katinka. 2004. "From Strength to Strength." *Parliament Magazine.* February 23.

Bergsten, C. Fred. 1975a. *Dilemmas of the Dollar: The Economics and Politics of U.S. International Monetary Policy.* New York: New York University Press.

———. 1975b. "New Urgency for International Monetary Reform." *Foreign Policy* 19.

———, ed. 1991. *International Adjustment and Financing: The Lessons of 1985–1991.* Washington, D.C.: Institute for International Economics.

———. 1997. "The Dollar and the Euro." *Foreign Affairs* 76, no. 4.

Bergsten, C. Fred, and John Williamson, eds. 2003. *Dollar Overvaluation in the World Economy.* Washington, D.C.: Institute for International Economics.

———, eds. 2004. *Dollar Adjustment: How Far? Against What?* Special Report 17. Washington: Institute for International Economics.

———. 2005. "The Euro and the Dollar." In *The Euro at Five: Ready for a Global Role?* ed. A. Posen. Washington, D.C.: Institute for International Economics.

Bernanke, Ben. 2005. "The Global Savings Glut and the U.S. Current Account Deficit." Sandbridge Lecture, Virginia Association of Economics. March 10.

Bertuch-Samuels, Axel, and Parmeshwar Ramlogan. 2007. "The Euro: Ever More Global." *Finance and Development* 44, no. 1: 46–49.

Borio, C. 1995. "The Structure of Credit to the Non-Government Sector and the Transmission Mechanism of Monetary Policy: A Cross-Country Comparison." Bank for International Settlements Working Papers No. 24. Basel: BIS.

Boughton, James M. 2001a. "Northwest of Suez: The 1956 Crisis and the IMF." *IMF Staff Papers* 48, no. 3: 425–46.

———. 2001b. *Silent Revolution: The International Monetary Fund, 1979–1989.* Washington, D.C.: International Monetary Fund.

Bouvier, J. 1967. *Les Rothschild.* Paris: Fayard.

Bowles, Paul. 2002. "Asia's Post-Crisis Regionalism: Bringing the State Back In, Keeping the (United) States Out." *Review of International Political Economy* 9, no 2: 244–70.

Bowles, Paul, and Baotai Wang. 2008. "The Rocky Road Ahead: China, the U.S., and the Future of the Dollar." *Review of International Political Economy* 15, no. 3: 335–53.

Bradsher, Keith. 2002. *High and Mighty: SUVs—the World's Most Dangerous Vehicles and How They Got That Way.* New York: Public Affairs.

Bresciani-Turroni, Costantino. 1918. *MittelEuropa: L' Imperoeconomico dell' Europa central.* Roma: "L'Universelle"Imprimerie Polyglotte.

Brinley, Thomas. 1973. *Migration and Economic Growth.* Cambridge: Cambridge University Press.

Buiter, Willem. 2006. "Dark Matter or Cold Fusion?" Goldman Sachs Global Economics Paper No. 136.

Burdekin, Richard. 2006. "China and the Depreciating U.S. Dollar." *Asia Pacific Issues* (East-West Center) 79 (January).

Burk, Kathleen. 1985. *Britain, America and the Sinews of War.* London: Allen and Unwin.

Burk, Kathleen, and Alec Cairncross. 1992. *Goodbye, Great Britain: The 1976 IMF Crisis.* New Haven: Yale University Press.

Caballero, Ricardo, Emmanuel Farhi, and Pierre-Olivier Gourinchas. 2006. "An Equilibrium Model of Global Imbalances and Low Interest Rates." National Bureau of Economic Research Working Paper 11996. Cambridge: NBER.

Calleo, David P. 1968. *Britain's Future.* New York: Horizon Press.

——. 1970. *The Atlantic Fantasy.* Baltimore: Johns Hopkins University Press.

——, ed. 1976. *Money and the Coming World Order.* New York: New York University Press.

——. 1982. *The Imperious Economy.* Cambridge: Harvard University Press.

——. 1987. *Beyond American Hegemony.* New York: Basic Books.

——. 1992. *The Bankrupting of America.* New York: Morrow.

——. 1999. "The Strategic Implications of the Euro." *Survival* 41, no. 1: 5–19.

——. 2001. *Rethinking Europe's Future.* Princeton: Princeton University Press.

Calleo, David P., and Benjamin M. Rowland. 1973. *America and the World Political Economy.* Bloomington: Indiana University Press.

Case, Karl E., John M. Quigley, and Robert J. Shiller. 2001. "Comparing Wealth Effects: The Stock Market versus the Housing Market." National Bureau of Economic Research Working Paper 8606. November. Cambridge: NBER.

Castellano, Marc. 1999. "Internationalization of the Yen: A Ministry of Finance Pipe Dream?" *JEI Report* 23A, 1–10.

Castles, Francis G. 1998. "The Really Big Trade-off: Home Ownership and the Welfare State in the New World and the Old." *Acta Politica* 33: 5–19.

Chamberlin, Jeffrey. 2004. "FY2005 Defense Budget: Frequently Asked Questions." *CRS Report for Congress.* July 12. Washington, D.C.: Congressional Research Service.

Chambers, Matthew, Carlos Garriga, and Don E. Schlagenhauf. 2007. "Accounting for Changes in the Homeownership Rate." Federal Reserve Bank of Atlanta Working Paper 2007–21. September.

Cheung, Yin-Wong, Menzie D. Chinn, and Eiji Fuji. 2007. "The Overvaluation of Renminbi Undervaluation." National Bureau of Economic Research Working Paper 12850. January. Cambridge: NBER.

Chin, Gregory, and Eric Helleiner. 2008. "China as a Creditor: A Rising Financial Power?" *Journal of International Affairs* 62, no. 1: 87–102

Chinn, Menzie, and Jeffrey Frankel. 2005. "Will the Euro Eventually Surpass the Dollar as Leading International Reserve Currency?" National Bureau of Economic Research Working Paper 11510. Cambridge: NBER.

Cipolla, Carlo. 1970. "Editor's Introduction." In *The Economic Decline of Empires,* ed. Carlo Cipolla. London: Methuen.

Clapham, John. 1944. *The Bank of England, a History.* Cambridge: Cambridge University Press.

Clark, William R. 2005. *Petrodollar Warfare, Oil, Iraq and the Future of the Dollar.* Gabriela Island, British Columbia: New Society Publishers.

Clayton, James L. 1972. "The Fiscal Cost of the Cold War to the United States: The First Twenty-Five Years, 1947–1971." *Western Political Quarterly* 25, no. 3.

Cleveland, Harold van Buren. 1990. "Europe in the Economic Crisis of Our Time: Macroeconomic Policies and Macroeconomic Constraints." In *Recasting Europe's Economies: National Strategies in the 1980s,* ed. David P. Calleo and Claudia Morgenstern. Lanham, Md.: University Press of America.

Cline, William. 2005. *The United States as a Debtor Nation.* Washington, D.C.: Institute for International Economics.

Cohen, Benjamin J. 1971a. *The Future of Sterling as an International Currency.* London: Macmillan.

——. 1971b. "The Seigniorage Gain of an International Currency: An Empirical Test." *Quarterly Journal of Economics* 85: 494–507.

——. 1979. "Europe's Money, America's Problem." *Foreign Policy* 35.

——. 1993. "The Triad and the Unholy Trinity: Lessons for the Pacific Region." In *Pacific Economic Relations in the 1990s: Cooperation or Conflict?* ed. Richard Higgott, Richard Leaver, and John Ravenhill, 133–58. Boulder, Colo.: Lynne Rienner.

——. 1998. *The Geography of Money.* Ithaca: Cornell University Press.

——. 2003. "Global Currency Rivalry: Can the Euro Ever Challenge the Dollar?" *Journal of Common Market Studies* 41, no. 4: 575–95.

——. 2004. *The Future of Money.* Princeton: Princeton University Press.

——. 2006a. "The Euro and Transatlantic Relations." In *Hard Power, Soft Power, and the Future of Transatlantic Relations,* ed. Thomas L. Ilgen, 73–89. Burlington, Vt.: Ashgate.

——. 2006b. "The Macrofoundations of Monetary Power." In *International Monetary Power,* ed. David Andrews. Ithaca: Cornell University Press.

——. 2008a. *Global Monetary Governance.* New York: Routledge.

——. 2008b. "The International Monetary System: Diffusion and Ambiguity." *International Affairs* 84, no. 3: 455–70.

Congressional Research Service. 1994. "Savings Rates: An International Comparison." *Report for Congress, 94–102E.* February. Washington, D.C.: CRS.

Cooper, Richard N. 1973. "The Future of the Dollar." *Foreign Policy* 11 (Summer).

——. 1975. "Prolegomena to the Choice of an International Monetary System." *International Organization* 29, no. 1: 63–98.

——. 2005. "Living with Global Imbalances: A Contrarian View." Institute for International Economics, *Policy Briefs* (November).

——. 2007. "Living with Global Imbalances." *Brookings Papers on Economic Activity* 2: 91–107.

Credit Suisse. 2007. "Mortgage Liquidity du Jour: Underestimated No More." June.

Daalder, Ivo H., and Michael E. O'Hanlon. 2000. *Winning Ugly—NATO's War to Save Kosovo.* Washington, D.C.: Brookings Institution.

de Cecco, Marcello. 1974. *Money and Empire.* Oxford: Blackwell.

de Gaulle, Charles. 1967. *Major Addresses, Statements, and Press Conferences, 3/17/ 64–1/16/67.* New York: Press and Information Division, French Embassy.

Department of the Treasury. 2007. *Foreign Portfolio Holdings of US Securities, June 2006.* Washington, D.C.: U.S. Government Printing Office.

Despres, Emile, Charles Kindleberger, and Walter Salant. 1970. "The Dollar and World Liquidity: A Minority View." In *Changing Patterns in Foreign Trade and Payments,* ed. Bela Balassa. New York: W. W. Norton.

Dewey, Davis Rich. 1922. *Financial History of the United States.* New York: Longmans.

Dooley, Howard J. 1989. "Great Britain's 'Last Battle' in the Middle East: Notes on Cabinet Planning during the Suez Crisis of 1956." *International History Review* 11, no. 3: 487–517.

Dooley, Michael, David Folkerts-Landau, and Peter Garber. 2003. "An Essay on the Revived Bretton Woods System." National Bureau of Economic Research Working Paper 9971. Cambridge: NBER.

——. 2005. *International Financial Stability.* New York: Deutsche Bank, Global Markets Research.

Dooley, Michael, and Peter Garber. 2005. "Is It 1958 or 1968? Three Notes on the Longevity of the Revised Bretton Woods System." *Brookings Papers on Economic Activity* 1: 147–87.

Economist. 2005. "The Great Thrift Shift: A Survey of the World Economy." *Economist* supplement (September 24).

Edwards, Sebastian. 2005. "Is the U.S. Current Account Deficit Sustainable? And If Not, How Costly Is Adjustment Likely to Be?" National Bureau of Economic Research Working Paper 11541. Cambridge: NBER.

Eichengreen, Barry. 2004. "The Dollar and the New Bretton Woods System." Henry Thorton Lecture delivered at the Case School of Business, December 15.

——. 2005a. "Comments and Discussion." *Brookings Papers on Economic Activity* 1: 188–94.

——. 2005b. "Sterling's Past, Dollar's Future: Historical Perspectives on Reserve Currency Competition." Mimeo, April.

——. 2006. *Global Imbalances and the Lessons of Bretton Woods.* Cambridge: MIT Press.

Einzig, Paul. 1935. *World Finance 1914–1935.* New York: Macmillan.

Ehrlich, Isaac. 2007. "The Mystery of Human Capital as Engine of Growth, or Why the US Became the Economic Superpower in the Twentieth Century." National Bureau of Economic Research Working Paper 12868. January. Cambridge: NBER.

ElBoghdady, Dina, and Sarah Cohen. "The Growing Foreclosure Crisis." *Washington Post,* January 17, 2009, A1.

Elliot, J. H. 2006. *Empires of the Atlantic World: Britain and Spain in America, 1492–1830.* New Haven: Yale University Press.

Ellis, Luci. 2008. "The Housing Meltdown: Why Did It Happen in the United States." Bank for International Settlements Working Papers No. 259. September. Basel: BIS.

Elwell, Craig K. 2006. "Foreign Outsourcing: Economic Implications and Policy Responses." Congressional Research Service Report RL32484. June 21. Washington, D.C.: CRS.

Englehart, Gary V. 2006. *Housing Trends among Baby Boomers.* Washington, D.C.: Research Institute for Housing America.

Essayyad, Musa, and Ibrahim Algahtani. 2005. "Policy Issues Related to the Substitution of the U.S. Dollar in Oil Pricing." *International Journal of Global Energy Issues* 23, no. 1: 71–92.

European Central Bank. 2008. "Review of the International Role of the Euro." Frankfurt: European Central Bank.

European Commission, DG Internal Market and Services. 2005. "The Costs and Benefits of Integration of EU Mortgage Markets." August. Brussels: European Commission.

European Mortgage Federation. 2005. "Hypostat 2004: A Review of Europe's Housing and Mortgage Markets." Brussels: European Mortgage Federation.

Favell, Adrian. 2008. *Eurostars and Eurocities: Free Movement and Mobility in an Integrating Europe.* Oxford: Blackwell.

Federal Home Loan Mortgage Corporation. 2006. *Annual Report.* Washington, D.C.: FHLMC.

Federal National Mortgage Agency. 2006. *Annual Report.* Washington, D.C.: FNMA.

Federal Reserve. 2008. *Flow of Funds of the United States: Second Quarter 2008.* September. Washington, D.C.: U.S. Federal Reserve.

Feldstein, Martin. 1993. "The Dollar and the Trade Deficit in the 1980s: A Personal View." National Bureau of Economic Research Working Paper 4325. Cambridge: NBER.

Fielding, Jeremy. 1999. "Coping with Decline: US Policy toward the British Defense Reviews of 1966." *Diplomatic History* 23, no. 4: 633–56.

Flandreau, Marc. 2004. *The Glitter of Gold.* Oxford: Oxford University Press.

Flandreau, Marc, and Clemens Jobst. 2005. "The Empirics of International Currencies: Evidence from the 19th Century." Mimeo, November.

Fogli, Alessandra, and Fabrizio Perri. 2007. "The 'Great Moderation' of the US External Imbalance." European University Institute Working Paper. March. Florence: European University Institute.

Foxwell, H. S. 1912. *Papers on Current Finance.* London: Macmillan.

Frank, Ellen. 2003. "The Surprising Resilience of the US Dollar." *Review of Radical Political Economics* 35, no. 3: 248–54.

Frankel, Jeffrey. 2006. "Could the Twin Deficits Jeopardize US Hegemony?" *Journal of Policy Modeling* 28, no. 6: 653–63.

Friedman, Milton. 1968. "The Role of Monetary Policy." *American Economic Review* 58, no. 1: 157–203.

Galati, Gabrielle, and Philip Wooldridge. 2006. "The Euro as a Reserve Currency: A Challenge to the Pre-eminence of the US Dollar?" Bank for International Settlements Working Papers No. 218. Basel: BIS.

Gavin, Francis. 2004. *Gold, Dollars, and Power: The Politics of International Monetary Relations, 1958–1971.* Chapel Hill: University of North Carolina Press.

Genberg, Hans, Robert McCauley, Tung Chul Park, and Avinash Persaud. 2005. "Official Reserves and Currency Management in Asia: Myth, Reality and the Future." Geneva Reports on the World Economy 7. Geneva: International Center for Monetary and Banking Studies.

Gilpin, Robert. 1981. *War and Change in World Politics.* Cambridge: Cambridge University Press.

———. 1987. *The Political Economy of International Monetary Relations.* Princeton: Princeton University Press.

———. 2001. *Global Political Economy: Understanding the International Economic Order.* Princeton: Princeton University Press.

Goldberg, Linda, and Eleanor Wiske Dillon. 2007. "Why a Dollar Depreciation May Not Close the U.S. Trade Deficit." Federal Reserve Bank of New York, *Current Issues in Economics and Finance* 13, no. 5. June.

Goldstein, Morris, and Nicholas Lardy. 2005. "China's Role in the Revived Bretton Woods System: A Case of Mistaken Identity." Institute for International Economics Working Paper 05–2. March. Washington, D.C.: Institute for International Economics.

———. 2007. "China's Exchange Rate Policy: An Overview of Some Key Issues." Conference on China's Exchange Rate Policy, Institute for International Economics, October 19.

Gourinchas, Pierre-Olivier, and Hélène Rey. 2005. "*From World Banker to World Venture Capitalist: US External Adjustment and the Exorbitant Privilege.*" National Bureau of Economic Research Working Paper 11563. August. Cambridge: NBER.

Gowa, Joanne. 1984a. *Closing the Gold Window.* Ithaca: Cornell University Press.

———. 1984b. "Hegemons, IOs, and Markets: The Case of the Substitution Account." *International Organization* 38, no. 4: 661–83.

Gray, H. Peter. 2004. *The Exhaustion of the Dollar.* New York: Palgrave.

Green, Michael Jonathan. 2001. *Japan's Reluctant Realism: Foreign Policy Challenges in an Era of Uncertain Power.* New York: Palgrave.

Greenspan, Alan. 2007. *The Age of Turbulence.* New York: Penguin.

Greenspan, Alan, and James Kennedy. 2007. "Sources and Uses of Equity Extracted from Homes." Federal Reserve Bank, FEDS research paper 2007–20. Washington, D.C.: Federal Reserve.

Grimes, William. 2008. *Currency and Contest in East Asia: The Great Power Politics of Financial Regionalism.* Ithaca: Cornell University Press.

Gros, Daniel. 2006. "Why the U.S. Current Account Deficit Is Not Sustainable."
    *International Finance* 9, no. 2.
Grubel, Herbert. 1964. "The Costs and Benefits of Being the World's Banker."
    *National Banking Review* 2, no. 2: 189–212.
——. 1969. "The Distribution of Seigniorage from International Liquidity
    Creation." In *Monetary Problems of the International Economy*, ed. Robert A.
    Mundell and Alexander K. Swoboda. Chicago: University of Chicago Press.
Hale, David D., and Lyric Hughes Hale. 2008. "Reconsidering Revaluation: The
    Wrong Approach to the U.S.-Chinese Trade Imbalance." *Foreign Affairs* 87, no. 1.
Hamilton, Daniel S., and Joseph P. Quinlan. 2007. "The Transatlantic Economy
    2006." Washington, D.C.: Center for Transatlantic Relations.
Harvard University Joint Center for Housing Studies. 2008. *The State of the Nation's
    Housing.* Cambridge: Harvard University.
Hausman, Jerry, and Ephraim Leibtag. 2004. "CPI Bias from Supercenters: Does the
    BLS Know That Wal-Mart Exists?" National Bureau of Economic Affairs
    Working Paper 10712. Cambridge: NBER.
Haussmann, Ricardo, and Federico Sturzenegger. 2006. "Global Imbalances or Bad
    Accounting? The Missing Dark Matter in the Wealth of Nations." Harvard
    Center for International Development Working Paper 124. January.
Hayek, Frederich A. 1978. *The Constitution of Liberty.* Chicago: University of
    Chicago Press.
Helleiner, Eric. 1994. *States and the Reemergence of Global Finance.* Ithaca: Cornell
    University Press.
——. 1999. "State Power and the Regulation of Illicit Activity in Global Finance." In
    *The Illicit Global Economy and State Power*, ed. R. Friman and P. Andreas. New
    York: Rowman and Littlefield.
——. 2003a. "Dollarization Diplomacy: US Policy towards Latin America Coming
    Full Circle?" *Review of International Political Economy* 10, no. 3: 406–29.
——. 2003b. *The Making of National Money.* Ithaca: Cornell University Press.
——. 2006a. "Below the State: Micro-level Monetary Power." In *International
    Monetary Power*, ed. David Andrews. New York: Cornell University Press.
——. 2006b. *Towards North American Monetary Union?* Montreal: McGill-Queen's
    University Press.
——. 2008. "Political Determinants of International Currencies: What Future for
    the US Dollar?" *Review of International Political Economy* 15, no. 3: 354–78.
Henning, C. Randall. 1987. *Macroeconomic Diplomacy in the 1980s.* London: Croom
    Helm.
——. 1998. "Systemic Conflict and Regional Monetary Integration: The Case of
    Europe." *International Organization* 52: 537–74.
Henning, C. Randall, and Pier Carlo. 2000. *Transatlantic Perspectives on the Euro.*
    Washington, D.C.: Brookings Institute.
——. 2000. "US-EU Relations after the Inception of the Monetary Union:

Cooperation or Rivalry?" In *Transatlantic Perspectives on the Euro*, ed. C. Randall Henning and Pier Carlo Padoan. Washington, D.C.: Brookings Institute.

———. 2006. "The Exchange Rate Weapon and Macroeconomic Conflict." In *International Monetary Power*, ed. D. Andrews. Ithaca: Cornell University Press.

Hirsch, Fred. 1969. *Money International: Economics and Politics of World Money.* New York: Doubleday.

Hirschman, Albert O. 1980. *National Power and the Structure of Foreign Trade.* Berkeley: University of California Press.

Holbrooke, Richard C. 1998. *To End a War.* New York: Random House.

Huntington, Samuel P. 1989. "The U.S.—Decline or Renewal?" *Foreign Affairs* 67, no. 1.

Ikenberry, John. 2008. "The Rise of China and the Future of the West: Can the Liberal System Survive?" *Foreign Affairs* (January–February).

Ingham, Geoffrey. 1984. *Capitalism Divided? The City and Industry in British Social Development.* London: Macmillan.

International Monetary Fund. 2003. "Deflation: Determinants, Risks, and Policy Options—Findings of an Interdepartmental Task Force." Washington, D.C.: IMF.

———. 2004. *World Economic Outlook.* September. Washington, D.C.: IMF.

———. 2007. *World Economic Outlook.* April. Washington, D.C.: IMF.

James, Harold. 1996. *International Monetary Cooperation since Bretton Woods.* New York: Oxford University Press.

———. 2006. *The Roman Predicament: How the Rules of International Order Create the Politics of Empire.* Princeton: Princeton University Press.

Johnman, Lewis. 1989. "Defending the Pound: The Economics of the Suez Crisis, 1956." In *Post-War Britain, 1945–64: Themes and Perspectives,* ed. Anthony Gorst, Lewis Johnman, and W. Scott Lewis. London: Pinter Publishers.

Johnson, Juliet. 2008. "Forbidden Fruit: Russia's Uneasy Relationship with the Dollar." *Review of International Political Economy* 15, no. 3: 379–98.

Jones, Ronald W. 1975. "Presumption and the Transfer Problem." *Journal of International Economics* 5: 263–74.

Kamin, Steven B., Mario Marazzi, and John W. Schindler. 2004. "Is China 'Exporting Deflation'?" *International Finance Discussion Paper 791.* Washington, D.C.: Board of Governors of the Federal Reserve System.

Karlik, John R. 1968. "The Costs and Benefits of Being a Reserve-Currency Country." In *The Open Economy: Essays on International Trade and Finance,* ed. Peter Kenen and Roger Lawrence. New York: Columbia University Press.

Katada, Saori N. 2002. "Japan and Asian Monetary Regionalisation: Cultivating a New Regional Leadership after the Asian Financial Crisis." *Geopolitics* 7, no. 1: 85–112.

———. 2008. "From a Supporter to a Challenger? Japan's Currency Leadership in Dollar-Dominated East Asia." *Review of International Political Economy* 15, no. 3: 399–417.

Katzenstein, Peter. 2005. *A World of Regions: Asia and Europe in the American Imperium.* Ithaca: Cornell University Press.

Kawasaki, Tsuyoshi. 1992. "Structural Transformation in the US-Japanese Economic Relationship." In *Power, Economics, and Security,* ed. Henry Bienen. Boulder, Colo.: Westview.

Kemeny, Jim. 1980. "Home Ownership and Privatisation." *International Journal of Urban and Regional Research* 4, no. 3: 372–88.

———. 2005. "'The Really Big Trade-Off' between Home Ownership and Welfare: Castles' Evaluation of the 1980 Thesis, and a Reformulation 25 Years On." *Housing, Theory, and Society* 22, no. 2: 59–75.

Kenen, Peter B. 1973. "Convertibility and Consolidation: A Survey of Options for Reform." *American Economic Review* 63, no. 2.

———. 2005. "Stabilizing the International Monetary System." *Journal of Policy Modeling* 27: 487–93.

Kennedy, Paul. 1987. *The Rise and Fall of the Great Powers.* New York: Random House.

Kenworthy, Lane. 2002. "Corporatism and Unemployment in the 1980s and 1990s." *American Sociological Review* 67, no. 3: 367–88.

Keohane, Robert. 1982. "Inflation and the Decline of American Power." In *Political Economy of International and Domestic Monetary Relations,* ed. Raymond E. Lombra and Willard E. White. Ames: Iowa State University Press.

———. 1984. *After Hegemony: Cooperation and Discord in the World Political Economy.* Princeton: Princeton University Press.

Keynes, John Maynard. 1971 [1930]. *A Treatise on Money: The Applied Theory of Money.* Cambridge: Cambridge University Press.

Kindleberger, Charles. 1967. *The Politics of International Money and World Language.* Essays in International Finance 61. Princeton: International Finance Section, Princeton University.

———. 1970. *Power and Money: The Politics of International Economics and the Economics of International Politics.* New York: Basic Books.

———. 1973. *The World in Depression, 1929–1939.* Berkeley: University of California Press.

———. 1976. "Systems of International Economic Organization." In *Money and the Coming World Order,* ed. David P. Calleo. New York: Lehrman Institute.

———. 1996. *World Economic Primacy 1500–1990.* New York: Oxford University Press.

Kirschen, E. S. 1974. "The American External Seigniorage." *European Economic Review* 5: 355–78.

Kirshner, Jonathan. 1995. *Currency and Coercion: The Political Economy of International Monetary Power.* Princeton: Princeton University Press.

———. 2000. "Rationalist Explanations for War?" *Security Studies* 10, no. 1: 143–50.

———. 2003. "States, Markets, and Great Power Relations in the Pacific: Some Realist

Expectations." In *International Relations Theory and the Asia Pacific,* ed. G. John Ikenberry and Michael Mastanduno. New York: Columbia University Press.

———. 2006. "Currency and Coercion in the Twenty-first Century." In *International Monetary Power,* ed. David Andrews. New York: Cornell University Press.

———. 2007a. *Appeasing Bankers: Financial Caution on the Road to War.* Princeton: Princeton University Press.

———. 2007b. "Money, Capital, and Cooperation in the Asia Pacific Region." In *The Uses of Institutions: U.S., Japan, and Governance in East Asia,* ed. G. John Ikenberry and Takashi Inoguchi. New York: Palgrave Macmillan.

Klug, Adam, and Gregor Smith. 1999. "Suez and Sterling, 1956." *Explorations in Economic History* 36, no. 3: 181–203.

Kotlikoff, Lawrence, Hans Fehr, and Sabine Jokisch. 2003. *"The Developed World's Demographic Transition—The Roles of Capital Flows, Immigration, and Policy."* Mimeo, October.

Kotlikoff, Lawrence, and Niall Ferguson. 2003. "Going Critical." *National Interest* (Fall).

Krasner, Stephen. 1978. "United States Commercial and Monetary Policy." In *Between Power and Plenty: Foreign Economic Policies of Advanced Industrial States,* ed. Peter Katzenstein. Madison: University of Wisconsin Press.

Krugman, Paul. 1984. "The International Role of the Dollar: Theory and Prospect." In *Exchange Rate Theory and Practice,* ed. J. Bilson and R. Marston. Chicago: University of Chicago.

———. 1991. "Has the Adjustment Worked?" *Policy Analysis in International Economics* 34. Washington, D.C.: Institute for International Economics.

———. 2007. "Will There Be a Dollar Crisis?" *Economic Policy* 51: 437–67.

Kunz, Diane B. 1991. *The Economic Diplomacy of the Suez Crisis.* Chapel Hill: University of North Carolina Press.

Kupchan, Charles. 2002. *The End of the American Era: U.S. Foreign Policy and the Geopolitics of the Twenty-first Century.* New York: Knopf.

Kuznets, Simon. 1967. *Secular Movements in Production and Prices.* New York: Augustus Kelly.

Kwan, C. H. 2001. *Yen Bloc: Toward Economic Integration in Asia.* Washington, D.C.: Brookings Institution.

Lawrence, Robert Z. 1994. "Rude Awakening: The End of the American Dream." *International Economic Insights* (January–February).

Lescure, J. 1912. "Les marches financiers de Berlin et Paris et la crise franco-allemande de julliet-octobre 1911." *Revue Economique Internationale.*

Leverett, Flynt. 2008. "Black Is the New Green." *National Interest* (January–February).

Lim, Ewe-Ghee. 2006. "The Euro's Challenge to the Dollar." IMF Working Paper 06/153. Washington, D.C.: International Monetary Fund.

Liss, Jodi. 2008. "Making Monetary Mischief." *World Policy Journal* (Winter): 29–38.

Litfin, Karen. 1997. "Sovereignty in World Ecopolitics." *Mershon International Studies Review* 41, no. 2: 167–204.

Ludwig, A., and T. Slok. 2002. "Impact of Changes in Stock Prices and House Prices on Consumption in OECD Countries." IMF Working Paper 02/01. January. Washington, D.C.: International Monetary Fund.

Makin, John H. 1971. "Swaps and Roosa Bonds as an Index of the Cost of Cooperation in the 'Crisis Zone.'" *Quarterly Journal of Economics* 85, no. 2.

McKinnon, Ronald I. 1969. *Private and Official International Money: The Case for the Dollar.* Essays in International Finance 74. Princeton: International Finance Section, Princeton University.

McKinnon, Ronald I., and Kenichi Ohno. 1997. *Dollar and Yen: Resolving Economic Conflict between the United States and Japan.* Cambridge: MIT Press.

——. 2005a. *Exchange Rates under the East Asian Dollar Standard: Living with Conflicted Virtue.* Cambridge: MIT Press.

——. 2005b. "Trapped by the International Dollar Standard." *Journal of Policy Modeling* 27, no. 4: 477–86.

——. 2005c. "The World Dollar Standard and Globalization, New Rules for the Game?" Stanford University. September.

——. 2006. "China's New Exchange Rate Policy: Will China Follow Japan into a Liquidity Trap?" *Economists' Voice* 3, no. 2.

——. 2007a. "Japan's Deflationary Hangover: Wage Stagnation and the Syndrome of the Ever Weaker Yen." *Singapore Economic Review* (December).

——. 2007b. "The Transfer Problem in Reducing the U.S. Current Account Deficit." *Journal of Policy Modeling* 29, no. 5: 669–75.

——. 2007c. "Why China Should Keep Its Dollar Peg." *International Finance* 10, no. 1: 43–70.

McNamara, Kathleen, and Sophie Meunier. 2002. "Between National Sovereignty and International Power: What External Voice for the Euro." *International Affairs* 78, no. 4: 849–68.

McNamara, Kathleen. 2008. "A Rivalry in the Making? The Euro and International Monetary Power." *Review of International Political Economy* 15, no. 3: 439–59.

Mead, Walter Russell. 1987. *Mortal Splendor.* Boston: Houghton Mifflin.

Momani, Bessma. 2008. "Gulf Cooperation Council Oil Exporters and the Future of the Dollar." *New Political Economy* 13, no. 3: 293–314.

Mundell, Robert. 1971. *The Dollar and the Policy Mix.* Essays in International Finance 85. Princeton: International Finance Section, Princeton University.

Murphy, R. Taggart. 2006. "East Asia's Dollars." *New Left Review* 40: 39–64.

Murray, Justin, and Marc Labonte. 2005. "Foreign Holdings of Federal Debt." *CRS Report* RS22331. November 23. Washington, D.C.: Congressional Research Service.

Mussa, Michael. 2005. "Sustaining Growth While Reducing External Imbalances." In *The United States and the World Economy,* ed. C. Fred Bergsten. Washington, D.C.: Institute for International Economics.

Nau, Henry R. 1990. *The Myth of America's Decline: Leading the World Economy into the 1990s.* New York: Oxford University Press.

Newhouse, John. 1971. *U.S. Troops in Europe: Issues, Costs, and Choices.* Washington, D.C.: Brookings Institution.

Nitzan, Jonathan. 1998. "Differential Accumulation: Towards a New Political Economy of Capital." *Review of International Political Economy* 5, no. 2: 169–216.

Nogaro, Bertrand. 1912. "Les banques d'émission et leur évolution contemporaine." *Revue économique internationale* 9: 475–94.

Noyes, A. D. 1909. *Forty Years of American Finance.* London: Putnam.

Nye, Joseph S. 1990. *Bound to Lead: The Changing Nature of American Power.* New York: Basic Books.

———. 2004. *Soft Power: The Means to Success in World Politics.* New York: Public Affairs.

Obstfeld, Maurice, and Kenneth Rogoff. 2004. "The Unsustainable US Current Account Position Revisited." *National Bureau of Economic Research* Working Paper 10869. Cambridge: NBER.

Olson, Mancur. 1982. *The Rise and Decline of Nations.* New Haven: Yale University Press.

Organisation for Economic Cooperation and Development. 2005a. *OECD Factbook.* *http://www.sourceOECD.org.* Paris: OECD.

———. 2005b. *OECD in Figures: Statistics on Member Countries.* Paris: OECD.

Oye, Kenneth A. 1992. *Economic Discrimination and Political Exchange: World Political Economy in the 1930s and 1980s.* Princeton: Princeton University Press.

Palyi, Melchior. 1961. *Inflation Primer.* Chicago: H. Regnery.

Papaioannou, Elias, and Richard Portes. 2008. "The International Role of the Euro: A Status Report." *European Economy, Economic Papers* 317. April.

Pape, Robert. 2005. "Soft Balancing against the United States." *International Security* 30, no. 1: 7–45.

Pascha, Werner. 2007. "The Role of Regional Financial Arrangements and Monetary Integration in East Asia and Europe in Relations with the United States." *Pacific Review* 20, no. 3: 423–46.

Paul, T. V. 2005. "Soft Balancing in the Age of U.S. Primacy." *International Security* 30, no. 1: 46–71.

Persaud, Avinash. 2004. "When Currency Empires Fall." Lecture presented at Gresham College, London (available at http://www.gresham.ac.uk).

Peyrefitte, Alain. 2003. *C'était de Gaulle.* Paris: Galliard.

Posen, Adam. 2008. "Why the Euro Will Not Rival the Dollar." *International Finance* 11, no. 1: 75–100.

Powell, Colin L. 1993. "U.S. Forces: Challenges Ahead." *Foreign Affairs* 72, no. 5: 32–45.

Qiao, Hong. 2007. "Exchange Rates and Trade Balances under the Dollar Standard." *Journal of Policy Modeling* 29, no. 5: 765–82.

Reich, Robert B. 1991. *The Work of Nations: Preparing Ourselves for 21st Century Capitalism.* New York: Knopf.

Reinhart, Carmen. 2000. "The Mirage of Floating Exchange Rates." *American Economic Review* 90: 65–70.

Reinhardt, Carmen, and Kenneth Rogoff. 2008. "Is the 2007 U.S. Sub-Prime Financial Crisis So Different? An International Historical Comparison." Paper presented at the American Economics Association annual meeting. January 6.

Roach, Stephen. 2003. "The World Economy at the Crossroads." Speech at the Boao Forum for Asia. November 2.

———. 2005. "Think Again: Alan Greenspan." *Foreign Policy* (January–February).

Roosa, Robert V., and Fred Hirsch. 1966. *Reserves, Reserve Currencies, and Vehicle Currencies: An Argument.* Essays in International Finance 54. Princeton: International Finance Section, Princeton University.

Rosecrance, Richard, ed. 1979. *America as an Ordinary Country.* Ithaca: Cornell University Press.

Roubini, Nouriel, and Brad Setser. 2005. "Will the Bretton Woods 2 Regime Unravel Soon?" Mimeo. February.

Rowland, Benjamin, ed. 1976. *Balance of Power or Hegemony: The Interwar Monetary System.* New York: New York University Press.

Rubin, Robert, and Jacob Weisberg. 2003. *In an Uncertain World: Tough Choices from Wall Street to Washington.* New York: Random House.

Rueff, Jacques. 1967. *Balance of Payments: Proposals for the Resolution of the Most Pressing World Economic Problem of Our Time.* New York: Macmillan.

———. 1972. *The Monetary Sin of the West.* New York: Macmillan.

Rueff, Jacques, and Fred Hirsch. 1965. *The Role and the Rule of Gold.* Essays in International Finance 47. Princeton: International Finance Section, Princeton University.

Russett, Bruce. 1985. "The Mysterious Case of U.S. Hegemony; or, Is Mark Twain Really Dead?" *International Organization* 38, no. 2: 207–31.

Salant, William A. 1964. "The Reserve Currency Role of the Dollar: Blessings or Burden to the United States?" *Review of Economics and Statistics* 46, no. 2.

Sayers, R. 1976. *The Bank of England, 1891–1944.* Cambridge: Cambridge University Press.

Schinasi, Garry. 2005. "Financial Architecture of the Eurozone at Five." In *The Euro at Five,* ed. Adam Posen. Washington, D.C.: Institute for International Economics.

Schwartz, Anna J. 1997. "From Obscurity to Notoriety: A Biography of the Exchange Stabilization Fund." *Journal of Money, Credit, and Banking* 29, no. 2: 135–53.

Schwartz, Herman. 2003. "Hobson's Voice: American Internationalism, Asian Development, and Global Macroeconomic Imbalances." *Journal of Post-Keynesian Economics* 25, no. 2: 331–51.

Schwartz, Herman. 2009. *Subprime Nation: American Power, Global Capital, and the Housing Bubble.* Ithaca: Cornell University Press.

Schwartz, Herman, and Leonard Seabrooke, eds. 2009. *The Politics of Housing Booms and Busts.* Basingstoke: Palgrave.

Setser, Brad. 2008. *Sovereign Wealth and Sovereign Power.* Council Special Report no. 37. September. New York: Council on Foreign Relations.

Shannon, H. A. 1950. "The Sterling Balances and the Sterling Area." *Economic Journal* 60.

Shiller, Robert J. 2000. *Irrational Exuberance.* Princeton: Princeton University Press.

Smith, Adam. 1976 [1776]. *Wealth of Nations.* Chicago: University of Chicago Press.

Sohmen, Egon. 1969. *Flexible Exchange Rates.* Chicago: University of Chicago Press.

Sorokina, Olga, Anthony Webb, and Dan Muldoon. 2008. "Pension Wealth and Income: 1992, 1998, and 2004." Boston College Center for Retirement Research Issue in Brief, IB-8–1.

Spiro, David. 1999. *The Hidden Hand of American Hegemony.* Ithaca: Cornell University Press.

Sprague, O. M. W. 1908. "The American Crisis in 1907." *Economic Journal* 18, no. 71: 353–72.

———. 1910. *History of Crises under the National Banking System.* Washington, D.C.: Government Printing Office.

Stasavage, David. 2003. *Public Debt and the Birth of the Democratic State.* Cambridge: Cambridge University Press.

Stein, Herbert A. 1996. *The Fiscal Revolution in America.* Washington, D.C.: American Enterprise Institute.

Stockholm International Peace Research Institute. 2005. *SIPRI Yearbook 2005: Armaments, Disarmament, and International Security.* Stockholm: Almquist and Wiksell.

Strange, Susan. 1971a. "The Politics of International Currencies." *World Politics* 23, no. 2.

———. 1971b. *Sterling and British Policy: A Political Study of an International Currency in Decline.* London: Oxford University Press.

———. 1972. "The Dollar Crisis 1971." *International Affairs* 48, no. 2: 191–216.

———. 1976. *International Monetary Relations.* London: Oxford University Press.

———. 1986. *Casino Capitalism.* Oxford: Blackwell.

———. 1987. "The Persistent Myth of Lost Hegemony." *International Organization* 41, no. 4: 551–74.

———. 1988. *States and Markets.* New York: Basil Blackwell.

———. 1990. "Finance, Information, and Power." *Review of International Studies* 16, no. 3: 259–74.

———. 1994. "Finance and Capitalism: The City's Imperial Role Yesterday and Today." *Review of International Studies* 20, no. 4.

Summers, Lawrence H. 2004. *The U.S. Current Account Deficit and the Global Economy.* Washington, D.C.: Per Jacobsson Foundation.

Swodoba, Alexandre. 1969. "Vehicle Currencies in the Foreign Exchange Market:

The Case of the Dollar." In *The International Market for Foreign Exchange,* ed. R. Aliber. New York: Praeger.

——, ed. 1971. *L'Union monétaire en Europe.* Geneva: Institute Universitaire de Hautes Études Internationales.

Tavlas, George. 1997. "The International Use of the US Dollar: An Optimum Currency Area Perspective." *World Economy* 20, no. 6: 709–47.

Taylor, John. 1993. "Discretion versus Policy Rules in Practice." *Carnegie-Rochester Conference Series on Public Policy* 39: 195–214.

——. 2007. *Global Financial Warriors: The Untold Story of International Finance in the Post-9/11 World.* New York: W. W. Norton.

Thompson, Helen. 2007. "Debt and Power: The United States' Debt in Historical Perspective." *International Relations* 21, no. 3: 305–23.

Treverton, Gregory F. 1978. *The "Dollar Drain" and American Forces in Germany: Managing the Political Economics of Alliance.* Athens: Ohio University Press.

Triffin, Robert. 1960. *Gold and the Dollar Crisis: The Future of Convertibility.* New Haven: Yale University Press.

——. 1966. *The World Money Maze.* New Haven: Yale University Press.

——. 1978–79. "The International Role and the Fate of the Dollar." *Foreign Affairs* (Winter): 269–86.

——. 1988. "Discussion." In *The European Monetary System,* ed. Francesco Giavazzi, Stefano Micossi, and Marcus Miller. Cambridge: Cambridge University Press.

Truman, Edwin M. 2005a. "The Euro and Prospects for Policy Coordination." In *The Euro at Five,* ed. Adam Posen. Washington, D.C.: Institute for International Economics.

——. 2005b. "Reflections." *Federal Reserve Bank of St. Louis Review* 87, no. 2.

Truman, Edwin, and Anna Wong. 2006. "The Case for an International Reserve Diversification Standard." *Working Paper* 06–2. Washington, D.C.: Institute for International Economics.

Underhill, Paco. 2004. *Call of the Mall.* New York: Simon and Schuster.

U.S. Government. 1997. *The Economic Report of the President.* Washington, D.C.: U.S. Government Printing Office.

——. 1998. *The Economic Report of the President.* Washington, D.C.: U.S. Government Printing Office.

——. 1999. *The Economic Report of the President.* Washington, D.C.: U.S. Government Printing Office.

——. 2000. *The Economic Report of the President.* Washington, D.C.: U.S. Government Printing Office.

——. 2007. *The Economic Report of the President.* Washington, D.C.: U.S. Government Printing Office.

United States Department of State. 1998. *Foreign Relations of the United States 1964–1998.* Vol. 8. Washington, D.C.: U.S. Government Printing Office.

U.S. Treasury Department. 2008. *Report on Foreign Portfolio Holdings of U.S.*

*Securities as of June 30, 2007.* Washington, D.C.: U.S. Government Printing Office.

Volcker, Paul. 1979. *Federal Reserve Bulletin 65.* November.

von Lumm, Carl. 1912. "Mesures complementaires de la politique d'escompte." *Revue economique internationale.*

Wachtel, Paul. 2006. "Understanding the Old and New Bretton Woods." Paper at "In Search of a New Bretton Woods: Reserve Currencies and Global Imbalances" conference, Florence, October 20.

Wade, Robert Hunter. 2003. "The Invisible Hand of the American Empire." *Ethics and International Affairs* 17, no. 2: 77–88.

Walras, Leon. 1954. *Elements of Pure Economics.* Translated by William Jaffe. Homewood, Ill.: Irwin.

Walter, Andrew. 1991. *World Power and World Money: The Role of Hegemony and International Monetary Order.* New York: St. Martin's.

———. 2006. "Domestic Sources of International Monetary Leadership." In *International Monetary Power,* ed. David Andrews. Ithaca: Cornell University Press.

Walter, Norbert. 1999. "The Euro: Second to (N)one." *German Issues* 23.

Waltz, Kenneth. 1979. *Theory of International Politics.* Reading, Mass.: Addison-Wesley.

Warnock, Francis E., and Veronica Cacdac Warnock. 2006. "International Capital Flows and U.S. Interest Rates." FRB International Finance Discussion Paper No. 840. September. Washington, D.C.: Federal Reserve Board.

Wilson, Shaun. 2006. "Not My Taxes! Explaining Tax Resistance and Its Implications for Australia's Welfare State." *Australian Journal of Political Science* 41, no. 4: 517–35.

Wolf, Martin. 2008. *Fixing Global Finance.* Baltimore: Johns Hopkins University Press.

Wooldridge, Philip. 2006. "The Changing Composition of Official Reserves." *Bank for International Settlements Quarterly Review.* September. Basel: BIS.

World Bank. 2002. "China Is Becoming the World's Manufacturing Powerhouse." *Transition Newsletter.*

Wyplosz, Charles. 1999. "An International Role for the Euro?" In *European Capital Markets with a Single Currency,* ed. Jean Dermine and Pierre Hillion, 76–104. New York: Oxford University Press.

———. 2003. "Exchange Rate Policy of the Euro Area." Briefing Notes to the Committee for Economic and Monetary Affairs of the European Parliament. Fourth quarter.

Yang, Denise. 2002. "China: Exporting More Deflation." *Global Economic Forum.* New York: Morgan Stanley.

Zhang Dingmin. 2007. "Beyond Borders." *China Business Weekly* (16–22 May), 1–2.

Zimmermann, Hubert. 2002. *Money and Security: Troops, Monetary Policy and West*

*Germany's Relations with the United States and Britain, 1950–1971.* Washington, D.C.: German Historical Institute; Cambridge: Cambridge University Press.

——. 2004. "Ever Challenging the Buck? The Euro and the Question of Power in International Monetary Governance." In *Governing the EMU,* ed. Francisco Torres, Amy Verdun, and Hubert Zimmerman. Florence: European University Institute.

# INDEX